CORPORATION TAX FOR STUDENTS

Second edition

H. C. D. RANKIN and D. M. CATTERALL

First published in 1985 by
Van Nostrand Reinhold (UK) Co. Ltd
Molly Millars Lane, Wokingham, Berkshire, England

Typeset in 10 on 11 pt Plantin by
Kelly Typesetting Ltd, Bradford-on-Avon, Wiltshire

Printed and bound in Great Britain by
Billing & Sons Ltd, Worcester

Library of Congress Cataloging in Publication Data

Rankin, H. C. D.
  Corporation tax for students.

  Includes index.
  1. Corporations—Taxation—Great Britain.   2. Tax
accounting—Great Britain.   I. Catterall, D. M.   II. Title.
HD2753.G7R36   1985   657'.46'0941   85-3272
ISBN 0-85258-242-0

British Library Cataloguing in Publication Data

Rankin, H. C. D.
  Corporation tax for students—2nd ed.
  1. Corporations—Taxation—Great Britain
  I. Title.   II. Catterall, D. M.
  336.24'3'0941   HD2753.G7

  ISBN 0-85258-242-0

The law is stated as at 1 February 1985.

CONTENTS

PREFACE

This is the second edition, completely up-dated and enlarged, of H. C. D. Rankin's *Corporation Tax for Students*, published in 1977. This edition, as was the first, is intended for students studying for the examinations of accountancy and other professional bodies and those of universities and colleges.

The opportunity has been taken in preparing this edition of adding new chapters on Capital Allowances and the Foreign Element. The treatment of losses has been completely reshaped and a large amount of new material has been included in Chapter 1, The Computation of Profit. Many more examples in amplification of the text have been added and, as well as questions of final examination standard at the end of each chapter, a selection of examination questions (with worked solutions by the authors) from the final examinations of the Institute of Chartered Accountants of Scotland, the Institute of Chartered Accountants in England and Wales and the Chartered Association of Certified Accountants is included at the end of the book.

It is hoped that the book will be found sufficiently rigorous in theory and practice to be a useful refresher for members of accountancy and other bodies looking for an overview of the principles of corporation tax.

Many people assisted in various ways in the writing and preparation of the text. They all have our sincere thanks and gratitude. In particular, Geraldine Lord, Irene McKain, Jean Roberts and Joyce Spencer typed our manuscripts with great skill; Roger Leslie BSc, CA, ATII, Ernst and Whinney, Bob Harris BCom, CA, McLellan Harris & Co, Alan Reid LLB, CA, FTII, KMG Thomson McLintock and Gavin Morton BA, CA, KMG Thomson McLintock read all or part of the text and made many helpful suggestions which are incorporated. Needless to say any remaining shortcomings are our sole responsibility.

We would like to thank the Institute of Chartered Accountants in England and Wales and the Chartered Association of Certified Accountants for their ready permission to use examination questions published by them. In particular, we thank the Institute of Chartered Accountants of Scotland for its permission to use examination questions and other questions and materials used in the Education Department and for its assistance in preparing the book for publication.

The first edition of this book has been used with success by many thousands of students in the UK and elsewhere. The authors hope that many more new readers will find understanding and examination success in reading and studying the present publication.

H. C. D. Rankin

D. M. Cattcrall

ABBREVIATIONS

ACT	Advance Corporation Tax
AP	Accounting Period
CA	Court of Appeal
CAA 1968	Capital Allowances Act 1968
CFC	Controlled Foreign Company
CGT	Capital Gains Tax
CGTA 1979	Capital Gains Taxes Act 1979
CT	Corporation Tax
FA	Finance Act
FII	Franked Invesment Income
FY	Financial Year
FYA	First Year Allowance
IBA	Industrial Buildings Allowance
IT	Income Tax
Para.	Paragraph
QBD	Queen's Bench Division
S and Ss	Section and Sections
Sch.	Schedule
TA 1970	Income and Corporation Taxes Act 1970
Taxes Act 1970	Income and Corporation Taxes Act 1970
TC	Tax case
TMA 1970	Taxes Management Act 1970
UFII	Unfranked Investment Income
WDA	Writing Down Allowance
WDV	Written Down Value

CHAPTER 1

THE COMPUTATION OF PROFIT

1.1 INTRODUCTION

Until the passing of the Finance Act 1965 the taxation of companies was part of the income tax code which charged both individuals and corporations to tax. In 1965 corporation tax imposed a charge on the profits of companies distinct and separate from the income tax charge on individuals. In addition when a company distributed profits to its shareholders it paid an additional amount of income tax. This later feature is a characteristic of what is called the 'classical system' of corporation tax, but since it was shortlived, and in any case something of a novelty in UK taxation when it was introduced in 1965, the significance of the description 'classical system' for our purpose is to distinguish it from the 'imputation system' which was legislated for in 1972 and remains with us.

The classical system made it more expensive to distribute profits than to retain them; the imputation system is in theory neutral as between the taxation of distributed and retained profits and achieves this by charging all profits of a company at the same rate regardless of the destination of these profits. Neutrality is not, however, always achieved in the practical working out of the system. In both systems one can see very obviously the pre-1965 income tax origins of corporation tax. Even superficially a corporation tax computation bears the marks of income tax:

A Company Ltd
Corporation tax computation for the year ended 31 March 1986.

	£000
Schedule D Case I	500
Schedule D Case III	6
Schedule D Case V	1
Schedule A	2
Unfranked investment income	2
Chargeable gains (abated)	13
Total profits	524
Less Charges on income	14
Profits chargeable	510
Corporation tax payable:	
Financial year 1985, 40%	204

From this it will be seen that a corporation tax computation retains many of the familiar names and titles of income tax and indeed income tax principles, with important variations, are applied in arriving at the amounts included in each of the schedules of the computation. However there are differences from income tax; two important differences are the inclusion of 'chargeable gains' in the profit total (these would be taxed under capital gains tax if they arose to an individual taxpayer) and the fact that an assessment on a company is made on its chargeable profits and not under each separate schedule of income as is the case for income tax.

The imputation system of corporation tax is described in detail in Chapter 3. The system requires that at the time a company pays a dividend it pays to the Inland Revenue an amount of tax, called advance corporation tax. From the company's point of view this payment is, as its name suggests, a payment in advance of its ultimate corporation tax liability. When the time comes to compute or pay the corporation tax, for example the figure of £204,000 above, any payment which the company has made in advance, the advance corporation tax, is deducted, and only the net amount, the so-called 'mainstream corporation tax', i.e. what is not paid in advance, is paid to the Inland Revenue. It follows that in the imputation system the payment of a dividend does not increase the amount of the tax payable on a company's profits but only determines the time at which a part of the corporation tax is paid. This will hold true as long as the distributing company enjoys profits which are charged to corporation tax. If for any reason there are no profits chargeable to corporation tax so that there is nothing against which to set the advance corporation tax, the latter payment may come to have some of the appearances of a tax cost of making distributions in the face of the theoretical basis of the system.

1.2 THE CHARGE TO CORPORATION TAX

Corporation tax is charged on
  (a) Companies resident in the United Kingdom,
  (b) Companies which are not resident in the United Kingdom but which carry on a trade in the United Kingdom through a branch or agency.
The taxation of non-resident companies is dealt with in Chapter 7.

The term company is defined in Section 526(5) Taxes Act 1970 as any body corporate or unincorporated association. An example of an unincorporated association is a members' club, such as a golf club. Much of such a club's income is not taxable in so far as it is what is called 'mutual income', income which arises from its trading relationshps with its members. But where, for example, the club receives interest on bank deposits or other investments this will be chargeable to corporation tax and not income tax.

1.3 ACCOUNTING PERIODS

Corporation tax assessments are made for accounting periods and are based on the profits of the same accounting periods. This is in contrast to income tax where assessments are made for fiscal years and are commonly based on the income and profits of business accounts ending in previous fiscal years.

Very often a company's own accounting year is its accounting period for corporation tax. Thus the basis of assessment for corporation tax may be described as a current year basis.

Example 1
Company A Ltd prepares accounts for the 12 months to 31 December 1983. The Inspector of Taxes will make a corporation tax assessment on the profits of A Ltd for the accounting period commencing on 1 January 1983 and ending on 31 December 1983.

Where the company does not prepare a twelve month account reference has to be made to the definition of an accounting period which is provided in S.247 TA 1970.

(1) An accounting period begins:
(a) when the previous accounting period comes to an end,
(b) when a company comes within the charge to corporation tax perhaps for the first time, on becoming resident in the United Kingdom or commencing to trade or acquiring some other source of income (S.247(2) TA 1970).

(2) An accounting period ends on the earliest of the following events, viz:
(a) The expiry of twelve months from the beginning of the accounting period;
    — the effect of this is that no accounting period can be longer than twelve months,
(b) a date to which the company makes up its accounts,
(c) the company beginning or ceasing to trade,
    — an illustration of an accounting period ending when a trade begins is given below (Example 2),
(d) the company beginning or ceasing to be United Kingdom resident,
(e) the company ceasing to be within the charge to corporation tax;
    — if a company in its lifetime becomes exempt from corporation tax, for example, on becoming a charity, an accounting period will end at that time.

Apart and distinct from the above rules an accounting period ends at the commencement of the winding-up of a company and thereafter annually at the anniversary of the commencement of the winding-up (S.247(7) TA 1970).

Example 2

On 16 March 1984 Blank Ltd was formed with an authorized share capital of 100,000 ordinary shares of £1 each. On 28 April 1984 the shares were subscribed for and on 2 May 1984 Blank Ltd placed most of the subscription moneys on deposit account with Noland Bank. The company commenced trading on 1 July 1984. Accounts are to be prepared to 30 September each year.

The accounting periods are as follows:

(a) 2 May 1984 to 30 June 1984

The accounting period begins on 2 May 1984 when the company acquires a source of income—namely the deposit account (see 1(b) above).

The accounting periods ends on 30 June which is the day preceding that on which trading commences (see 2(c) above).

(b) 1 July 1984 to 30 September 1984

This accounting period begins on 1 July on the day following the end of the previous accounting period (see 1(a) above).

The accounting period ends on 30 September, the date to which the company prepares its accounts (see 2(b) above).

(c) Each year to 30 September thereafter will be an accounting period for corporation tax purposes (see 2(b) above).

Example 3

Cort Ltd commenced trading on 1 July 1980 and made up accounts annually to 30 June. On 1 July 1982 the whole of the share capital of Cort Ltd was acquired by Mar Ltd which prepared accounts to 30 September. It was decided that Cort Ltd would have the same accounting date as its parent company and so accounts were prepared for Cort Ltd for the 15 month period from 1 July 1982 to 30 September 1983 and thereafter to 30 September each year.

The corporation tax accounting periods for Cort Ltd are as follows:

(a) The period of 12 months to 30 June 1981
(b) The period of 12 months to 30 June 1982

In both (a) and (b) the corporation tax accounting period follows the company's own accounting year. (see 2(b) above).

(c) The period of 12 months to 30 June 1983—S.247(3)(a) provides that an accounting period may not exceed 12 months in length (see 2(a) above).

(d) The period of 3 months to 30 September 1983—the remaining 3 months will form a separate accounting period which ends on the company's own accounting date (see 2(b) above).

(e) Thereafter each 12 month period beginning with the year to 30 September 1984 (see 2(b) above).

1.4 FINANCIAL YEARS

Corporation tax is charged for financial years at rates which are generally fixed annually in the Finance Act, in arrear. A financial year begins on 1 April in one year and ends on 31 March the next year, and is identified by the year in which it *begins*. Thus the financial year 1984 begins on 1 April 1984 and ends on 31 March 1985.

As we have seen, corporation tax assessments are made for specific accounting periods and in most cases the corporation tax accounting period will be the same as the period for which the company prepares accounts. If the accounting period runs from say 1 January 1985 to 31 December 1985, part of the accounting period is within Financial Year 1984 (i.e. the year from 1 April 1984 to 31 March 1985) and part of the accounting period is within Financial Year 1985 (i.e. the year from 1 April 1985 to 31 March 1986). In this case it is necessary to apportion the profits of the accounting period on a time basis between the financial years. The rate of tax for each financial year will then be applied to that part of the profits so apportioned (S.243(3) TA 1970).

Example 4
Assume that the accounts of AS Ltd show profits of £360,000 for the year to 31 December 1984 and £540,000 for the year to 31 December 1985, The rates of tax applicable for financial years 1983, 1984 and 1985 are 50%, 45% and 40% respectively.

The corporation tax payable will be calculated as follows:

	£
(i) *Accounting Period 1.1.84 to 31.12.84*	
Financial year 1983	
(1 January 1984 to 31 March 1984)	
£360,000 × 3/12 = 90,000 at 50%	45,000
Financial year 1984	
(1 April 1984 to 31 December 1984)	
£360,000 × 9/12 = 270,000 at 45%	121,500
Corporation tax payable	166,500

	£
(ii) *Accounting Period 1.1.85 to 31.12.85*	
Financial year 1984	
(1 January 1985 to 31 March 1985)	
£540,000 × 3/12 = 135,000 at 45%	60,750
Financial year 1985	
(1 April 1985 to 31 December 1985)	
£540,000 × 9/12 = 405,000 at 40%	162,000
Corporation tax payable	222,750

1.5 COMPUTATION OF PROFITS: Application of Income Tax Principles

Section 250, Taxes Act 1970 provides that for the purposes of corporation tax, income is to be computed in accordance with income tax
principles. This means, for example, that all the statutory and case law
rules about allowable deductions in arriving at trading profits for income
tax will apply in arriving at Schedule D Case I profits assessable to
corporation tax.

Subsection (3) of Section 250, Taxes Act 1970 puts the matter as
follows:

> Accordingly for purposes of corporation tax income shall be computed,
> and the assessment shall be made, under the like Schedules and Cases as
> apply for purposes of income tax, and in accordance with the provisions
> applicable to those Schedules and Cases, but (subject to the provisions of
> Corporation Tax Acts) the amounts so computed for the several sources of
> income, if more than one, together with any amount to be included in
> respect of chargeable gains, shall be aggregated to arrive at the total profits.

We would thus expect to find in a corporation tax computation a listing
of the company's income taxable under the various schedules and cases.
There is given in Appendix 1 a suggested layout for any corporation tax
computation showing not just items dealt with in this chapter but also
matters such as loss relief which are dealt with later in the book. You may
find it useful to refer to this form while studying the contents of this book
and indeed while carrying out any type of corporation tax calculation.

It is not proposed to discuss here all the income tax principles which
may apply to companies. Readers should refer to any standard work on
income tax. There are, however, a number of points which have special
significance for corporation tax computations and these are dealt with
below.

1.5.1 Schedule D Case I

Basis of Assessment
As we have seen when considering accounting periods, the basis of
assessment for corporation tax is the profits of the current year. This is in
contrast to the charge to income tax on a continuing business carried on
by a sole trader or partnership where the basis of assessment is the profits
for the accounting period that ended in the previous fiscal year.

Interest Payments
In the computation of the Schedule D Case I profits of a sole trader or
partnership all interest is generally allowable as a deduction so long as it is
incurred wholly and exclusively for the purposes of the trade. As regards
bank interest paid by a company and overdraft interest in particular this
is an allowable deduction for Schedule D Case I purposes. Other interest,
such as debenture interest may be deducted from total profits as a 'charge

on income' (see 1.7 below) but is not an allowable expense for Schedule D Case I purposes.

Capital Allowances

The capital allowances to which a company is entitled are calculated in the normal way by reference to the Capital Allowances Act 1968 and subsequent Finance Acts (see Chapter 2). For an individual taxpayer capital allowances are deducted *from* the Schedule D Case I profits when charging these profits to income tax. In the case of a company the capital allowances are normally treated in every respect like trading expenses and are deducted *in arriving at* the Schedule D Case I profit. This apparently small practical difference between the two taxes has a significant effect in certain situations, for example where losses arise. In the same way balancing charges arising to a company are treated as trading receipts and are *included* in the Schedule D Case I profits.

Example 5

The accounts of Sunspin Ltd show a net profit of £122,000 after deducting depreciation of £5,000 and debenture interest of £10,000. It is ascertained that the company is entitled to a writing down allowance of £1,725 and a first year allowance of £8,000. A balancing charge of £2,000 arises on the sale of the Managing Director's car.

The Schedule D Case I computation will be as follows:

	£	£
Profit per accounts		122,000
Add: Depreciation	5,000	
Debenture interest	10,000	15,000
		137,000
Deduct: Capital allowances		
WDA	1,725	
FYA	8,000	9,725
		127,275
Add: Balancing charge		2,000
Schedule D Case I profit		129,275

1.5.2 Schedule D Case III

It is an income tax principle that interest assessed under Schedule D Case III (interest received gross) is the interest arising in the basis period. The term 'arising' means the crediting of interest in the taxpayer's account in the books of a bank or other debtor. This income tax principle applies for corporation tax also and only interest *arising* in the corporation tax accounting period will be included under Schedule D Case III in the company's computation of total profits. It follows that any interest which a company may have accrued at the year end is not brought into the corporation tax computation.

Example 6
The accounts of Tacker Ltd include a credit of £6,350 in respect of bank deposit account interest. This is made up as follows:

	£
Received in accounting period	6,000
Interest accrued at end of accounting period	350
	6,350

If the net profit shown in the profit and loss account is £100,000, the Schedule D Case I computation will proceed as follows:

	£
Profit per accounts	100,000
Deduct: Deposit account interest	6,350
Schedule D Case I profit	93,650

The Schedule D Case III figure to be included in the corporation tax computation will be £6,000, since this is the amount of interest that arose in the accounting period.

You will note from this example that the amount of interest which is deducted in arriving at the Schedule D Case I profit is not necessarily the same figure as will be included in the corporation tax computation under the Case III heading.

1.5.3 Income from which income tax has been deducted

Certain types of interest received by an individual for example interest from government securities are received net of basic rate income tax. These types of interest, when received by a company, are known as unfranked investment income. The term unfranked investment income is not defined in the legislation but is commonly used to distinguish such income from franked investment income which is described below. To say that income is unfranked means that the profits out of which the income has been paid have not been 'franked' or charged to corporation tax. The loan interest or charge on income has been deducted from the total profits of the paying company before arriving at profits chargeable to corporation tax and is thus paid out of profits *before* tax.

A company in receipt of unfranked investment income receives an amount net of basic rate tax. It is, however, the gross amount of unfranked income that is included in its total profits in the corporation tax computation.

Example 7
In the year to 31 March 1985 the company has adjusted trading profits of
£65,000 and receives debenture interest of £700.

The corporation tax computation for Dragon Ltd will take the following
form:

	£
Schedule D Case I	65,000
Unfranked investment income	
$700 \times \dfrac{100}{70}$	1,000
Total profits	66,000

It will be seen that the gross amount of debenture interest of £1,000 has
been included in the computation although only £700 was received.

It has been stated earlier that the only tax chargeable on companies is
corporation tax. However, in the case of <u>unfranked</u> investment income
the income has already suffered income tax by deduction at source. It
follows that some means must be provided to give the company relief for
the income tax that has been deducted by the payer.

There are three possible ways whereby the company may obtain this
relief:-

(a) By setting off income tax suffered against income tax which the
    company hs deducted from loan interest, debenture interest or any
    other 'charge' which it may have paid during the accounting
    period. See 1.8 'Accounting for income tax'.
(b) By setting off the income tax suffered against the corporation tax
    payable for the same accounting period (see Example 9).
(c) If the two former possibilities are not applicable the income tax
    suffered will be repaid to the company, when the corporation tax
    computation has been agreed with the Inspector of Taxes.

Example 8
We have seen in Example 7 that the total profits of Dragon Ltd for the year
ended 31 March 1985 are £66,000.
If we assume a corporation tax rate of 30%, the corporation tax payable by
Dragon Ltd will be:

	£
£66,000 × 30%	19,800
Less: Income tax suffered by deduction on	
unfranked investment income	300
Corporation tax payable	19,500

Thus Dragon Ltd has obtained relief for the £300 income tax deducted at
source from the debenture interest by deducting it from the corporation tax
payable.

Example 9
Assume that as a result of utilizing trading losses surrendered under the group relief provisions (see Chapter 4) Dragon Ltd has no profits liable to corporation tax.

In these circumstances there is no corporation tax liability against which to set the income tax suffered and therefore the company will be entitled to have the income tax of £300 repaid. (S.240(5) TA 1970).

In certain circumstances a company may have a corporation tax liability of an amount which is smaller than the amount of income tax suffered by deduction at source. In this case the company will obtain relief for the income tax suffered:

Firstly by set off against the corporation tax liability; and
Secondly by repayment of the balance.

Example 10
Mainsell Ltd receives unfranked investment income of £1,400 (net) in its accounting year to 31 March 1983. The gross amount of the unfranked investment income, £2,000 will be included in the corporation tax computation leaving £600 of income tax suffered, for which relief must be obtained.

Mainsell's corporation tax liability for the year to 31 March 1983 has been agreed at £450 (after application of loss relief).

Relief for the income tax deducted from the unfranked investment income is obtained as follows:

	£
Income tax suffered	600
Set off against	
corporation tax liability	450
Balance to be repaid to company	150

You may be aware that from 6 April 1985 bank deposit account interest received by an *individual* will be received under deduction of income tax, i.e. net. However, companies will continue to receive bank deposit account interest gross, and therefore this type of income will not be treated as unfranked investment income of a company.

1.5.4 Building society interest

When an individual taxpayer receives building society interest it has to be grossed up at the basic rate of tax for the fiscal year in which the interest is received. The gross sum is then included in his total income for income tax purposes. Similarly when a company receives building society interest this is treated as having been received net of basic rate income tax. Accordingly when calculating the amount of building society interest to be included in the corporation tax computation the interest received must be grossed up by reference to the basic rate of income tax currently in force. (Multiplied by 100/70 when the basic rate of income tax is 30%). The credit for the income tax suffered may then be deducted from the corporation tax payable or repaid to the company. The credit *may not* be set against income tax which the company has itself retained under the provisions of Schedule 20 FA 1972 (see 1.7 below). The possibility of repayment distinguishes the company position from that of an individual. An individual taxpayer cannot receive a repayment of the income tax which is treated as deducted from building society interest (S.343 TA 1970).

1.5.5. Distributions received

Dividends and other distributions received from UK resident companies are not included in the calculation of profits chargeable to corporation tax (S.239 TA 1970). The question of how this income is treated for taxation purposes is dealt with in Chapter 3.

1.6 COMPUTATION OF PROFITS: Application of Capital Gains Tax Principles

The total profits of a company for corporation tax include chargeable gains which if realized by an individual would be charged to capital gains tax. Such chargeable gains are to be computed on the basis of the rules which apply for capital gains tax (S.265(2) TA 1970). Any allowable capital losses will be deducted in arriving at the amount of gains to be included in total profits. Such losses may be losses of the current accounting period or losses brought forward from earlier accounting periods. Although there are extensive provisions for relieving trading losses, which are described in Chapter 4, the rules for the relief of capital losses are much more restrictive. The company may set-off a capital loss against gains of the current accounting period and may carry forward the balance of the loss for set-off against gains arising in future accounting periods. There are no provisions for set off of capital losses against any profits other than chargeable gains. Likewise there are no provisions which permit a company to carry back a capital loss for set-off against the chargeable gains of earlier accounting periods.

The maximum capital gains tax liability on chargeable gains realized by an individual is 30%. In order to apply an effective rate of 30% to chargeable gains arising to companies it is necessary to reduce (or abate) the gain liable to corporation tax. Thus for the financial year 1984 the amount of chargeable gain to be included in the corporation tax computation is reduced by 1/3 and so only 2/3 of the gain is brought into the computation. This proportion will be charged to corporation tax at the normal rate in force for the relevant financial year.

The fractions by which chargeable gains are to be abated are given below for all financial years from 1983 to 1986:

Financial Year	Reducing Fraction
1983	2/5
1984	1/3
1985	1/4
1986	1/7

Example 11

Morgan Ltd disposed of three chargeable assets in its accounting year to 31 March 1985. Capital gains and losses are as follows:

	£
Asset No. 1 — gain	10,600
Asset No. 2 — gain	3,400
Asset No. 3 — loss	4,000
The net gain is £10,000	
Tax computation is:	
Chargeable gains	10,000
Less: 10,000 × 1/3	3,333
	―――
Chargeable gain	6,667

Corporation tax on chargeable gain of £6,667 will be
$$£6,667 \times 45\% = \quad £3,000$$
Note that the tax on the abated chargeable gains, £3,000, is 30% of the unabated chargeable gains.

After the one third abatement has been applied the reduced gain is charged at 45%. In certain circumstances a company's income is liable to what is called a small company rate of corporation tax at a lower rate of 30 per cent instead of the normal rate. The lower rate may *never* be applied to chargeable gains. The chargeable gains will always be charged to corporation tax at the full rate.

A change in the rate of corporation tax means that the fraction used to abate the chargeable gains will change. Where different fractions are in force for different parts of the accounting period in which the chargeable gain is realized the gain is apportioned between the different parts on a time basis and the appropriate fraction applied to the apportioned amount (S.93 FA 1972).

Example 12

Hanoverian Ltd realizes a chargeable gain of £28,000 in its accounting period of twelve months ended 31 December 1986.
The relevant rate of tax are:

	FY 1985	FY 1986
Corporation tax	40%	35%
Abatement of chargeable gains	1/4	1/7

Corporation tax on the chargeable gain is as follows:

Financial year 1985
1.1.86–31.3.86

	£
£28,000 × 3/12	7,000

Gain	7,000
Less: Abatement £7,000 × 1/4	1,750
	5,250

Corporation tax payable:	
£5,250 × 40%	2,100

Financial year 1986
1.4.86–31.12.86

	£
£28,000 × 9/12	21,000

Gain	21,000
Less: Abatement £21,000 × 1/7	3,000
	18,000

Corporation tax payable:	
18,000 × 35%	6,300

So far we have been considering the nature of the total profits of a company for corporation tax purposes. It will, however, be seen from the pro forma in Appendix 1 that certain deductions may be made in calculating the profits chargeable to corporation tax. The deductions which may be made under the heading of 'Charges' are considered below.

1.7 CHARGES ON INCOME

Charges are defined as:

(a) any yearly interest, annuity or other annual payment, e.g. royalties;
(b) any other interest paid to a bank, stockbroker or discount house carrying on business in the UK (S.248 TA 1970).

The definition excludes any payment which is deductible as an expense in computing the Case I profit or any other kind of profit. In particular bank overdraft interest is commonly deductible in computing trading profits for the purposes of corporation tax and in such cases will not be treated as a charge. All other types of interest, for example debenture interest, will be added back in arriving at the Case I liability and will then be deducted from total profits (including the chargeable gains) so long as the interest payments meet certain conditions. The conditions which must be satisfied for the deduction of interest as a charge and for the deduction of any other type of annual payment are briefly as follows:

(i)   The charges must be ultimately borne by the company claiming relief for the payment. Thus if a parent company were to debit interest to the receivable account of a subsidiary the interest could not be said to be 'ultimately borne' by the parent company.

(ii)   A charge cannot be deducted from the company's total profits until it has actually been paid. Interest in the accounts of a company will commonly include interest accrued or payable. These accrued amounts will not be deductible as charges.

Example 13
In the year ended 30 September 1983 the trading profit in the accounts of Cobber Ltd is arrived at after deducting royalties of £3,000 for the use of certain patented processes. The figure of £3,000 is made up as follows:

	Gross amounts
	£
Royalties paid in year	2,000
Add: Accrued year ended 30.9.83	2,500
	4,500
Less: Accrued year ended 30.9.82	1,500
	3,000

In computing the amount of the Schedule D Case I profits for the year ended 30 September 1983 the royalties of £3,000 will be added back.
The amount deductible from total profits under the heading of Charges on Income will be the gross amount of the royalties *actually paid* — i.e. £2,000.

(iii) The definition of a charge includes a covenanted donation to a charity which can continue for more than three years, for example a four year deed of covenant. A charitable deed of covenant is broadly an agreement between say company A and charity X whereby company A undertakes to pay the charity a fixed sum for a specified number of years.

A purely gratuitous payment (other than one under the terms of a four year deed of covenant) cannot be a charge.

1.7.1 Excess charges

A distinction is frequently drawn in practice between payments of debenture interest, royalties, etc., called trade charges and covenanted donations to charities called non-trade charges. The importance of this distinction arises when a company pays charges in a particular period which exceed the total profits, leaving a certain amount of charges for that accounting period which can not be utilized at that time.

Example 14
Freedland Ltd is a manufacturing company which prepares accounts to 31 December. In the year to 31 December 1983 the company has total profits of £5,000. In the same period the company paid the following charges:

	£
Payments under deed of covenant to charity	6,000
Debenture interest	1,000

The corporation tax computation will proceed as follows:

	£	£
Total profits		5,000
Less: Charges		
Deed of covenant to charity	6,000	
Debenture interest	1,000	
	7,000	
Limited to		5,000
Profits chargeable to corporation tax		Nil

The amount of unrelieved charges = £7,000 − £5,000 = £2,000, is called an 'excess of charges'.

Where there is an excess of charges over total profits the balance can be carried forward and set off against future *trading* profits but only in so far as the charges were incurred wholly and exclusively for the purposes of the trade. That is to say only in so far as they are trade charges (S.177(8) TA 1970).

Thus 'trade charges' can be carried forward but 'non-trade charges' can not be carried forward. In this situation it is clearly beneficial for a company to set non-trade charges paid in a particular accounting period against the total profits for that accounting period in priority to trade charges, since the balance of the non-trade charges can not be utilized in future years.

Example 15
In Example 14 Freedland Ltd had unrelieved charges of £2,000 for the accounting period ended on 31 December 1983. This figure may be

analysed as follows:

	£	£
Payments under deed of covenant	6,000	
Less: set against total profits	5,000	
		1,000
Debenture interest		1,000
Unrelieved charges		2,000

The payment under deed of covenant is not a trade charge and so the company will be unable to carry forward the unused amount of £1,000. The company will therefore not obtain relief for this payment.

The debenture interest is a trade charge and so the figure of £1,000 may be carried forward under the provisions of S.177(8).

One further point should be noted regarding the carry forward of excess charges. In subsequent years these charges are to be considered as trading expenses and are set off against trading profits in arriving at the Schedule D Case I amount; they may *not* be set against the total profits. Thus in any corporation tax computation it is necessary to distinguish between charges brought forward and charges paid in the relevant accounting period.

Example 16

Greenland Ltd has the following results for the two years ended 31 March 1984:

	Year ended 31.3.83 £	Year ended 31.3.84 £
Adjusted trading profits	1,250	10,000
Chargeable gains (abated)	2,000	3,000
Payment under deed of covenant to charity	4,000	4,000
Debenture interest	2,500	2,500

Profits chargeable to Corporation Tax will be calculated as follows:

Year ended 31.3.83

	£	£
Schedule D Case I		1,250
Chargeable gain (abated)		2,000
		3,250
Less: Charges		
Charity	4,000	
Debenture interest	2,500	
	6,500	

	£	
Limited to		3,250
		———
Profits chargeable to corporation tax		Nil
		———

Charges carried forward S.177(8) TA 1970 £2,500 (note that the unutilized portion of the payment under deed of covenant to charity may *not* be carried forward.

Year ended 31.3.84

	£	£
Trading profits		10,000
Less: Charges brought		
forward (S.177(8))		2,500
		———
Schedule D Case I		7,500
Chargeable gains (abated)		3,000
		———
		10,500
Less: Charges paid in		
current year:		
Charity	4,000	
Debenture interest	2,500	
	———	
		6,500
		———
Profits chargeable to		
corporation tax		4,000
		———

1.7.2 Deduction of income tax from charges paid

When a company pays debenture interest, royalties or similar charges on income it must deduct income tax at the basic rate for the year in which the payment is made (Ss.53 and 54 TA 1970). The tax which is deducted from the payments made is accounted for in the manner described below.

This procedure of 'deduction of tax at source' is a long-standing method of collection of income tax. In deducting income tax from payments in this way and accounting for that tax to the Inland Revenue, companies are acting a tax collectors.

Example 17
Blueland Ltd is a manufacturing company which prepares accounts to 31 December each year. In the year to 31 December 1983 the company has an obligation to pay debenture interest of £10,000.

On making the payment of £10,000 Blueland Ltd must deduct income tax at the basic rate and thus £7,000 will go to the debenture holders and £3,000 is accounted for to the Inland Revenue.

It is common, in company accounts and elsewhere, to talk about an amount of charges having been paid, referring to a gross amount. You should remember that this gross amount is in two parts: one part which is paid to the individual creditor and the other part which is accounted for to the Inland Revenue. Nevertheless it is the gross amount which is deducted in the corporation tax computation.

1.8 ACCOUNTING FOR INCOME TAX

We have seen that income tax is deducted at source by companies from payments of loan interest and other charges and that the income tax is then paid to the Inland Reveue. The arrangements whereby the company notifies the Revenue of the amounts of income tax deducted from each charge, or 'relevant payment' are set out in Sch. 20 FA 1972.

A company makes a return of relevant payments made by it in each return period. A return period is:

(a) Each complete quarter of the calendar year falling within the company's accounting period, i.e. each of the periods of 3 months ending with 31 March, 30 June, 30 September and 31 December.

(b) If the company does not prepare its accounts to a quarter date then the period from the beginning of the company's own accounting period to the next quarter date forms a separate return period and likewise the period from the last quarter date to the end of the company's own accounting period forms another return period.

Example 18
Accounts are prepared by Fotheringholt Ltd for its year ended 31 August 1984. For Schedule 20 Finance Act 1972 purposes the return periods will be as follows:
1 September 1983—30 September 1983
  — period from commencement of accounting period to next quarter date
1 October 1983—31 December 1983
  — quarterly return period
1 January 1984—31 March 1984
  — quarterly return period
1 April 1984—30 June 1984
  — quarterly return period
1 July 1984—31 August 1984
  — period from last quarter date to end of company's own accounting period.

A company will make a return on a form called a CT61 to the Collector of Taxes within 14 days of the end of each return period and pay over any income tax which is due within the same time.

The company is liable to pay to the Collector, income tax at the basic rate which has been deducted from relevant payments made. However, the company may claim on form CT61 to set off against this income tax, any income tax which the company itself has suffered by deduction from its unfranked investment income (Para. 5 Sch. 20 FA 1972).

Example 19
Sumac Ltd prepares accounts to 31 December each year. In the return period running from 1 January 1984 to 31 March 1984 the following transactions take place:

10 February 1984 pays patent royalties
(net) of £3,500 (tax deducted £1,500)
26 February 1984 receives debenture interest
(net) of £1,400 (tax suffered £600)

Sumac Ltd may set off the income tax suffered of £600 against the income tax of £1,500 which it has deducted from the patent royalties paid on 10 February 1984. The amount of income tax payable to the Collector of Taxes is thus reduced to £900 (i.e. £1,500 less £600), payable fourteen days after the end of the return period, i.e. by 14 April 1984.

If a company pays income tax to the Collector of Taxes in respect of a relevant payment in one return period and then in a subsequent return period within the same accounting period it suffers income tax by deduction from unfranked investment income which it receives, the company may claim a repayment of income tax on the form CT61.

Example 20
Brinog Ltd prepares accounts to 31 March each year. On 16 April 1984 Brinog Ltd has an obligation to pay loan interest of £9,000. On 17 August it has the right to receive debenture interest of £6,000

Return period 1.4.84—30.6.84
A payment of £6,300 is sent to the lender. This represents the £9,000 due less income tax of £2,700 (30% of £9,000).
The income tax of £2,700 is paid to the Collector on 14.7.84

Return period 1.7.84—30.9.84
Company is entitled to receive debenture interest of £6,000 but actually receives a payment of £4,200 being the amount remaining after deduction of income tax (at 30%) of £1,800.
At this point the overall position is as follows:

	£
Income tax deducted from relevant payments	2,700
Income tax suffered by deduction from debenture interest	1,800
Net amount due to Inland Revenue	900

Since the company paid the collector £2,700 at the end of the first return period a repayment is made to the company as follows:

	£
Income tax paid to Collector of Taxes 14.7.84	2,700
Net income tax due to Revenue	900
Therefore repayment to be made by Collector	1,800

1.9 RATES OF CORPORATION TAX

For the financial years 1973 to 1983 the rates of corporation tax for one particular year have been fixed in the Finance Act passed in the following year. Thus the rates for financial year 1982 were announced in the budget speech of March 1983 and enacted in the first Finance Act of 1983.

In 1984 the Chancellor of the Exchequer took the unusual step of announcing the rates of corporation tax for the financial years 1983 to 1986. These are set out below:

Financial year	Rate of tax	Small company rate	Marginal relief fraction
1983	50%	30%	1/20
1984	45%	30%	3/80
1985	40%	30%	1/40
1986	35%	30%	1/80

The small company rate is applied to companies whose *profits* as specifically defined in S.95 FA 1972, fall below certain limits. The matter of the small company rate and the marginal relief fraction is discussed immediately below.

Small Company Rate
It is generally recognized that smaller companies must look to internal sources to finance their development. Because such small companies have limited access to capital other than those profits which they themselves can generate, the legislation provides in S.95 FA 1972, for a lower than normal rate of corporation tax to be charged on those companies.

For the financial years 1983 to 1986 it is provided that if a company has *profits* for a twelve month accounting period of not more than £100,000 then the *income* of the company will be charged at the small company rate.

The term *profits* for the small company rate is defined as:
Profits chargeable to corporation tax plus franked investment income.

Any franked investment income which a company receives from a 51% subsidiary and which if the companies elected would be group income (see Chapter 5) is ignored—i.e. is not included in the total of franked investment income to be added to chargeable profits (S.95(7) FA 1972).

The term *income* is the same for small company rate purposes as for general purposes, namely:
Profits chargeable to corporation tax less chargeable gains included therein (S.85(6) FA 1972).

The significance of deducting chargeable gains is that they are taxed at the full corporation tax rate. The thinking behind excluding chargeable gains from the small company rate is that chargeable gains included in total profits already benefit from an abatement and it is not desired to give further relief for such gains by the application of a lower rate of corporation tax.

You will note that the small company rate applies whenever profits are below a certain figure. In the nature of things small companies will make small profits and will benefit from the reduced rate. But there is no theoretical reason why a large company, or indeed a company of any size should not benefit from the application of the small rate if its profits are not in excess of the limit.

Example 21
Singo Ltd has the following results for the year ended 31 March 1984.

	£
Schedule D Case I	42,500
Schedule D Case III	1,000
Schedule A	2,000
Abated chargeable gain	1,500
Debenture interest paid	3,000
Franked investment income	12,000

The *profits* as defined in S.95(7) FA 1972 are

	£
Schedule D Case I	42,500
Schedule D Case III	1,000
Schedule A	2,000
Chargeable gain	1,500
Total profits	47,000
Less: Charges	3,000
Profits chargeable to corporation tax	44,000
Add: Franked investment income	12,000
'Profits' as defined in (S.95(7) FA 1972)	56,000

Since the *profits* do not exceed £100,000 the *income* will be charged at the small company rate of 30%. The abated portion of the chargeable gains is *always* charged to corporation tax at the full rate.

The company's *income* is:

	£
Profit chargeable to Corporation Tax	44,000
Less: Chargeable gain	1,500
'Income' (S.85(6) FA 1971)	42,500

The corporation tax payable is:

	£
£42,500 at 30%	12,750
£1,500 (chargeable gain) at 50%	750
	13,500

Where the accounting period is less than twelve months the figure of £100,000 will be proportionately reduced. Thus if the accounting period of Singo Ltd in Example 21 was six months in length, the small company rate would only apply if the 'profits' were less than $6/12 \times £100,000 = £50,000$.

One further anti-avoidance provision applies to stop the splitting up of a company's business among several companies in order that each benefits from the lower rate. If a company has one or more associated companies the limit of £100,000 must be reduced by dividing the limit by one plus the number of associated companies that the company has. Thus if a company has 2 associated companies the small company relief limit becomes:

$$\frac{100,000}{1 + 2} = £33,333 \text{ (S.95(3) FA 1972)}$$

For these purposes one company is an associated company of another if one of them has control of the other, or if both are under the control of the same company or person. Any associated company which has been dormant throughout the relevant accounting period is disregarded.

Marginal Small Companies Relief

We have seen that the small companies rate of corporation tax does not apply to companies whose profits exceed £100,000. In order to lessen the impact of the differential between the small companies rate and the normal rate S.95(2) FA 1972 provides a method of increasing the rate gradually for companies with profits exceeding £100,000 but less than £500.000.

In order to achieve this graduation the following method is applied:

(i) Charge the *income* at the normal full rate (the abated chargeable gains will be taxable at this rate in any case).
(ii) Deduct from the corporation tax so computed an amount calculated in accordance with a formula contained in the legislation (S.95(2) FA 1972 and S.27(2) FA 1976).

For Financial Year 1984 the formula is as follows:

$$\frac{3}{80} (M - P) \times \frac{I}{P}$$

In this formula:

M is the 'Upper Relevant Amount' i.e. £500,000
P is the amount of the 'profits' (as defined above)
I is the amount of the 'income' (as defined above)

Example 22

Pandate Ltd prepares accounts to 31 March each year and the results for the year ended 31 March 1985 are as follows:

	£
Schedule D Case I	230,000
Unfranked investment income	3,000
Chargeable gain (abated)	10,000
Franked investment income	40,000
Debenture interest paid	5,000

	£
The total profits liable to corporation tax are:	
Schedule D Case I	230,000
Unfranked investment income	3,000
Chargeable gain	10,000
	243,000
Less: Charges	5,000
Profits chargeable to corporation tax	238,000

The S.95(2) 'profits' for marginal small companies relief purposes are:

	£
Profits chargeable to corporation tax	238,000
Add: Franked investment income	40,000
	278,000

The company's 'income' is:

	£
Profits chargeable to corporation tax	238,000
Less: Chargeable gain	10,000
	228,000

The corporation tax payable is calculated as follows:

	£
£238,000 × 45%	107,000

Less: Marginal small companies relief:

$$\frac{3}{80}(M - P) \times \frac{I}{P}$$

$$= \frac{3}{80}(500{,}000 - 278{,}000) \times \frac{228{,}000}{278{,}000} \qquad 6{,}828$$

Corporation tax payable	100,272

As with the small companies relief there are anti-avoidance provisions dealing with accounting periods of less than 12 months and associated companies.

If in Example 22 the accounting period of Pandate Ltd was 9 months in length instead of 12 months the Upper Relevant Maximum amount would become £375,000 (£500,000 × 9/12) and the Lower Relevant Maximum amount would be £75,000 (£100,000 × 9/12).

If Pandate Ltd had three associated companies and none were dormant then the Upper and Lower Relevant Maximum amounts applicable for a 12 month accounting period would become £125,000 (£500,000 ÷ (1 + 3)) and £25,000 (£100,000 ÷ (1 + 3)).

1.10 DATES FOR PAYMENT OF CORPORATION TAX

In general the corporation tax assessed for an accounting period is payable within nine months of the end of that accounting period or, if it is later, thirty days from the date of issue of the notice of assessment (S.243(4) TA 1970).

The general rule regarding payment of corporation tax does not apply to companies which were within the charge to income tax on the profits of a trade before the financial year 1965. Prior to the introduction of corporation tax these companies paid income tax under Schedule D Case I and assessments were normally on a preceeding year basis. Thus the 1965/66 income tax assessment of a company, say X Ltd with annual accounts ending on 30 June would have as its basis period the year ended 30 June 1964. Income tax charged in this assessment was due on 1 January 1966 and so there was a gap of 18 months between the end of the accounting period and the payment of tax.

Section 244 TA 1970 provides that where a company conducts a trade and was within the charge to income tax in respect of that trade prior to 1 April 1965 the same interval of time should elapse between the end of an accounting period and the due date for payment of corporation tax as lay between the end of the basis period for 1965/66 and 1 January 1966. Thus X Ltd will be entitled to retain the 18 month gap between the end of its accounting period and the date of payment of corporation tax for so long as it continues to carry on the same trade. This will be so whether or not the accounting periods of the company continue to end on 30 June each year.

Example 23
Green Ltd is a trading company established in 1950. Accounts were prepared to 30 September each year down to 30 September 1975. Thereafter it prepared accounts annually to 31 December beginning with accounts for a period of 15 months to 31 December 1976.

For all accounting periods ending on 31 September the due date for payment of corporation tax is 1 January, 15 months later.

For the three month accounting period running from 1 October 1976 to 31 December 1976 the due date for payment is 1 April 1978, 15 months later. For all subsequent accounting periods to 31 December the due date is also 1 April, 15 months later.

1.11 GENERAL ADMINISTRATIVE PROVISIONS

The general administrative provisions regarding appeals against assessments to tax and payments to account (S.55 TMA 1970) apply to corporation tax. Where a taxpayer disagrees with the amount of an assessment he appeals against the assessment within thirty days of the date of issue of the notice of assessment. The appeal will be to the General Commissioners unless the taxpayer elects to bring the appeal before the Special Commissioners. If the taxpayer wishes to postpone all or part of the tax charged by the assessment he must make a claim to the Inspector, again within 30 days of the date of issue of the notice of assessment.

1.12 INTEREST ON OVERDUE CORPORATION TAX

Corporation tax is payable generally nine months from the end of the relevant accounting period or thirty days from the date of issue of the notice of assessment if this is later. For some trading companies the period of time from the end of the accounting period to the date for payment of tax is longer (see 1.10 above).

All of the above dates for payment are called normal due dates. Where a company has appealed against an assessment and at the same time claimed to postpone payment of some part of the tax charged, the due date for payment is different for tax postponed and for tax not postponed.

(a) Tax postponed is due after the Commissioners have heard the appeal on the assessment and determined the matter in dispute. An agreement with the Inspector of Taxes after the company has appealed against an assessment has the same force in law as a hearing and determination by Commissioners (S.55(7) and (9) TMA 1970). Following a determination by Commissioners (or its equivalent) the Inspector issues a notice of the tax payable and this is treated from the point of view of due dates for payment as if it were an assessment issued on the date the Inspector issues his notice. This means that corporation tax which is postponed is due thirty days from the date of the notice if this is later than the normal due date.

(b) As regards the payment to account, i.e., the tax not postponed, this is due thirty days after the Inspector has agreed to the amount to be postponed which is, by corollary, the amount to be paid to account (S.55(6) TMA 1970).

The date from which interest on unpaid corporation tax runs is called the reckonable date (S.86(1), TMA 1970). If a company does not appeal against an assessment or appeals against an assessment but does not claim to postpone any of the tax charged, the normal due date is the reckonable date and interest runs from that date.

If, however, the company appeals against an assessment, and claims to postpone tax, interest on tax postponed and tax not postponed will run from the reckonable date in accordance with the following rule.

Where an appeal has been made with a claim to postponement, the reckonable date is the later of the normal due date which would have applied if there had been no appeal and the earlier of two other dates. The two others dates (of which the earlier is relevant) are the due date (which refers to tax postponed or not postponed) and the 'table date'. The table date for corporation tax is a date six months after the nine months (or longer period for companies trading before 1985) following the end of the accounting period (S.86(4), TMA 1970).

Example 24

Moreover Ltd was incorporated in 1970 and makes up its accounts annually to 31 March each year. With respect to the year ended 31 March 1984, the following dates are relevant to the payment of corporation tax and interest on unpaid tax:

> Normal due date: 31 December 1984
> Table date: 30 June 1985

The company has appealed against an assessment for the accounting period ended 31 March 1984 on which corporation tax payable is £150,000. The company claims to postpone payment of £30,000 of the tax charged; accordingly the tax not postponed, or the payment to account, is £120,000. After correspondence and discussions with the Inspector the total tax payable on the assessment is agreed at £170,000 and the Inspector issues a notice showing a balance due of £50,000 (£30,000 postponed, plus £20,000 additional tax due).

The relevant dates are as follows:

Date of issue of original assessment	30 November 1984
Date of appeal and claim to postponement	1 December 1984
Date of Inspector's agreement to the amount of tax to be postponed	18 January 1985
Date of issue of notice for balance of tax following agreement with Inspector	12 July 1985

Interest runs from the reckonable dates which are as follows:

Tax postponed

The due date is 11 August 1985 (30 days from the date of issue of notice for balance of tax). The table date (a fixed date) is 30 June 1985. The earlier date is 30 June 1985.

The reckonable date is the later of the normal due date (had there been no appeal)—31 December 1984, and the earlier of the due date and table date—30 June 1985. Since 30 June 1985 is later, this is the reckonable date.

Tax not postponed

The due date is 17 February 1985 (30 days from date of Inspector's agreement—S.55(6)(a), TMA 1970). The table date, as before, is 30 June 1985. The earlier date of these two dates is 17 February 1985.

The reckonable date is the later of the normal due date, had there been no appeal—31 December 1984, and the earlier of the due and table dates, 17 February 1985. 17 February 1985, being later, is the reckonable date.

Additional tax

The balance of the corporation tax due, £50,000, is made up of £30,000, the tax postponed, and an additional amount of tax which was not charged in the notice of assessment isued on 30 November 1984, £20,000. The reckonable date in the case of the additional tax is to be computed as if the additional tax had been included in the original assessment and postponed. It follows that both the due date for payment and the reckonable date are as for tax postponed, namely 11 August 1985 and 30 June 1985 respectively. This means that we have a somewhat strange situation where interest runs from a date which is earlier than the due date for payment (Ss.55(9) and 86(3)(aa) TMA 1979).

Interest on overdue tax is not allowable as a deduction for corporation tax purposes.

1.13 REPAYMENT SUPPLEMENTS

A repayment of corporation tax by the Inland Revenue made more than twelve months after the 'material date' carries with it a repayment supplement, which is an amount of tax-free interest (S.48(1) and (2), F.(2)A. 1975). Interest is paid only for complete tax months and runs from the 6th of the month following the date 12 months after the 'material date'. Tax months begin on the 6th of one month and end on the 5th of the following month (S.47(2), F.(2)A. 1975). To qualify for a supplement the repayment must be in excess of £100 (S.48(2), F.(2)A. 1975).

The 'material date' means the normal due date for payment of tax, nine months from the end of the accounting period (or longer period in the case of a pre-1965 company) (S.48(9), F.(2)A. 1975).

If corporation tax for an accounting period was paid more than a year after the material date, interest on a subsequent repayment runs only from the 6th of the calendar month after the next anniversary of the material date.

Example 25

(a) Y Ltd pays corporation tax of £80,000 for the accounting period ended 31 December 1984, on its normal due date (the material date), 1 January 1986. By reason of a S.177(2) TA 1970 loss claim, £50,000 of the tax for the accounting period ended 31 December 1984 is repaid on 5 August 1987. The £50,000 will be supplemented by a payment of interest in respect of the period 6 January 1987, to 5 August 1987.

(b) If Y Ltd had not paid its £80,000 corporation tax liability until 5 January 1987 (more than 12 months after the material date), no interest supplement would be payable if the repayment was on 5 August 1987 (since interest runs from the next anniversary of the material date).

(c) If, as in (b) above, the corporation tax liability had been paid on 5 January 1987, but the repayment by the Revenue was not made until 5 September 1988, interest would be paid for the period 6 January 1988 to 5 September 1988.

Question 1

Exer Sighs Ltd is a company which has been manufacturing keep-fit equipment since 1960. The following is a summary of its profit and loss account for the year ended 31 March 1984:

	£
Trading profit	75,075
Add: Other income	9,000
	84,075
Deduct: Charges (gross)	7,000
Profit before taxation	77,075

Notes:
(1) Trading profit was arrived at after charging:
   (a) Directors' fees   £45,000
   (b) Depreciation   £11,625
   (c) Loss on sale of machine   £650
(2) Other income consisted of:
   (a) Franked investment income of £2,000 received in September 1983 from a holding of preference shares in Running Boards Ltd.
   (b) Deposit account interest £300.
   (c) Debenture interest of £6,200 (gross) received from Upton Downies Ltd.
   (d) Building Society interest £500.
(3) Charges comprised:
   (a) Annual payment to a charity under a four year deed of covenant £2,000.
   (b) Loan interest of £5,000. This is payable in two instalments on 30 September and 31 March each year. The payment due on 31 March 1984 was not made until 10 April 1984.
The company disposed of a small office unit on 2 February 1984 and a chargeable gain of £56,000 arises.
The capital allowances for the year ended 31 March 1984 have been calculated at £26,350.
Required:
Calculate the corporation tax payable in respect of the accounting period ended 31 March 1984 and state the date by which the tax should be paid.

CHAPTER 2

CAPITAL ALLOWANCES

2.1 PRINCIPLES OF CAPITAL ALLOWANCES

The general prohibition against the deduction of capital expenditure in computing Schedule D Case I profits (S.130(f), TA 1970) applies in particular to depreciation charged in a company's accounts. Accounting depreciation traditionally seeks to spread the cost of assets over the years and is an approximate financial measure of the physical deterioration of assets through their limited lives.

In the computation of Schedule D Case I profits for corporation tax purposes the disallowed accounting depreciation is replaced by a complex and highly detailed system of capital allowances. As previously stated such allowances are normally treated for corporation tax as trading expenses and if in the operation of the rules a balancing charge arises such a charge is treated as trading income (S.73(2) CAA 1968).

Capital allowances incorporate two elements: depreciation proper of the familiar accounting kind and an economic element which seeks to offer an incentive to investment usually in the form of accelerated rates at which the cost of assets is written off. The allowances are also selective. All assets do not qualify for allowances; and certain assets only qualify if they are of a certain size or are located in certain parts of the country.

Reliefs for capital expenditure fall broadly into two systems, that instituted in 1945 which provides relief for expenditure on industrial buidings and structures and that legislated for in 1971 which established the modern framework for reliefs in respect of plant and machinery. Outside of these two systems there exists a wide range of specific reliefs for particular kinds of capital expenditure.

The method of computation and description of allowances and elements of the computation differ as between the industrial buildings and plant and machinery systems. The industrial buildings system employs the 'straight line method' of computing allowances, i.e. a fixed percentage of cost each year; the plant and machinery system adopts the 'reducing balance method' of calculating allowances, i.e. a fixed percentage of the written down value of plant and machinery year by year. In the year of expenditure the industrial buildings system grants an 'initial allowance' in respect of new unused buildings to the first purchaser; in the first year of expenditure the plant and machinery system grants a 'first year allowance' to the purchaser of both new and secondhand plant and machinery. As part of a review which is taking place of allowances for capital expenditure both 'initial allowances' and 'first year allowances' will no longer be available in respect of expenditure on or after 1 April 1986.

2.2 INDUSTRIAL BUILDINGS ALLOWANCES

The industrial buildings system of capital allowances applies to:

(a) Industrial buildings or structures as defined in Section 7 Capital Allowances Act 1968, see 2.3 below,
(b) Hotels qualifying for relief in terms of Section 38, Finance Act 1978 (expenditure after 11 April 1978) see 2.4 below,
(c) Small and very small workshops, see 2.5 below,
(d) Commercial buildings in enterprise zones (areas designated by the government for special economic incentives) see 2.6 below.

2.3 INDUSTRIAL BUILDINGS OR STRUCTURES

Qualifying Expenditure
The Capital Allowances Act 1968 provides relief to companies for expenditure on the construction of an industrial building or structure or in purchasing a new, unused industrial building or structure which is then used in a trade carried on by the company itself or by a tenant or sub-tenant of the company.

'Building or structure' is not defined in the legislation but an industrial building is among other things a building or structure in use for a trade carried on in a 'mill, factory or similar premises'. The most common type of industrial building qualifying for allowances is thus a factory. However the terms of S.7 CAA 1968 include buildings and structures in use in the following:

(a) Transport, dock, water and power generation activities;
(b) Tunnel and bridge undertakings;
(c) Manufacturing and processing;
(d) Raw materials and finished goods storage (but not by a retailer or wholesaler);
(e) The mineral extraction industry (including the oil industry);
(f) Farming and forestry services;
(g) Agricultural contracting;
(h) The fishing industry.

Structure in the phrase 'industrial buiding or structure' will include roads, tunnels, walls, car parks, loading platforms, piers and similar structures.
'*Building or structure*' includes a part of a building or structure and in this

way extensions and improvements to buildings qualify as industrial buildings as expenditure is incurred over the years (S.87(4) CAA 1968). The cost of preparing, cutting, tunnelling or levelling land is regarded as a part of the cost of construction of a building and is available for industrial buildings allowance. However in no case is expenditure on acquiring the land available for allowances and for the purpose of computing industrial buildings allowance the cost of the land on the one hand and the costs of construction of the building on the other have to be distinguished, see Example 1 below (S.17(1) CAA 1968).

Certain buildings are excluded from the definition of an industrial building (and it follows are not granted allowances); these are houses, retail shops and showrooms (S.7(3) CAA 1968).

The Capital Allowances Act 1968 also specifies hotels and offices in the list of buildings excluded from the definition of an industrial building. However in certain circumstances such buildings are granted allowances. Expenditure after 11 April 1978 on some hotels qualifies for industrial buildings allowance, see 2.2 'Qualifying Hotels' below. A drawing office which was ancillary to manufacturing elsewhere in a factory was held in CIR v. Lambhill Ironworks Limited 31TC 393 to be an industrial building. More generally an office which forms a part of a building may qualify for industrial buildings allowance in the circumstances described below.

Frequently in the construction or purchase of a manufacturing facility there will be included in one building both a manufacturing and a general office area. As a first principle the cost of constructing the manufacturing area will have allowances available and the office area, assuming it is of a general administrative character, will have no allowances available. Where, however, part of a building is an industrial building and part is not, as long as the cost of construction of the non-industrial part does not exceed 25% of the cost of the construction of the whole, the total costs of construction, including the costs of the non-industrial part, will be available for industrial buildings allowance (S.7(4) CA 1968).

All welfare premises, for example, a canteen or social club, are to be regarded as industrial buildings if they are used by employees in one of the activities and trades listed in Section 7 of the Capital Allowances Act 1968 which qualify a building as an industrial building, see list above. On the other hand a sports pavilion used by employees of a trade is an industrial building for the purpose of allowances whether or not the trade is in the qualifying list, e.g. a retail group will obtain industrial buidings allowance in respect of the costs of building a sports pavilion but not the costs of the employees' social club.

Example 1
Electronics Ltd purchased a five acre site for £30,000 in March 1984 and built a manufacturing unit costing in total £470,000. This cost was made up as follows:

	£
Architect's fees	30,000
Preparing land	50,000
Design office for electronic circuitry	60,000
General office and showroom	100,000
Manufacturing area	200,000
Car park, roads, walls, gate, etc.	30,000
Total	470,000

The amount available for industrial buildings allowance is as follows:

	£	
Architect's fees	30,000	Costs of construction will normally
Preparing land	50,000	include professional fees (excluding costs associated with acquisition of land), and the costs of preparing, etc. land.
Design office etc.	60,000	CIR v. Lambhill Ironworks Ltd
General office etc.	100,000	Does not exceed 25% of cost of whole building, £470,000 and accordingly an industrial buiding.
Manufacturing area	200,000	
Car park etc.	30,000	Structures
Available for IBA	470,000	

The cost of purchasing the land, £30,000, has no allowance available.

2.3.1 Initial Allowances

A company incurring expenditure on the construction of a new industrial building is entitled, in the accounting period in which the expenditure is incurred, to an initial allowance with respect to that expenditure. A company purchasing a new unused building from a *builder* is entitled to an initial allowance on the purchase price and the builder's costs of construction are ignored. (S.5(2) CAA 1968).

Example 2

Hearts Ltd purchases a new factory from Ace Builders Ltd in Hearts Ltd's accounting period ended 30 September 1984. The purchase price is £250,000, payable on 31 August 1984. The costs of construction by Ace Builders Limited were £200,000. Hearts Ltd is entitled to an initial allowance with respect to £250,000 in the AP ended 30 September 1984.

It has been assumed above and in what follows that the company incurring the expenditure will itself use the building in a qualifying trade. A landlord company may also incur expenditure which will qualify for allowances granted to the landlord if the building is used by a tenant in one of the qualifying trades.

It is important to note carefully that the initial allowance is granted only in respect of a *new* buiding; the purchaser of a used second-hand building obtains no initial allowance. The amount of the initial allowance has varied over the years since 1944 and depends on the date when the expenditure was incurred which in general terms means the date when the amounts of the expenditure became payable. The initial allowance in respect of expenditure on or after 10 March 1981 and before 14 March 1984 is 75%; in respect of expenditure on or after 14 March 1984 and before 1 April 1985 the allowance is 50%; on or after 1 April 1985 and before 1 April 1986, 25%. No initial allowance is granted in respect of expenditure on or after 1 April 1986. The rates of allowances from 6 April 1944 onwards are contained in Appendix 2.

For an initial allowance to be given it is not necessary for the building to be in use; it is sufficient that it will be used subsequently as an industrial building. If subsequently it is not used as an industrial building any initial allowance given is withdrawn (S.1(5) CAA 1968).

Example 3
Futronic Ltd makes up accounts annually to 31 December. It entered into a contract with a builder for the construction of a factory. The contract provided for progress payments were made as follows:

	£
Year ended 31 December 1980	75,000
Year ended 31 December 1981	
Pre 10 March 1981	100,000
Post 9 March 1981	90,000
Year ended 31 December 1982	220,000

The building was completed and brought into use in May 1983. Initial allowances available are as follows:

	£
AP ended 31 December 1980	
50% × £75,000	37,500
AP ended 31 December 1981	
50% × £100,000	50,000
75% × £90,000	67,500
AP ended 31 December 1982	
75% × £220,000	165,000

2.3.2 Writing Down Allowances

A company which incurs expenditure on the construction of a *new* industrial building (or purchases a *new* industrial building) is entitled to a writing down allowance on a straight line basis of 4% (expenditure on or after 6 November 1962) where the building is an industrial building at the end of the accounting period, i.e. is *in use* for a qualifying trade at the end of the accounting period. If the expenditure was incurred prior to 6 November 1962 the rate of writing down allowances is 2% (S.2(1) and (2)

CAA 1968). If the AP is less than twelve months in length the allowance is proportionately reduced (Ss.2(2) CAA 1968). Where a company incurs expenditure on a *used* second-hand building the writing down allowance is computed in a special way, see 2.3.6 below, 'purchaser of second-hand used industrial building'.

Notwithstanding that the writing down allowance is 4% (or 2%) of cost the amount of an annual writing down allowance cannot exceed the amount of the 'residue', i.e. the written down value of the expenditure—being the cost of the industrial building less the initial and writing down allowances previously granted (or notional allowances written off, see below). A writing down allowance continues to be given where an industrial building is temporarily disused (S.12 CAA 1968) but not where an industrial building is put to another non-qualifying use, e.g. as a retail outlet. In the latter case, that is where a building is put to non-qualifying uses, a notional writing down allowance, which is not deducted as a trading expense from trading profits, is deducted in arriving at the residue of the expenditure (S.4 CAA 1968). If notional allowances were not deducted a balancing allowance might arise when the building was sold and in this way an allowance effectively given for years during which it was in use other than as an industrial building; as to balancing allowances see 2.3.3 below.

Example 4

Clubs Ltd, a chemical processing company, constructed a factory costing £300,000 in the early 1970s. In the year ended 30 June 1971 and before the factory was operational it incurred expenditure of £250,000. In the subsequent six months' accounting period ended 31 December 1971 it incurred further expenditure of £50,000. The plant was in operation, i.e. brought into use, at the end of 1971. The initial allowance was 30% throughout the period of expenditure and the company has made up accounts to 31 December annually since the change of accounting date on 31 December 1971. Because of an economic recession the plant was not in use from 1 September 1979 to February 1984.

Initial and writing down allowances are as follows:

	£	Residue £
AP ended 30 June 1971		
Initial allowance 30% × £250,000	75,000	175,000
AP ended 31 December 1971		
Initial allowance 30% × £50,000	15,000	
(no proportional restriction of initial allowance)		
Writing down allowance		
4% × £300,000 £12,000		
Restricted to half	6,000	204,000

	£	Residue £
APs ended 31 December 1972 to 1988		
Writing down allowances		
17 years at £12,000 per annum	204,000	Nil
(allowances continue to be given during		
temporary disuse)		

Note: An initial allowance is granted in the AP in which the expenditure is incurred whether or not the building is in use at the end of the AP. In contrast writing down allowances are only available for the first time if the building is in use at the end of the relevant AP.

2.3.3 Balancing Adjustments

Where an industrial building is sold or demolished (and in other circumstances set out in S.3(1) CAA 1968) a balancing adjustment is made. A balancing adjustment may give rise to a deduction from profits or more usually an addition to profits. The object of a balancing adjustment is to allow over the period of use of the building the net cash cost to the company of the capital expenditure.

> **Example 5**
> Uno Ltd incurs expenditure on an industrial building costing £300,000. The company obtains allowances over the years of use of the building totalling £300,000. The building is sold for £400,000. The net cash cost to the company is thus nil; it has expended £300,000 and recovered £300,000. Since the net cash cost is nil the company is not entitled to any allowances and the balancing adjustment will seek to recover tax on the £300,000 of allowances granted over the years of use.
>
> The difference between the selling price of the building £400,000 and the cost of the building £300,000, the 'profit' on the sale of the building is a capital gain.

No balancing adjustment is made where a building is sold more than 25 years after it was first used (50 years if the expenditure was before 6 November 1962). It is important to recall that the definition of an industrial building includes a part of a building; it follows that in respect of an industrial building which may be a physical unity, a balancing adjustment may arise with respect to certain expenditure and not arise with respect to certain other expenditure.

> **Example 6**
> Spades Ltd, a long established engineering company which makes up accounts to 31 December each year incurred the following expenditure on an industrial building in the years indicated:
>
> | | £ |
> |---|---|
> | Year ended 31 December 1920 | 50,000 |
> | Year ended 31 December 1967 | 200,000 |

In the year ended 31 December 1984 the building was sold for £530,000. Of the latter sum £80,000 was in respect of land, and of the balance of £450,000, £150,000 on a just apportionment was attributable to the 1920 expenditure and £300,000 to the 1967 expenditure (Ss.77 and 81, CAA 1968). No balancing adjustment will arise with respect to the £150,000 apportionment to the 1920 expenditure since the 1920 expenditure was more than 50 years before the date of sale in 1984; a balancing adjustment will arise in respect of the 1967 expenditure since the date of sale in 1984 is not more than 25 years after 1967.

If the residue exceeds the sale price a balancing allowance is given of the difference (S.3(2) CAA 1968). A balancing allowance is deducted from trading income. If the sale price is more than the residue a balancing charge of the difference is made on the company (S.3(3) CAA 1968). A balancing charge is added to trading income. Because of initial allowances and inflation balancing charges frequently arise in more common transactions. There is no limit on the amount of a balancing allowance, but no balancing charge can exceed the amount of allowances given, i.e. balancing adjustments are only intended to recover any excessive allowances in the past (or to give extra allowances if the allowances have been too low in the past).

Example 7
Diamonds Ltd built a factory in 1966 at a cost of £200,000. The factory was in use (other than temporary disuse for one year) from 1966 until it was sold in 1983. The residue of expenditure for IBA purposes at the end of the AP prior to sale was nil; allowances granted to Diamonds Ltd since 1966 were thus £200,000. The sale price of the freehold (the heritage) was £400,000. Diamonds Ltd and the purchaser have agreed that of the £400,000, £100,000 was in respect of land and £300,000 in respect of the industrial building.

The balancing charge arising to Diamonds Ltd on the sale is:

	£	£
Residue before sale		Nil
Sale proceeds:		
Land and buildings	400,000	
Less: Land	100,000	300,000
Balancing charge		300,000
Restricted to allowances granted		200,000

Note: The excess of the sale proceeds of the land and buildings over the cost of these assets is a capital gain.

2.3.4 Special case of balancing adjustment

When a building is sold which at times during its use was an industrial building on which allowances were granted and at other times was not an industrial building, e.g. was in use as retail stores or offices, special rules apply to the balancing adjustment (S.3(4) and (5) CAA 1968).

Where the building is sold for *more* than the building cost a balancing charge is made which is the amount of the allowances granted.

In the unusual case where the building is sold for *less* than it cost, an adjustment is made to cost, to arrive at what the legislation calls 'adjusted net cost'. If the 'adjusted net cost' is more than the allowances which have been given a balancing allowance arises; if less a balancing charge is made.

'Adjusted net cost' means cost less the sale price, reduced in the proportion that the period of time for which allowances were granted bears to the whole period of use.

Example 8
Chess Ltd built a factory at a cost of £300,000 and sold it four years later for £250,000. For the first two years it was used as a factory and for the last two years it was used as a retail outlet. Industrial buildings alowances granted during its years of use as a factory total £174,000.

Since the building was used both as a factory qualifying for industrial buildings allowance and as a retail outlet which does not qualify for allowances the special balancing adjustment is appropriate; the building was sold for less than it cost and the balancing adjustment comprises the difference between adjusted net cost and allowances granted.

Adjusted net cost is as follows:

	£
Cost	300,000
Less: Sale price	250,000
Net cost	50,000
Reduced by factor 2/4	
Adjusted net cost	25,000

Balancing charge is excess of allowances granted over adjusted net cost:

Allowances granted	174,000
Less: Adjusted net cost	25,000
Balancing charge	149,000

2.3.5 Residue of Expenditure

Reference is made above to the residue of expenditure which consists of the costs of the industrial building less:

(a) any initial allowance,
(b) writing down allowances for periods of use,

(c) writing down allowances for periods of temporary disuse as an industrial building,
(d) notional allowances for periods of use otherwise than as an industrial building.

The so-called 'residue before sale' is the residue as at the end of the accounting period prior to the accounting period in which the industrial building is sold. The 'residue after sale' is the residue before sale plus the amount of a balancing charge which arises out of the sale or less the amount of a balancing allowance on the occasion of the sale. The notions of residue, and residue before and after sale are important when considering balancing adjustments generally and when computing industrial buildings allowances available to the purchaser of a second-hand, used industrial building. The position of the latter is considered immediately below.

2.3.6 Purchaser of second-hand used industrial building

The capital allowances which are granted to the purchaser of a second-hand, used industrial building differ greatly from those available to the purchaser (or constructor) of a new, unused building. As emphasised elsewhere in this chapter no initial allowance is available to the purchaser of a used industrial building and the writing down allowance which is annually 4% to the original purchaser is computed in a special way as regards the second-hand purchaser. The purpose of the latter computation is to write off the residue after sale by the 25th year after the building was first used. The computation proceeds as follows:

(a) Establish the 25 year period from the date the building was first used,
(b) Establish the time still to run of the above 25 year period from the date on which the building was sold,
(c) Compute a proportion of the residue after sale (obtained from the seller) which is the length of the accounting period of the purchaser (usually 1 year) over the period in (b) immediately above. The amount computed is the amount of the writing down allowance.

Example 9
Bridge Ltd makes up its accounts to 31 December each year. On 31 May 1975 in its accounting period ended 31 December 1975 it bought a new unused industrial building from a builder at a cost of £150,000 and brought it immediately into use. The building was used throughout by Bridge Ltd as an industrial building. On 30 November 1982 in the accounting period of Bridge Ltd ended 31 December 1982 it was sold to Backgammon Ltd in that company's twelve month accounting period ended 30 September 1983, for a price of £225,000.

The industrial buildings allowance available to Bridge Ltd and the residues before and after sale are as follows:

Bridge Ltd

	£	£
Cost		150,000
AP ended 31 December 1975		
Initial allowance 50%	75,000	
Writing down allowance 4%	6,000	
	81,000	
AP ended 31 December 1976 to		
AP ended 31 December 1981		
6 years at £6,000 per annum	36,000	117,000
Residue before sale		33,000
Sale price		225,000
Balancing charge		192,000
Restricted to allowances granted		117,000
Residue after sale:		
Residue before sale		33,000
Add: Balancing charge		117,000
		150,000

Backgammon Ltd

No initial allowance will be available to Backgammon Ltd.

The writing down allowance is calculated as follows:

(a) The 25 year period from the building's first use runs from 1 June 1975 to 31 May 2000.

(b) The time still to run of the period in paragraph (a) above from the date of sale, 30 November 1982, is 17 years 6 months.

(c) The proportion of the residue after sale, £150,000, which is the amount of the writing down allowance is:

$$\frac{\text{Length of AP of purchaser}}{\text{Period in (b) above}} = \frac{1 \text{ year}}{17\frac{1}{2} \text{ years}}$$

and the writing down allowance is $\dfrac{2}{35} \times £150,000 = £8,571$

On a second or subsequent sale of an industrial building the same principles and computations apply, the object being as before to write off the residue which each successive purchaser inherits over the remainder of the 25 year period since the building was first used by the first purchaser or constructor.

Example 10
Backgammon Ltd in the above example continues to use the building as an industrial building until it is sold on 28 February 1986 to Cribbage Ltd. Cribbage Ltd which has made up accounts to 30 June each year was taken over by the Games Group Ltd on 31 July 1985 and Cribbage Ltd will draw up its accounts to 31 March 1986 and annually to 31 March thereafter. The price paid by Cribbage Ltd for the building was £250,000.

The industrial buildings allowance available to Backgammon Ltd and the residue before and after sale are as follows:

	£
Residue after sale (Bridge Ltd)	150,000
Writing down allowances:	
AP ended 30 September 1983 to	
AP ended 30 September 1985	
3 years at £8,571 (previously computed)	25,713
Residue before sale	124,287
Sale price	250,000
Balancing charge	125,713
Restricted to allowances granted	25,713
Residue after sale:	
Residue before sale	124,287
Add: Balancing charge	25,713
Residue after sale	150,000

The industrial buildings allowances available to Cribbage Ltd are as follows:

(a) 25 year period as in Example 9 above ends on 31 May 2000
(b) The time still to run from the date of sale, 28 February 1986, is 14 years 3 months
(c) The proportion of the residue after sale, £150,000, which is the amount of the writing down allowance is:

$$= \frac{\text{Length of AP of purchaser}}{\text{Period in (b) above}}$$

$$= \frac{9 \text{ months}}{14 \text{ years 3 months}}$$

$$= \frac{9 \text{ months}}{171 \text{ months}}$$

and the writing down allowance is:

$$\frac{9}{171} \times £150,000 = £7,895$$

In the AP of 12 months ending 31 March 1987 and in subsequent years to 31 March the writing down allowance is:

$$\frac{1}{14\frac{1}{4}} \times £150,000, \text{ i.e. } £10,526.$$

2.4 QUALIFYING HOTELS

What has been described above is, in general terms, the relief for expenditure on industrial buildings introduced in 1945. From 1978 onwards the IBA system was extended, with modifications, to expenditure on qualifying hotels after 11 April 1978. The initial allowance in respect of qualifying hotel expenditure is 20%.

The extension of IBA to hotels was made with caution. It applies only to expenditure after 11 April 1978 and only to hotels which qualify by reason of size and type. As regards type of hotel the relief was intended to benefit tourist and not residential hotels; and as regards size the medium-sized and larger hotels were intended to benefit since ten letting bedrooms were required in order to qualify.

A qualifying hotel has the following characteristics (S.38 FA 1978):

(a) it is open for a minimum of four months in a 'season' of seven months from April to October inclusive,

(b) during the time it is open it has a minimum of ten letting bedrooms defined as private bedrooms not normally in the same occupation for more than a month,

(c) the services provided normally include breakfasts and evening meals, bed-making and cleaning of rooms.

If a hotel meets the above characteristics it obtains a 20% initial allowance on expenditure after 11 April 1978. The initial allowance applies as it does for IBA generally to the costs of construction or the purchase price of a new hotel; the purchaser of a second-hand, used hotel does not obtain an initial allowance. The costs of an extension or improvements to a qualifying hotel after 11 April 1978 will obtain initial allowances. Qualifying capital expenditure on which an initial allowance is granted also obtains a 4% per annum writing down allowance.

To establish whether the requirements regarding the number of bedrooms, seasonal opening, etc., are being met (and thus whether allowances are due in respect of certain expenditure) the legislation requires us to look at a period of 12 months which ends, usually, on the last day of the company's accounting period (S.38(4)(a) FA 1978).

Example 11

Scop Ltd, a company in the hotel business, has owned for many years a 50 bedroom tourist hotel open throughout the year. In the company's year to 31 October 1984 the company built an extension containing 6 bedrooms at a cost of £50,000.

Since Scop Ltd satisfied the requirements of a qualifying hotel for the 12 months ended 31 October 1984 (at least 10 letting bedrooms etc.) it will obtain an initial allowance and a writing down allowance in the year ended 31 October 1984 as follows

		£
Initial allowance	20% × £50,000	10,000
Writing down allowance	4% × £50,000	2,000

When a hotel is first used by a company after the beginning of the twelve month period in Example 11, the qualifying period is twelve months from the date of first use.

Example 12

In addition to the extension referred to in Example 11, Scop Ltd, in the year ended 31 October 1984, opens a new tourist hotel on 1 April 1984 which has 30 bedrooms, is open all year round, and cost £400,000. In assessing what industrial buildings allowances are available for the AP ended 31 October 1984 one is required to look at the characteristics of the hotel for the 12 months since it opened, i.e. the year beginning on 1 April 1984 and ended on 31 March 1985. Since the building meets the requirements of a qualifying hotel for this period IBA will be available for the AP ended 31 October 1984.

2.4.1 Writing down allowances

The normal writing down allowance, computed on the straight line basis, is available in respect of qualifying hotels. This is granted as in the case of industrial buildings generally, where the hotel is in use at the end of the AP. A writing down allowance continues to be given during temporary disuse as a hotel for two years after the end of the accounting period in which the hotel falls temporarily out of use.

2.4.2 Balancing adjustments

Balancing charges and allowance are computed on the sale of an hotel in the same manner as for other industrial buildings as described earlier in the chapter. A special computation requires to be made two years after an hotel ceases to be a qualifying hotel without being sold or disposed of, e.g. by becoming a residential hotel say, for the elderly. In such an instance the hotel is deemed to be sold at open market value and a computation made of the resulting balancing charge or allowance.

2.5 SMALL AND VERY SMALL WORKSHOPS

As part of a government policy to encourage small businesses certain small industrial buildings, called in Section 75 Finance Act 1980 small workshops, were granted enhanced rates of initial and writing down allowances.

A Finance Act 1980 small workshop was an industrial building whose gross internal floor space did not exced 2,500 square feet. Expenditure on small workshops after 26 March 1980 and before 27 March 1983 qualified for an initial allowance of up to 100%. Where part or all of this initial allowance was disclaimed the company was granted a writing down allowance of 25% on the part disclaimed.

A Finance Act 1982 very small workshop did not exceed 1,250 square feet in gross internal floor area. For expenditure after 26 March 1983, starting where the Finance Act 1980 provisions ended, and before 27 March 1985, the initial allowance and writing down allowance are, as before, up to 100% and 25% respectively.

2.6 ENTERPRISE ZONES

Enterprise zones are geographical areas of the country designated by the government and offering special financial and economic incentives to businesses to develop in these areas. Perhaps the most interesting incentive to businesses is freedom from local authority rates in the designated areas.

From the point of view of capital allowances and the industrial buildings allowance, expenditure on industrial buildings, qualifying hotels and commercial buildings in enterprise zones are integrated into the industrial buildings allowance scheme with, as for small workshops, an enhanced initial allowance of up to 100% and a writing down allowance of 25%. To qualify the expenditure must have been incurred on contracts entered into within ten years of the site being included in an enterprise zone (S.74(1) FA 1980).

In addition to industrial buildings and qualifying hotels, i.e. qualifying under the 1978 Finance Act as described above, the enhanced IBA applies to commercial buildings or structures. A commercial building or structure is defined in S.74(4) FA 1980 and means a building (other than an industrial building or qualifying hotel) used as an office, or used for the purpose of a trade, profession or vocation. It follows that for practical purposes all business and commercial properties qualify for allowances, including both hotels which obtain allowances as 'qualifying hotels' and those which while not qualifying under the 1978 Act, satisfy the definition of a commercial building.

2.7 PLANT AND MACHINERY

The second major system of capital allowances is that legislated for in 1971 in respect of capital expenditure on plant and machinery.

'Plant and machinery' is not defined in the legislation and because of the historically higher rates of allowances granted to capital expenditure on plant and machinery as opposed to that incurred for example on buildings, a large number of cases have come before the courts seeking to claim that certain expenditure was incurred on plant and machinery.

In the course of Lord Lindley's judgement in Yarmouth v. France CA 1887, 19 QBD, 647, a workmen's compensation case and not a tax case as such, he said, 'There is no definition of plant in the Act; but, in its ordinary sense includes whatever apparatus is used by a businessman for carrying on his business—not his stock in trade which he buys or makes for sale; but all goods and chattels fixed or moveable, live or dead, which he keeps for permanent employment in his business'.

This dictum had an important influence on subsequent cases. The modern trend in the development of the definition of plant and machinery has been to look at the 'function' of the expenditure, i.e. is the asset part of the apparatus for the carrying on of the business of the company.

The following have been held to be plant or machinery:

> Moveable office partitioning,
> A dry dock for the repair of ships,
> A swimming pool on a caravan site,
> A silo for delivering grain,
> Special lighting and fittings in licensed premises.

The items below have been held not to be plant or machinery:

> Prefabricated school buildings,
> A canopy over a petrol filling station,
> False ceilings to conceal pipes etc.,
> Ship converted as a floating restaurant,
> Electrical installation in retail store.

In the nature of things tax cases tend to consider the more out-of-the-way items of expenditure although of course they also establish a framework of definitions and principles. Within that framework are to be found all the machinery and equipment of manufacturing industry as well as furniture and fittings of offices and shops, e.g. desks, counters, chairs, etc., and motor vehicles such as buses, lorries and cars.

Expenditure on plant and machinery obtains two allowances, a first year allowance (which will not be available after 31 March 1986) and a writing down allowance.

2.7.1 First year allowances

For expenditure on plant and machinery after 22 March 1972 and before

14 March 1984 a first year allowance of up to 100% of the expenditure is granted (S.41 FA 1971).

Capital expenditure after 13 March 1984 and before 1 April 1985 obtains a first year allowance of up to 75%; capital expenditure on or after 1 April 1985 and before 1 April 1986 obtains an allowance of up to 50%; no first year allowance is granted on expenditure incurred on or after 1 April 1986.

Expenditure	Rate %
After 22 March 1972 and before 14 March 1984	100
After 13 March 1984 and before 1 April 1985	75
After 31 March 1985 and before 1 April 1986	50
After 31 March 1986	Nil

In order for a first year allowance to be granted it is not necessary for the item to be in use in the company's trade; it is sufficient that the expenditure has been incurred, i.e. the sum in question has become payable, and that the plant belongs to the company in the AP in which it claims the allowance. Plant on hire purchase is treated for this purpose as if it belonged to the company.

Within two years of the end of the relevant AP a company may disclaim a FYA completely or specify the reduced amount which it claims (S.41(3) FA 1971). The reason for this provision is to accommodate claims for first year allowance with other claims e.g. for group relief, and generally to permit companies to take the best advantage of the allowance.

Where a company decides to disclaim the whole of the FYA to which it is entitled in an accounting period the capital expenditure becomes part of what is called the 'qualifying expenditure' for the same accounting period and a 'writing down allowance' becomes available (S.59(4) FA 1984). If it disclaims a part of the first year allowance to which it is entitled the 'relevant portion' of the expenditure is included in 'qualifying expenditure' for the same accounting period (S.59(6) and (7) FA 1984). The relevant portion is that part of the capital expenditure which the amount of the first year allowance or allowances disclaimed bears to the full amount of the first year allowance or allowances available. If for example a company incurs capital expenditure of £10,000 with respect to which it is entitled to a first year allowance of 75%, £7,500, and it disclaims £1,875 of the latter entitlement, the amount which may be included in 'qualifying expenditure' immediately is:

$$\frac{\text{Amount of FYA disclaimed}}{\text{Amount of FYA available}} \times \text{expenditure}$$

$$= \frac{£1,875}{£7,500} \times £10,000$$

$$= £2,500$$

Finally, in contrast with the above situations, where a first year allowance of 75 or 50% is not disclaimed and is received in full the balance of the expenditure only forms part of qualifying expenditure in the *next* acounting period.

A first year allowance is available for purchases of both new and second-hand plant and machinery. In a few cases a first year allowance is not available. Motor cars, generally, do not obtain a first year allowance. An asset which is sold without having been used in the trade does not obtain a first year allowance, and if an allowance has been granted (there is no requirement at the time of purchase other than that the plant is 'for the purposes of the trade') it is withdrawn (S.41(2) FA 1971). If the unused asset is sold for a price less than the asset cost the difference is added to the 'qualifying expenditure' (and a writing down allowance becomes available) in the accounting period in which the sale is made (Para. 4 Sch. 8 FA 1971).

Although motor cars generally do not obtain first year allowances, the allowance is granted on expenditure on cars used for hire to, or carriage of, members of the public. Thus a car hire company, or taxi-hire company obtains first year allowance in respect of its fleet of cars. By way of contrast a manufacturing company which purchases cars for its sales force obtains no FYA. Although motor cars are usually denied FYA, it should be emphasised that lorries and vans obtain allowances in the usual way.

2.7.2 Writing down allowances

Where plant and machinery is or has been in use in a trade and the company has 'qualifying expenditure' a writing down allowance of 25% on a reducing balance basis is granted to the company.

For any accounting period ending after 13 March 1984 a company can disclaim a writing down allowance or claim a reduced allowance within two years from the end of an accounting period (S.442A FA 1971).

The government has stated that the Finance Act 1985 will contain a provision which will make writing down allowances available when expenditure is incurred, whether or not plant is in use. The provision will apply to accounting periods ending on or after 1 April 1985.

The writing down allowance is calculated on the amount of qualifying expenditure less the proceeds of assets sold. For this purpose assets are grouped, or 'pooled', and it is not usually necessary to identify any particular asset. The amount on which a writing down allowance is calculated is frequently called the 'pool' of expenditure. If on any occasion the sale price of assets should exceed qualifying expenditure a balancing charge arises, which is assessed to corporation tax as income.

The pool of qualifying expenditure on which allowances are calculated consists of the pool balance brought forward from the previous accounting period and expenditure becoming available for writing down allowances for the first time, less the disposal proceeds of items sold. This matter is perhaps best exhibited by way of an example (see Example 13 below), but at the time of writing the following is a brief analysis of the position prior to the passing of the Finance Act 1985.

(a) The over-riding principle is that only items of plant which are or have been in use in the trade may be included in the pool.

(b) In respect of purchases before 14 March 1984 (when the FYA could be up to 100%) in the AP in which a first year allowance is available, no writing down allowance is granted, and any balance remaining after a claim for a reduced first year allowance is included in the pool of the next AP (subject to the principle of use in (a) above).

(c) In respect of purchases after 13 March 1984 where a full first year allowance is granted the procedure in (b) above is followed and the remainder of the expenditure is taken into the pool in the next AP, subject to use as before.

(d) For purchases after 13 March 1984 where a first year allowance is disclaimed in its totality the expenditure is added to the pool for writing down allowance in the current AP subject to being in use (S.44(4) FA 1971 and S.59(4) FA 1984).

(e) For purchases after 13 March 1984 where a first year allowance is disclaimed in part, the 'relevant portion' (see above) of the expenditure is added to the pool for writing down allowance in the current AP subject to being in use (S.44(6) and (7) FA 1984).

Example 13

DR Ltd makes up accounts to 31 December each year and makes the following transactions in plant and machinery in the following year:

	£
Year ended 31 December 1982	
Pool balance 31 December 1981	30,000
Purchases October 1982	
80% FYA claimed	75,000
Year ended 31 December 1983	
Sales April 1983	10,000
Purchases November 1983	
30% FYA claimed	80,000
Year ended 31 December 1984	
Purchases January 1984	50,000
Purchases June 1984	25,000
	75,000
FYA claimed	50,000
Sales	20,000

The item purchased in the year ended 31 December 1982 was brought into use for the first time in May 1984. All other items were brought into use immediately after purchase.

The computations proceed as follows:
AP ended 31 December 1982

	FYA £	Pool £	Total £
Balance at 31 December 1981		30,000	
Purchases October 1982	75,000		
FYA 80%	60,000		60,000
WDA 25%		7,500	7,500
		.	
Balance of FYA expenditure	15,000		
Pool balance		22,500	
		.	
Total allowances			67,500

AP ended 31 December 1983

	FYA £	Pool £	Total £
Balance at 31 December 1982		22,500	
Purchases November 1983	80,000		
FYA 30%	24,000		24,000
Sales		(10,000)	
		12,500	
WDA 25%		3,125	3,125
Balance of FYA expenditure	56,000		
Pool balance		9,375	
Total allowances			27,125

AP ended 31 December 1984

	FYA £	Pool £	Total £
Balance at 31 December 1983		9,375	
Balance of FYA expenditure at 31 December 1983		5,600	
Purchases pre 14 March 1984	50,000		
Purchases post 13 March 1984	25,000		
	75,000		
FYA	(50,000)		50,000
Amount available for WDA:			
£25,000 × $\dfrac{£18,750}{£68,750}$ (Note 1)	(6,818)	6,818	
Balance of FYA expenditure for AP ended 31 December 1982 brought into use May 1984		15,000	
		87,193	
Sales		20,000	
		67,193	
WDA 25%		16,798	16,798
Balance of FYA expenditure c/f	18,182		
Pool Balance		50,395	
Total allowances			66,798

Notes:
(1) The 'relevant portion' of the post 13 March 1984 expenditure which may be included in the pool in AP ended 31 December 1984 is

$$\frac{\text{Amount of FYA disclaimed}}{\text{Amount of FYA available}}$$

The amount of FYA available is:
100% of £50,000	£50,000
75% of £25,000	£18,750
	£68,750

The amount of FYA claimed is £50,000 and the amount disclaimed is £18,750.

(2) Expenditure on plant in the year ended 31 December 1982 which is first used in the AP ended 31 December 1984 is brought into the pool in the latter AP, after deduction of the FYA claimed in the AP ended 31 December 1982, the year of purchase.

2.7.3 Disposal value

In the above analysis the pool of expenditure is arrived at after deduction of the sale proceeds of the plant. The 1971 legislation uses the phrase 'disposal value' and S.44(6) FA 1971 provides a description of disposal events. These include sale, demolition or destruction, the permanent loss of the plant, the permanent discontinuance of the trade and 'any other event'.

In no case can the disposal value exceed the capital expenditure incurred in the provision of the plant, i.e. the sale price included in the computation cannot exceed the cost of the plant in question. This is an instance where it is necessary to identify the sale of an item of plant with its purchase and the principle of pooling is not followed.

Example 14
Sally's Ltd makes up accounts to 31 March each year. At 31 March 1983 the balance on the pool of qualifying expenditure was £4,000. In the year ended 31 March 1984 the only transaction in plant or machinery was the sale of an item of plant for £6,000 which had cost £5,000 in the year ended 31 March 1982.

The computation for the year ended 31 March 1984 proceeds as follows:
AP ended 31 March 1984

	£
Pool balance at 31 December 1983	4,000
Sale of item restricted to cost	5,000
Balancing charge	1,000

The difference between the selling price of the plant, £6,000 and its cost, £5,000 is a capital gain and may be taxed accordingly.

2.7.4 Balancing allowances and permanent discontinuance of a trade

No first year allowances nor writing down allowances are given in the year in which a trade is permanently discontinued. The excess, if any, of qualifying expenditure over the disposal value, e.g. sale proceeds, is allowed as a balancing allowance.

Example 15
Leonard's Ltd makes up accounts each year to 30 September. The balance on the pool of qualifying expenditure at 30 September 1983 was £80,000. On 30 June 1984 the company ceased to trade and in the nine months AP ended 30 June 1984 the company made sales of plant totalling £40,000 and purchased plant costing £10.000.

AP ended 30 September 1984

	£
Pool balance at 30 September 1983	80,000
Purchases	10,000
	90,000
Sales	40,000
Balancing allowance	50,000

Note. An item which does not qualify for a first year allowance is included in qualifying expenditure in the AP of purchase (S.44(4) FA 1971). The expenditure of £10,000 above falls into this category.

2.7.5 Motor cars

As explained above in the context of first year allowances, motor cars generally do not obtain first year allowances. However as noted in Example 15 expenditure which does not obtain FYA's forms part of qualifying expenditure and as a consequence, in a continuing trade, is granted writing down allowances in the year of purchase.

Cars for the purpose of writing down allowances are divided into two classes, those costing £8,000 or less and those costing more than £8,000.

Each car costing more than £8,000 is held in a separate pool. The legislation asks us to consider that each car is in use in a separate trade and that the events of purchase and disposal in the actual trade take place in the deemed separate trade (Para. 10 Sch. 8 FA 1971).

The purpose of these provisions is to restrict the amount of the writing down allowance in respect of 'expensive' cars to £2,000 per annum, and the writing down allowance granted is the lesser of 25% of the balance on the separate pool or £2,000.

On the sale of the expensive car the separate trade is deemed to be permanently discontinued and it follows that in most cases an unrestricted balancing allowance arises.

Example 16

Chateau Ltd makes up accounts annually to 30 June. In the year ended 30 June 1983 the company purchased two cars, Car one costing £9,000 and Car Two costing £12,000. In the year ended 30 June 1985, Car one was sold for £4,000 and Car Two for £8,750.

The capital allowance computation proceeds as follows:

AP ended 30 June 1983

	Car One £	Car Two £	Total £
Purchases	9,000	12,000	
WDA at 25% restricted to	2,000	2,000	4,000
Pool balances	7,000	10,000	
Total allowances			4,000

AP ended 30 June 1984

	Car One £	Car Two £	Total £
Pool balance 30 June 1983	7,000	10,000	
WDA at 25%	1,750		1,750
WDA at 25% restricted to		2,000	2,000
Pool balances	5,250	8,000	
Total allowances			3,750

AP ended 30 June 1985

	Car One £	Car Two £
Pool balance 30 June 1984	5,250	8,000
Sale price	4,000	8,750
Balancing allowance	1,250	
Balancing charge		750

Cars costing less than £8,000, the second class into which cars are divided, are also kept in a separate pool as if in a separate and distinct trade (S.69 FA 1980). However, unlike the position with expensive cars, *all* cars costing less than £8,000 are kept in one pool and there is no restriction on the 25% writing down allowance. These provisions, tucked away rather oddly in the middle of complex provisions concerning restrictions on first year allowances granted to leasing companies, were intended to strike at features of the detailed operation of the pre-1980 rules which the Treasury then regarded as unsatisfactory.

Example 17
Halcyon Ltd in its year ended 31 December 1984 had the following transactions in plant or machinery:

	£
Purchase of lathe (second-hand)	20,000
Purchase of office computer	12,000
Purchase of desk	300
Purchase of Rover car	13,000
Purchase of two Ford Escorts	10,000
Sale of two Ford Cortinas purchased in 1981	3,000
Sale of plant	5,000

All items are in use in the AP ended 31 December 1984. Except for the Lathe purchased in January 1984, all transactions took place after 13 March 1984. Halcyon has disclaimed half of the first year allowances to which it is entitled. The balance on the general pool at 31 December 1983 is nil and on the car pool, £2,000
The computation of capital allowances for the AP ended 31 December 1984 is as shown opposite:

AP ended 31 December 1984

	FYA Pre 14 March 1984 £	FYA Post 13 March 1984 £	Pool £	Car Pool £	Rover Pool £	Total £
Pool balance 31 December 1983				2,000		
Purchases:						
Secondhand lathe	20,000					
Office computer		12,000				
Office desk		300				
Rover					13,000	
Escorts				10,000		
	(10,000)	12,300				
FYA 50%	(10,000)					10,000
FYA 37½%		(4,613)				4,613
£14,613						
$\frac{£14,613}{£29,225} \times £12,300$ (relevant portion)		(6,150)	6,150			
Sales:						
Cortinas				(3,000)		
Plant			(5,000)			
			1,150	9,000	13,000	
WDA 25%			288	2,250		2,538
WDA restricted					2,000	2,000
Balance of FYA expenditure	10,000	1,537				
Pool balances			862	6,750	11,000	
Total allowances						19,151

Notes
(1) The relevant portion of expenditure post 13 March 1984 takes account of the total of FYA's disclaimed and available in the accounting period including first year allowances disclaimed in respect of expenditure pre 14 March 1984.
(2) Without inclusion of a portion of the post 13 March 1984 expenditure in the pool in the accounting period ended 31 December 1984 a balancing charge of £5,000 would have arisen on the pool.

2.7.6 Hire Purchase

Instalments payable under a hire purchase agreement are regarded for accounting and capital allowances purposes as consisting of two elements, a capital element and a revenue element. The latter is described as the 'interest' or hire charge.

The financial analysis of a hire purchase agreement will have the following outline:

	£
Cash cost of asset	6,000
Deposit made at date of agreement (say)	1,200
	4,800
Interest say at 12%, £576 for two years, 2 × £576	1,152
Hire purchase price	5,952
Payable in 24 instalments of $\dfrac{5,952}{24}$ =	248

Each instalment of £248 is considered to comprise:

(a) Capital element $\dfrac{4,800}{24}$ =   £200

(b) Interest element $\dfrac{1,152}{24}$ =   £48

As soon as the hire purchase agreement is completed and the equipment has been brought into use a first year allowance is granted in respect of the whole of the capital expenditure which has either been made or is to be made in terms of the agreement. Thus if an agreement similar to that outlined above was made by a company after 13 March 1984 (say in October 1984) and the plant was brought into use the first year allowance would be as follows:

	£
Deposit	1,200
Instalments of capital 24 × £200	4,800
Cash cost	6,000
First year allowance 75% × £6,000	4,500

If the plant is not brought into use immediately a first year allowance would be granted in any accounting period only on the amount of the capital instalments actually due and payable in that AP.

Example 18
Indiana Ltd acquired on hire purchase a microcomputer for £6,000 in December 1984 in its accounting year ended 31 December 1984. The details of the purchase and the hire purchase agreement are set out immediately above this example. The deposit of £1,200 was paid on 15 December 1984 (the date of the agreement). The first of the 24 instalments was payable in January 1985 and the computer was only brought into use in February 1985.

In the accounting period ended 31 December 1984, Indiana Ltd is entitled to a first year allowance of 75% of £1,200, i.e. £900, and in the accounting period ended 31 December 1985 to a first year allowance of 75% of £4,800, i.e. £3,600.

2.7.7 Building alterations and machinery demolition

Alterations of buildings incidental to the installations of plant or machinery qualify for plant or machinery capital allowances (S.45 CAA 1968 and Para.15(2) Sch.8 FA 1971).

If a company incurs costs on demolishing plant or machinery which is then replaced by other plant the cost of the replacement plant or machinery for the purposes of capital allowances is increased by the costs of demolition. If not replaced the costs of demolition of plant form part of qualifying expenditure in the AP in which the demolition occurs and thus qualify for writing down allowances (Para.14 Sch.8 FA 1971).

2.7.8 Subsidies and investment grants

In the common case of investment grants (at 15% and 20%) payable under the Industrial Development Act 1982 the amount of the grant is not deducted from capital expenditure for the purposes of capital allowances generally (and other reliefs contained in Part I of the Capital Allowances Act 1968).

Example 19

Hero Ltd in its AP of twelve months ended 31 December 1983 incurred expenditure on a new borer costing £30,000. Hero Ltd is in a special development area and obtained a 20% investment grant.

The net cost to Hero Ltd of the borer is £30,000—20% × £30,000, £24,000. However Hero Ltd obtains a 100% first year allowance with respect to £30,000, a FYA of £30,000.

Other than investment grants under the Industrial Development Act 1972 subsidies by the Crown or any government or public or local authority are deductible from capital expenditure and only the net cost qualifies for allowances (S.84 CAA 1968 and Para.15(5) Sch.8 FA 1971).

2.7.9 Lessors of Plant and Machinery

Reference was made in 2.7.1 to the fact that a car hire company or taxi hire company obtains first year allowances in respect of its fleet of cars. These latter companies are examples of lessors of plant or machinery who obtain first year allowances in respect of the items of plant etc. which they hire or lease.

A first year allowance is only granted in respect of machinery or plant for leasing if it meets a range of conditions as to use for a 'requisite period', a period of four years from the date it is brought into use by the lessor company, e.g., it begins to hire out the plant. The 'requisite period' ends if e.g. the plant is sold before the end of the four years (S.64(1) and 98) FA 1980).

The more common types of uses which are a condition for the grant of first year allowances are as follows:

(a) The plant is leased to a company for the purposes of a trade (not a leasing trade) and the lessee company would have obtained a first year allowance had it bought the item itself e.g. a leasing company leases a computer to a manufacturing company. A first year allowance will be available to the lessor company because had the manufacturing lessee company incurred the expenditure it would have obtained one. On the other hand no first year allowance is granted on cars which are leased long-term to a trading company, by the same logic.

(b) The plant or machinery has been purchased for short-term leasing. Short-term leasing or hire means that, for example, a car is not hired to the same person for more than twenty-nine consecutive days or for more than eighty-nine days in any period of twelve months (S.64(3) FA 1980). This covers the case of the taxi-hire company which purchases a taxi.

(c) Also covered is the case of a lessor company which leases an item of plant to a lessee company which uses it for a short-term leasing trade e.g. a plant hire company leases from a leasing company earth-moving equipment which in turn the plant hire company hires out on short hires. In this case the leasing company obtains the allowance. The leasing company must be a UK resident or its trade must be a UK trade.

(d) Ships and aircraft which are let on charter are also qualifying uses subject to further conditions.

Where expenditure on plant and machinery by a lessor company does not qualify for a first year allowance it is placed in a pool in the same manner as cars costing up to £8,000 and obtains a 25% writing down allowance. Expenditure which does qualify will enter the general pool in the normal way.

If in the requisite period of four years a non-qualifying use supervenes upon a qualifying use there is a balancing charge of the amount of the 'excess relief' in the accounting period in which the change occurs. 'Excess relief' is the difference between the reliefs granted for qualifying use over what they would otherwise have been for non-qualifying use. The balancing charge which arises in this fashion in an accounting period is treated as expenditure in the next accounting period and goes into the separate pool referred to above (S.66 FA 1980).

In the case of machinery or plant leased to non resident companies which do not use the plant etc. for the purposes of a UK trade and where the lease is not a short-term lease, the writing down allowance is 10% not 25%. Such internationally leased assets are placed in a separate pool (S.70 and Sch.11 FA 1982). If the plant hired under the foreign lease is not used for a qualifying purpose the requisite period is extended from four to ten years.

2.8 OTHER RELIEFS FOR CAPITAL EXPENDITURE

We have considered earlier in this chapter outlines of the two main reliefs for capital expenditure, the industrial buildings allowance and capital allowances for plant and machinery. We shall look briefly at a further range of reliefs for specific kinds of capital expenditure as follows:

> Agricultural land and buildings
> Scientific research
> Know-how
> Patent rights.

In addition to this list there are reliefs for capital expenditure in connection with mines, oil wells and mineral depletion (a particularly complex set of reliefs which is under review), cemeteries and crematoria, and dredging. These reliefs are not considered here.

Although certain of the reliefs contain echoes of the main reliefs they are best seen at the time of writing as distinct, ad hoc reliefs. As an outcome of the government's review it seems likely that they will become in due course a more integral part of the general structures as they apply to industrial buildings and plant or machinery.

2.9 AGRICULTURAL LAND AND BUILDINGS

Certain building and other expenditure by a company which owns or leases agricultural or forestry land in the UK is granted an initial allowance of 20% and a writing down allowance of 10% on the straight line basis over 8 years beginning with the year in which the expenditure is incurred (S.68 CAA 1968).

The government has announced that the Finance Act 1985 will contain provisions to reduce the initial allowance to nil and the writing down allowance to 4% from 1 April 1986.

Example 20
Cheviot Ltd builds a cottage costing £30,000 for occupation by a farm worker on the farm which it owns in the company's accounting year ended 31 December 1984. The allowances granted to the company in its AP ended 31 December 1984 are as follows:

	£
Initial allowance 20%	6,000
Writing down allowance 10%	3,000
	9,000

In each of the seven subsequent accounting periods Cheviot Ltd obtains a writing down allowance of £3,000. If any of the accounting periods are less than twelve months in length the writing down allowance for that AP is proportionately reduced. The initial allowance is not reduced in this way and the aggregate amount of the writing down allowances over time (80% of the expenditure) is not affected.

A company can, within two years of the end of the relevant accounting period, disclaim the initial allowance or require it to be reduced to a specified amount. No similar provision obtains for disclaiming the writing down allowance. If the initial allowance is disclaimed in total then a writing down allowance of 10% on the straight line basis is given for the ten years beginning with the year of the expenditure.

If a reduced amount is claimed the period of years over which writing down allowances are granted is increased in accordance with a formula as follows:

Example 21
Company requires reduction of initial allowance to 15%. Remaining percentage of expenditure to be relieved is 85%. Years over which 85% of expenditure is relieved is $(85/100) \times 10$ years, ie, 8½ years. The annual amount of the allowance remains at 100% per annum for eight years, the balance of the allowance being taken in the ninth year (S.68(3A) CAA 1968).

When the land to which the capital expenditure refers is sold (or more generally the interest in the land is transferred) no balancing adjustments arise to the owner or tenant who incurred the expenditure, and the new owner or tenant then usually becomes entitled to any of the allowances still to be given. Needless to say this is significantly different from the position in the case of the major systems of capital allowances.

The relief for agricultural land and buildings expenditure is the only relief which we discuss in this chapter which is not treated as a trading expense for corporation tax purposes. Described as being made 'by way of discharge or repayment of tax' it is to be deducted in the first instance from agricultural or forestry income. If it cannot be wholly relieved against such income in an accounting period the company can claim to set off the excess of the relief against total profits of that accounting period and the preceding accounting period in a manner similar to, but not identical with, relief for trading losses; any excess relief can also be carried forward for set-off against agricultural or forestry income only, in subsequent accounting periods (Ss.68 and 74 CAA 1968). Relief under Section 254 Taxes Act (set-off against a surplus of franked investment income) is also available. The latter relief is fully explained in relation to trading losses in Chapter 4, and applies similarly to agricultural buildings allowances.

2.10 SCIENTIFIC RESEARCH

Capital expenditure on scientific research related to a trade carried on by a company is allowed a scientific research allowance of 100% (S.91 CAA 1968).

There are no provisions, as, for example, in the case of first year allowances, for disclaiming the allowance or claiming a reduced allowance. In any particular case the alternatives are:

(a) To have the full 100% allowance granted,
(b) To seek no allowance,
(c) To claim or be granted an industrial buildings allowance or plant or machinery allowance.

Scientific research means 'any activities in the fields of natural or applied science for the extension of knowledge' and includes scientific research which may lead to or facilitate an *extension* of a trade and any medical research specially related to workers' welfare in that trade. Thus if a company manufacturing bagpipes were to incur capital research expenditure into the manufacture of electronic bagpipes this would be of a kind to lead to or facilitate an extension of that company's trade and would, other things being equal, qualify for a scientific research allowance without the company having to show that it was its intention to manufacture such an instrument. Again a brewery company might incur capital expenditure to undertake medical research into alcoholism among brewery workers and be allowed the relief.

In order to qualify the expenditure must be on scientific research from the outset. It is not possible to transfer expenditure made at one time for another purpose (e.g. manufacture) to scientific research at a later time, and claim a scientific research allowance. On the other hand it is possible to incur capital expenditure on scientific research and claim the allowance and later transfer the assets to another purpose without losing the benefit of the original claim.

As long as the expenditure is capital and the expenditure is on scientific research related to the company's trade the nature of the asset, e.g. building or plant is immaterial. Thus qualifying assets may include laboratories, offices for research workers, plant and machinery including cars, aircraft and boats, prototype and pilot plant down to the time of testing, land, roads and other buildings and works, etc.

The allowance is granted as a trading expense in the accounting period in which the expenditure is incurred.

When the asset is sold, either

(a) the excess of the sale price and the amount of the allowance over the expenditure, or
(b) the amount of the allowance if less than the excess in (a) is treated as a trading receipt in the accounting period of sale (S.92(2) CAA 1968).

The above somewhat unfamiliar formulations have the same outcome as a balancing charge computation in the context of plant or machinery allowances where a first year allowance of 100% is granted and the disposal value cannot exceed cost.

Example 22
Scores Ltd, an electronics company, purchased a second-hand building for research into robotics. The cost of the building was £300,000 and a further £50,000 in alterations required by the research project was expended. The expenditure was incurred in the company's accounting period of twelve months ended 31 December 1981. In the year ended 31 December 1984 the building was sold. We shall consider the taxation implications of a sale of the building for (a) £250,000 and (b) £400,000.

In the accounting period ended 31 December 1981 the company would be allowed a scientific research allowance of £350,000.

(a) In the year ended 31 December 1984 there would be treated as a trading receipt:

		£
Sale price		250,000
Allowance		350,000
		600,000
Less: Expenditure		350,000
Excess		250,000

(b) In this instance the following would be treated as a trading receipt:

		£
Sale price		400,000
Allowance		350,000
		750,000
Less: Expenditure		350,000
Excess		400,000

Amount of allowance, £350,000, is less than excess of £400,000 and accordingly the amount of the allowance, £350,000, is the amount of the trading receipt.

2.11 KNOW-HOW

A company which purchases 'know-how' for use in its trade is entitled at the time of writing to an annual allowance of one-sixth for six years beginning with the accounting period in which the expenditure is incurred (S.386 TA 1970). The government has indicated that the Finance Act 1985 will contain provisions to alter the allowance to 25% using the reducing balance method.

Know-how is secret industrial information and techniques which either may not be capable of being patented or which it is not desired to patent; a separate relief is available for the purchase of patent rights. Receipts from sales of know-how are treated usually as trading receipts (S.386(2) TA 1970.

Example 23
North Ltd pays £60,000 to South Inc. a US company for certain secret manufacturing processes. The payment is made in North Ltd's accounting year ended 30 June 1983. North Ltd will be allowed a writing down allowance of £10,000 annually for the years ending 1983 to 1988. In the year ended 30 June 1985 North Ltd sold certain of these processes to Regulus Ltd for £12,000. In its AP ended 30 June 1985 North Ltd will have a trading receipt of £12,000 and North Ltd's allowances continue as before down to 1988. Regulus Ltd will be entitled to a writing down allowance in respect of its purchase.

2.12 PATENT RIGHTS

A company incurring capital expenditure on patent rights to be used in its trade is allowed a writing down allowance over a maximum period of seventeen years, which may be reduced if the rights have a lesser number of years to run (S.378 TA 1970). The writing down allowance commences in the AP in which the expenditure is incurred. The government has announced its intention of altering the relief to a 25% writing down allowance on the reducing balance method.

Question 2

Davy Jones Ltd, which manufactures steel lockers, completed an extension to its existing factory in February 1984. The total cost of the project, excluding items eligible for capital allowances as plant and machinery, was £142,000 made up as follows:

	£
Cost of additional land	20,000
Legal fees re above	1,000
Production area	84,000
New drawing office	8,100
Canteen and kitchen	14,600
Toilets	2,200
Works manager's office	6,300
Storerooms	2,800
Architect's fees	3,000
	142,000

The company makes up its accounts to 31 March annually and the relevant details relating to industrial buildings allowances on the factory at 31 March 1983 were:-

Year of expenditure	Allowable cost £	Residue of expenditure £
Year ended 31 March 1959	14,800	5,920
Year ended 31 March 1970	8,600	2,494
Year ended 31 March 1976	12,800	2,304
Year ended 31 March 1981	2,100	798

In April 1984 the company was acquired by Lockstock and Barrel Ltd which manufactures safes. Consideration is being given to the transfer of Davy Jones Ltd's activities to the premises of Lockstock and Barrel Ltd where there is spare capacity. The redundant factory would then be sold. A firm of chartered surveyors has indicated that the whole factory might sell for £400,000.

Required:

(1) Calculate the industrial buildings allowances due to Davy Jones Ltd for the year ended 31 March 1984.

(2) Prepare notes for a meeting with the accountant of Lockstock and Barrel Ltd to discuss the taxation implications of the possible sale of the Davy Jones Ltd factory indicating any further information which might be required.

Institute of Chartered Accountants of Scotland
Question 8, Part I Examination
September 1983 (amended)

CHAPTER 3

THE IMPUTATION SYSTEM

3.1 THE PRINCIPLES OF THE IMPUTATION SYSTEM

The imputation system of corporation tax is so called because part of the corporation tax paid by a company is ascribed or 'imputed' to shareholders and is treated as satisfying the basic rate tax liability on distributions received from the company. The mechanics for giving effect to the system are as follows:

(a) When a company distributes profits by way of dividend (or other so-called 'qualifying distribution') the company pays to the Revenue a sum called Advance Corporation Tax or ACT. The amount of advance corporation tax payable is computed by applying to the amount of the dividend a fraction which is fixed in successive finance acts for each financial year. The rate of ACT has remained at 3/7 since 1 April 1979.

The fractions are determined in practice by the basic rate of income tax in the corresponding fiscal year and such that when the basic rate of income tax is applied to the amount of a dividend plus the relative advance corporation tax, the amount so computed is the same a the amount of advance corporation tax. There is no theoretical reason why in an imputation system of corporation tax, the basic rate of income tax and the ACT rate should be related in this way, see 3.11

Example 1

A company pays a dividend of £70,000 in July 1984 when the rate of advance corporation tax is 3/7 and the basic rate of income tax, for 1984–85, is 30 per cent.

	£
The amount of the dividend	70,000
Plus the relative ACT, 3/7 × £70,000	30,000
Totals	100,000
Basic rate income tax of 30% applied to £100,000 is	30,000

which equals the amount of advance corporation tax.

(b) Payments of advance corporation tax by a company are what the name suggests. They are payments of corporation tax in advance of the normal due dates for payment of the tax. Payments of ACT in respect of distributions made in an accounting period are deducted, subject to certain restrictions, from the corporation tax charge on the profits of that accounting period in arriving at the corporation tax liability payable on the normal due date.

Example 2
The profits chargeable to corporation tax for a company's twelve month accounting period ended 31 March 1984 are £800,000. The company was formed in 1968 and accordingly the normal due date for payment of corporation tax for the accounting period ended 31 March 1984 is 31 December 1984. The rate of corporation tax for financial year 1983 is 50%. In July 1983 the company paid a dividend of £56,000 in respect of the year ended 31 March 1983. The rate of advance corporation tax for financial year 1983 is 3/7.

AP ended 31 March 1984
            Corporation tax payable £800,000 × 50% = £400,000

Advance corporation tax
The rate of advance corporation tax is 3/7. When this is applied to a dividend of £56,000 the result is an amount of ACT of £24,000. The payment of advance corporation tax of £24,000 is treated as extinguishing a part of the corporation tax liability for the year in which the dividend is *paid* regardless of the year for which it is expressed to be paid. Thus the amount of corporation tax payable on 31 December 1984 is as follows:

Corporation tax payable on 31 December 1984

	£
Corporation tax on profits for year ended 31 March 1984	400,000
Less: Advance corporation tax	24,000
Payable on due date	376,000

The net amount payable on the due date £376,000 is sometimes called 'mainstream corporation tax'.

(c) A United Kingdom resident person who receives a qualifying distribution from a company, receives in addition to the dividend what is called a tax credit which equals the amount of advance corporation tax paid by the company on making the distribution. The tax credit is not a sum of money, but as the name suggests, is a credit which an individual taxpayer can set off against his income tax liability on his total income for the fiscal year in which the dividend is received. An individual is liable to income tax on the amount of the dividend he receives plus the tax credit. Since 'advance corporation tax' and 'tax credit' are the same amount the total on which an individual is charged to income tax is the equivalent of the £100,000 in Example 1.

Example 3
A United Kingdom resident individual receives in January 1984 a dividend of £140 on his holding of ordinary shares in a United Kingdom company. The amount to be included in the income tax computation of the individual

is the amount of the dividend—£140 plus a tax credit of 3/7, the rate of advance corporation tax for the financial year 1983:

	£
Dividend	140
Tax credit 3/7 × £140	60
	200

Income tax is calculated on the total income of the individual including the dividend plus the tax credit, but the tax credit is set off against his income tax liability for 1983–84. This liability will be arrived at after deducting the personal allowances to which he is entitled. If in fact the taxpayer has no liability to income tax or a liability which is less than £60, the whole of the tax credit of £60 or the difference between the income tax liability and £60 is repaid to the taxpayer by the Inland Revenue.

3.2 THE NATURE OF DISTRIBUTIONS

Whenever a company makes a qualifying distribution it must account for advance corporation tax to the Revenue at the appropriate rate. The administrative arrangements for payment of advance corporation tax are discussed in 3.9 towards the end of this chapter. Almost all distributions are qualifying distributions. They are not deductible from profits in a corporation tax computation.

The definition of a distribution for the purposes of payment of advance corporation tax and for corporation tax generally, goes far beyond the payment of an ordinary or preference dividend. The intentions of the legislators in the extensive provisions of Ss.233–237, TA 1970 and Sch.22 FA 1972 are twofold. On the one hand is the intention to prevent profits reaching the taxpayer in a capital form and thus not liable to income tax, and on the other is the intention to prevent 'disguised' dividends reaching shareholders in the shape of interest.

Excluded from the definition of distribution for the purposes of corporation tax and advance corporation tax are distributions made in respect of shares in the course of the winding-up or liquidation of a company. Such distributions are capital and from the point of view of a shareholder represent disposals of his shares for capital gains tax purposes (S.233(1), TA 1970).

Most distributions for corporation tax fall into one of three broad categories:

(a) The first category of distribution involves the transfer of cash or other assets of the company to a shareholder. This category includes the normal kind of ordinary or preference dividend.
(b) The second category embraces repayments or reductions of share capital coupled with a bonus issue of shares, before or after the reduction. If the bonus issue of shares is made after reduction the

amount of the distribution is the amount treated as paid up on the bonus issue of shares. If the reduction follows the bonus issue the amount of the distribution is the reduction.

The second category also includes bonus issues of redeemable shares or securities. In this instance the bonus shares themselves are the distribution.

(c) The third category of distribution consists of interest payable in exceptional circumstances on loan stock and debentures. As we have already seen a payment of interest is usually a charge on income from which income tax is deducted at source, and which is deductible from total profits in a corporation tax computation.

The more important distributions included in each of the three categories are described below.

3.2.1 Distributions of cash or other assets

Dividends, including so-called capital dividends, are distributions. A capital dividend is a dividend which is described as such and which is paid out of a company's capital profits. The distinction between a capital dividend and any other kind of dividend has no significance for taxation.

Generally, any other distribution to shareholders of cash or other assets of the company will be a distribution for tax. However, if the shareholders pay in full for the assets transferred to them if, as the legislation says, the company has received 'new consideration' for the assets, then there is no distribution. 'New consideration' is defined in S.237(1) TA 1970 and means consideration not provided directly or indirectly out of the assets of the company.

Example 4

(a) ABC Ltd owns 20% of the shares of X Ltd. The shares in X Ltd are transferred to the shareholders of ABC Ltd and the revenue reserve of ABC Ltd debited. No payment or other new consideration is given by ABC shareholders for the transfer. Accordingly the transfer of X Ltd shares to ABC shareholders is a distribution for tax.

(b) The shares in X Ltd have a market value of 50p per share. If ABC shareholders were to pay ABC Ltd 50p a share then the shareholders have provided new consideration equal to the value of the shares transferred and accordingly the transfer is not a distribution.

(c) In (b) above, the shareholders of ABC paid the full market price for the asset they received from ABC Ltd. If they had paid less than the full market price then S.233(3) TA 1970 provides that the difference between the market value of the asset and the new consideration is a distribution. Thus if they had paid 30p per share when the shares in X Ltd had a market value as before of 50p per share, 20p per share would constitute a distribution.

Example 5

PQR Ltd buys a building from an individual shareholder for £80,000, when the market value of the building is £50,000. The difference between the value of the asset transferred by the company, i.e. cash of £80,000 and the new consideration received by the company, that is the building having a value of £50,000, is a distribution.

No payment of cash which is a repayment of capital is a distribution.

Example 6

A company has a share capital of 100,000 ordinary shares of £1 all subscribed in cash. In a scheme of reduction of capital the company reduces the shares to 100,000 ordinary shares of 50p and repays 50p on each share. The repayment is not a distribution. From the shareholder's point of view it is a part disposal of his shares for capital gains tax purposes.

The general principle that any transfer of an asset for less than full consideration by a company to a shareholder is a distribution is set aside where the shareholder is the parent, or the fellow subsidiary of the company making the transfer (S.233(3) TA 1970). For this purpose a subsidiary is a company of which more than 50% of the ordinary share capital is owned by its parent. Such a subsidiary is called in the Taxes Act a '51% subsidiary' (S.532 TA 1970).

Example 7

Vax Ltd is the 51 per cent subsidiary of Quad Ltd. Vax Ltd transfers to Quad Ltd at book value of £100,000 a building with a market value of £500,000. Because Quad Ltd is Vax's parent there is no distribution on the transfer of the building from Vax to Quad for less than full consideration.

3.2.2 Bonus issues coupled with repayment of capital and bonus issues of redeemable capital

A straightforward bonus issue of shares is not a distribution, and as we have seen in Example 6, a repayment or reduction of capital is not a distribution. It is only when a bonus issue is coupled with a repayment of capital that a distribution may arise.

(a) If a company repays ordinary share capital and at the same time or later makes a bonus issue of shares, the amount treated as paid up on the bonus issue is a distribution unless the bonus is declared more than ten years after the repayment (S.234 TA 1970 and Para.5 Sch.22 FA 1972). A repayment of preference shares is excluded from these provsions. In the case of a closely held family company the 'ten-year exception' does not apply and a bonus issue at any time following a repayment of capital after 6 April 1965 is a distribution.

Example 8

OPQ Ltd with a share capital of £250,000 in £1 ordinary shares, all subscribed in cash, and a revenue reserve of £80,000 repays 25p on each £1 ordinary share. The repayment of 25p is not a distribution. The total amount repaid is £62,500. Shortly afterwards OPQ makes a bonus issue of ordinary shares totalling £62,500, debiting revenue reserve with £62,500. A bonus issue of this kind, coupled as here, with a reduction of capital, is a distribution. Without special legislation it would be possible for shareholders by this means to receive the revenue reserves of a company in a capital form. Presumably after ten years the relationship between the reduction and the bonus is too remote to concern the legislators.

(b) A repayment of share capital is not a distribution. However, where a repayment follows an earlier bonus issue of shares made after 6 April 1965, the amount of the repayment is a distribution unless the repayment is made more than ten years after the bonus issue of capital (S.235 TA 1970 and Para.6 Sch.22 FA 1972). As before the 'ten-year exception' does not apply to a closely held family company. Thus a bonus issue of shares preceded or followed by a reduction of share capital may give rise to a distribution for tax purposes.

(c) Finally in this category the issue to shareholders or debenture holders of bonus redeemable share capital or bonus securities, e.g. bonus debentures or loan stock, is a distribution. The significant characteristic of this kind of distribution is that the bonus issues are redeemable. The amount of the distribution is the amount of the bonus redeemable capital.

Bonus redeemable shares or securities are in the small group of distributions which are 'non-qualifying' for advance corporation tax purposes. No advance corporation tax is payable in respect of such distributions.

Example 9
A company makes an issue of 50,000 bonus redeemable preference shares of £1 each and debits its revenue reserve with £50,000. The company has made a non-qualifying distribution of £50,000. No advance corporation tax is payable by the company. Shareholders in receipt of the bonus shares are liable to higher rate taxes only in respect of their respective shares of £50,000. No addition is made for a tax credit since the distribution is non-qualifying.

It has already been seen in (b) above that a repayment of a bonus issue of shares is a distribution. It follows therefore that the redemption of bonus redeemable shares, being a repayment of share capital gives rise to a further distribution. In the latter case the distribution is a qualifying one giving rise to a payment of advance corporation tax. The legislation in S.87(6) FA 1972 provides for the set-off of income tax suffered on the issue of the bonus redeemable shares against the tax suffered on the redemption.

3.2.3 Interest payments in certain circumstances

The following is a summary of the more usual cases where interest payable on loan stock or debentures may be found in this third category of distributions:

(a) Interest on bonus redeemable securities of the kind which are themselves distributions,

(b) Interest on debentures or other securities which are convertible into shares or carry a right to receive shares,

(c) Interest which depends to any extent on the results of the company,

(d) Interest which is in excess of a reasonable commercial rate; only the amount in excess of a reasonable commercial rate is a distribution.

The interest payments outlined in paragraphs (a) and (b) above will not generally be treated as distributions where the recipient is a company within the charge to corporation tax. Thus the impact of paragraphs (a) and (b) will be restricted to interest payments to shareholders who are individuals.

In addition, interest payments within paragraph (c) will not be treated as distributions where the recipient is a company unless the obligation was entered into before 9 March 1982 (or 1 July 1982 if negotiations had commenced before 9 March 1982), the principal is £100,000 or less, and the principal and interest are repayable within five years.

Example 10

A company proposes to accept a loan of £500,000 from a friend of a shareholder. The alternative rates of interest proposed are:

(a) 20% per annum. HM Inspector of Taxes considers that 20% is a reasonable commercial rate.

(b) 25% per annum.

(c) 15% per annum and 30% if profits exceed £40,000.

As regards alternative (a) the whole of the interest paid of 20 per cent is a charge on income deductible from total profits. No part is a distribution.

Since alternative (b) is interest in excess of a reasonable commercial rate the excess interest, 5%, is a distribution. The part of the interest which is considered to be at a reasonable commercial rate, 20%, is a charge on income (Para.3(2) Sch.22 FA 1972).

The whole amount of interest paid under alternative (c), 15% or, when profits exceed £400,000, 30%, is a distribution. This should be contrasted with the position under alternative (b) where only the excess over a commercial rate is a distribution.

3.2.4 Purchase by a company of its own shares

A repayment of share capital is not a distribution (S.233(2)(b) FA 1970). If, however, in terms of the Companies Act 1981, a company purchases its own shares, there is, subject to an important exception described below, a distribution of the excess of the purchase price over the amount originally subscribed for the shares.

Example 11

Joy Ltd purchased from S, an individual shareholder, 10,000 of its shares for a sum of £35,000. The original subscription for the shares was £10,000. On the basis that the transaction does not meet the conditions described below a distribution arises as follows:

	£
Purchase price	35,000
Original subscription	10,000
Distribution	25,000

Since the amount of the distribution, with the addition of the tax credit of three-sevenths, is taxed as income in the hands of S, a purchase by a company of its own shares from an individual shareholder is unlikely to be attractive in these circumstances.

In a case where an *unquoted trading company* purchases its own shares from a shareholder, and provided other conditions are satisfied, the purchase will not be a distribution but will be within the normal charge to capital gains tax (S.53 and Sch.9 FA 1982). The other conditions are as follows:

(1) The reason why the company wishes to purchase its own shares must fall into one of two categories:
   (a) A shareholder is faced with a Capital Transfer Tax liability arising on a death and cannot meet this liability without undue hardship unless he sells his shares, or
   (b) The company wishes to purchase its shares wholly or mainly to benefit the trade.

When the legislation was first introduced there were considerable doubts expressed as to the types of situation in which a company could argue that it wished to purchase its own shares in order to benefit its trade. The Inland Revenue have indicated in a Statement of Practice that they will accept that the purchase of its shares would benefit a company's trade in the following sets of circumstances:

(i) a dissident shareholder is having an adverse effect on the running of the company's trade.
(ii) the majority shareholder is retiring to make way for new management.
(iii) an outside shareholder is withdrawing his investment.
(iv) the personal representatives of a shareholder who has died do not wish to keep the shares.

In all four circumstances the shareholder would normally be expected to dispose of the whole of his holding.

If the reason for the purchase of the shares is to meet a capital transfer tax liability, there are no further conditions to be satisfied. However if the reason for the purchase is within 1(b) above the legislation requires a further four main conditions to be satisfied:

(2) The vendor must be resident and ordinarily resident in the United Kingdom in the year of assessment in which the shares are purchased

(3) In most cases the vendor must have owned the shares throughout the period of five years ending with the date of purchase. Periods of ownership by a spouse will be aggregated with the period of ownership by the shareholder so long as the shares were transferred by the vendor to this spouse when they were living together.

(4) As a result of the purchase of the shares by the company the vendor's interest in the company must be substantially reduced, i.e. reduced by at least 25%. When considering this condition one must have regard to the holdings of the shareholders 'associates', such as the vendor's husband or wife and parents or minor children. Where the vendor owns shares in more than one company there must be a substantial reduction in his interest in the group as a whole.

(5) After the purchase of the shares by the company the vendor must no longer be 'connected' with the company or any other company in the same 51% group. Broadly, a person will be treated as 'connected' with the company if he, together with his associates, owns more than 30% of the issued share capital.

In the case of both (4) and (5) it should be borne in mind that the Revenue Statement of Practice goes further than the legislation and envisages that the shareholder will generally dispose of the whole of his holding.

The legislation provides that the purchase of its shares by a company msut not form part of a scheme or arrangement which has as one of its main purposes the avoidance of tax (S.53(1) FA 1982).

Where there are doubts about whether a particular transaction satisfies the conditions of S.53 it is possible to apply to the Board of Inland Revenue for clearance (Para.10 Sch.9 FA 1982).

3.2.5 Demergers

In another set of circumstances the legislation has stepped in to prevent what would otherwise be a distribution being so treated. The circumstances are as follows:

Suppose company A owns all the shares of its subsidiary company, B. In A's balance sheet appears an asset which is its shareholding in company B. Suppose then it is desired to 'demerge' company B, that is, it is desired that company B no longer be a subsidiary of company A but have an independent existence, not, it should be stressed, independent of its ultimate owners, the shareholders of company A, but independent of its legal owner, its parent company A. One way to achieve this would be for company A to simply hand over its shares in company B to its (company A's) shareholders pro rata with their shareholding.

Without special relieving provisions such a transfer would be a qualifying distribution by the company and income in the hands of the shareholders.

However in the above and other similar circumstances Sch.18 FA 1980 provides that such a distribution will be an 'exempt' distribution, i.e. no

ACT is payable and the distribution is not income of the demerging company's shareholder.

The general condition for the application of the relieving provisions is that a company is seeking to demerge its 75% subsidiaries, i.e. those subsidiaries in which it owns 75% or more of the ordinary share capital.

3.3 QUALIFYING AND NON-QUALIFYING DISTRIBUTIONS

All except one of the distributions within the three categories of distribution in 3.2 above are qualifying distributions and require that an amount of advance corporation tax should be accounted for. The solitary exception was an issue of bonus redeemable shares or securities—which is a non-qualifying distribution.

There is only one other kind of non-qualifying distribution. This is where a company X receives a non-qualifying distribution of the kind referred to above, say bonus redeemable preference shares, from company Y in respect of shares which company X holds in company Y. Company X then has an asset, the bonus shares in Y, which it transfers to its shareholders. This transfer in these special circumstances will be a non-qualifying distribution by company X (S.84(4) FA 1972).

3.4 FRANKED INVESTMENT INCOME

A United Kingdom resident person who receives a dividend or other qualifying distribution from a United Kingdom company is entitled to a tax credit. The amount of the credit is equal to the advance corporation tax paid by the company in respect of the dividend.

When such a dividend is received by a company the total of the dividend and the tax credit is called *franked investment income*.

Example 12
VB Ltd prepares accounts to 30 September each year. It received a dividend from a United Kingdom company of £35,000 in August 1984.

Amount of franked investment income

	£
Dividend received	35,000
Tax credit 3/7 × £35,000	15,000
Franked investment income	50,000

Franked investment income is so called because the income out of which the dividend has been paid has been charged or 'franked' with corporation tax. The distribution in short has been made out of post-tax profits. Franked investment income should be distinguished from unfranked investment income (income received by a company from which income tax has been deducted at source) described in 1.5.3. Franked investment income is not charged to corporation tax in the hands of the company receiving it. The income is regarded as having already suffered corporation tax.

A company receiving FII is entitled to a tax credit in the same way as an individual but the uses to which the tax credit may be put are peculiar to companies.

(a) The tax credit in franked investment income may be set off against the liability of the company to pay advance corporation tax on its own qualifying distributions made in the accounting period in which the FII is received, or in subsequent accounting periods, see 3.5.
(b) The tax credit may, *in one particular case*, be repaid to the company. This will be discussed in section 4.6.

3.5 FRANKED PAYMENTS

When considering the general principles of the imputation system it was seen that a company making a qualifying distribution must account to the Revenue for advance corporation tax at the rate of 3/7 of the amount of the distribution. The sum of the distribution plus the ACT is called a *franked payment*.

Example 13
VB Ltd pays a dividend of £105,000 in July 1984.
Amount of franked payment

	£
Qualifying distribution July 1984	105,000
Advance corporation tax 3/7 × £105,000	45,000
Franked payment	150,000

Advance corporation tax may be calculated in one of two ways:

(i) By applying the appropriate *fraction* to the amount of the dividend or
(ii) By taking the appropriate *percentage* of the franked payment.

Example 14
In Example 13 the two ways in which the advance corporation tax could be calculated are:
(a) 3/7 × £105,000 = £45,000
(b) 30% × £150,000 = £45,000

If, instead of applying the fraction 3/7, we thought in terms of a fraction 30/70 we would note, as a matter of practice, that:
(a) The numerator of the ACT fraction is the same as the basic rate of income tax for the corresponding fiscal year, e.g. 30/70 is effectively

the advance corporation tax proportion for the financial year 1984 and 30% is the basic rate of income tax for 1984/85.

(b) The numerator of the ACT fraction (for 3/7 read 30/70) expressed as a percentage and applied to the amount of a franked payment yields the amount of advance corporation tax required.

We have talked above in terms of the company 'accounting to the Revenue for advance corporation tax' rather than 'paying ACT'. The reason for the distinction is that the company will not necessarily have to pay to the Revenue the full amount of ACT on the distribution. If the company receives franked investment income during the accounting period in which the franked payment is made, the FII will be set against the franked payment and the company is only required to pay advance corporation tax on the *excess* of franked payments over franked investment income.

Example 15

In Examples 12 and 13 VB Ltd paid a dividend of £105,000 in July 1984 and received a dividend of £35,000 in August 1984.

The amount of ACT payable on the July distribution is calculated as follows:

	£
Franked payment	150,000
Less: Franked investment income	50,000
Excess of franked payment over FII	100,000
ACT payable	
£100,000 × 30% =	30,000

Note: It is important that the computation proceeds in this way by setting off franked investment income against franked payments, and not setting off credits against ACT amounts. This is because where the advance corporation tax rate changes a computation on the basis of a direct set-off of credits against ACT will yield an incorrect answer.

3.6 SET-OFF OF ADVANCE CORPORATION TAX

We have already mentioned in this chapter that advance corporation tax is, quite simply, a payment in advance; that is to say, a payment made during, or close to the end of an accounting period before the actual corporation tax liability for that accounting period has been determined. One might expect that the full amount of the ACT paid in respect of a particular accounting period would as a matter of course be set-off against the corporation tax liability as subsequently determined, but this is not always the case. In certain circumstances the legislation restricts the amount of advance corporation tax that may be deducted in arriving at the company's mainstream corporation tax liability.

3.6.1 Set-off of advance corporation tax against corporation tax on income

Section 85(1) Finance Act 1972 permits the set-off of ACT against a company's liability to corporation tax on its income. It will be recalled that corporation tax is payable by a company on its *profits*; however it is only the liability on its *income* that may be reduced by the application of advance corporation tax.

The company's 'income' comprises the profits chargeable to corporation tax less the chargeable gains. Thus the company's corporation tax liability on its chargeable gains may never be reduced by the offset of advance corporation tax.

Example 16

Manvix Ltd has the following results for the accounting period ended 31 March 1984:

	£
Schedule D Case I	30,000
Chargeable gains (abated)	50,000
Charges paid	20,000
Franked payments	30,000
Advance corporation tax paid	9,000

ACT computation for AP ended 31 March 1984

	£
Schedule D Case I	30,000
Chargeable gains	50,000
	80,000
Less: Charges paid	20,000
Profits chargeable	60,000

Corporation tax payable:

Income:	
£60,000–£50,000=£10,000×30% =	3,000
Less: ACT restricted to	3,000
	Nil
Chargeable gains: £50,000 × 50%	25,000
Corporation tax payable	25,000

Note: ACT of £9,000 was paid during the accounting period but only £3,000 has been set off against the corporation tax liability. The remaining £6,000 is termed 'surplus advance corporation tax'. The uses to which surplus advance corporation tax can be put will be dealt with in Section 3.7.

3.6.2 Restriction of advance corporation tax set-off

There is a further restriction on the amount of advance corporation tax that may be set off against the company's liability to corporation tax on its income. This restriction is dealt with in sub-section (2) of S.85 FA 1972 which states that the maximum ACT set-off permissible is an amount which when added to a qualifying distribution equals the *income* of the company.

The restriction in S.85(2) may be put another way by saying that if the company made franked payments during the accounting period of an amount equal to its income then the ACT that would be payable in respect of those franked payments represents the maximum amount of advance corporation tax that may be set off against the company's corporation tax liability.

Example 17
Rulers Ltd has income of £600,000 in the year ended 31 March 1984.
The company paid a dividend of £770,000 on 10 December 1983 and accounted for advance corporation tax of £330,000 on 13 January 1984.
Corporation tax on the profits is:
$$£600,000 \times 50\% = £300,000$$
The maximum ACT that may be set off against the corporation tax liability is calculated as follows:

The income is £600,000. If the company made franked payments of £600,000 the advance corporation tax payable would be £600,000 × 30% = £180,000
Therefore the maximum advance corporation tax that may be set off under S.85(2) FA 1972 is £180,000.

It can be seen that the restriction contained in S.85(2) can be reduced to a very simple rule which will always apply so long as the basic rate of income tax is 30% and the rate of advance corporation tax is 3/7. This rule is as follows:
The maximum amount of advance corporation tax that can be set off in arriving at the company's mainstream corporation tax liability is an amount equal to 30% of the company's income.

The application of this restriction should be considered as a matter of course in any corporation tax computation. This may be done by looking at two figures:

(a) Take 30% of the income of the company for the accounting period,
(b) Take 30% of the franked payments, less the franked investment income for the accounting period.

If (a) is greater than (b) then no restriction is called for. If, however, (b) is greater than (a) then there must be a restriction of the amount of advance corporation tax that may be deducted in arriving at the mainstream corporation tax liability.

Example 18

The results of Hoppers Ltd for the year ended 31 March 1984 are as follows:

	£
Schedule D Case I	560,000
Schedule A	5,000
Chargeable gains (abated)	20,000
Charges paid	85,000
Franked payments made	510,000
FII received	15,000

Corporation tax computation for AP ended 31 March 1984

	£	£
Schedule D Case I		560,000
Schedule A		5,000
Chargeable gains		20,000
		585,000
Less: Charges		85,000
Profits chargeable to corporation tax		500,000
Corporation tax payable		
£500,000 × 50%		250,000
Less: ACT		
Franked payments	510,000	
Less: FII	150,000	
Excess	495,000	
ACT paid by company:		
£495,000 × 30% = £148,500:		
ACT set off restricted to income		
(i.e. £500,000 — £20,000 =		
£480,000) × 30% = £144,000		144,000
Mainstream corporation tax payable		106,000

Note: The company paid advance corporation tax of £148,500 but has been permitted to set off only £144,000. There is thus a surplus of ACT of £4,500.

We have tried to simplify the S.85(2) restriction by saying that in order to decide whether a restriction is necessary you should compare the advance corporation tax paid with the figure resulting from multiplying the income of the company by 30%. This statement only applies so long as the basic rate of income tax remains at 30% and the ACT rate remains at 3/7. If for example the rate of income tax was reduced to 25% and consequently the advance corporation tax rate was reduced to 25/75 then you would multiply by 25% instead of 30%.

Example 19

The computation of profits chargeable to corporation tax for Skippers Ltd for a year ended 31 March is as follows:

	£
Schedule D Case I	72,000
Schedule A	4,000
Chargeable gain (abated)	6,000
	82,000
Less: Charges	12,000
Profits chargeable to corporation tax	70,000

Assume the following rates of tax:
Income tax, basic rate: 25%
ACT 25/75 or 1/3
Corporation tax—small companies: 30%
        —others: 35%

Assume also that the company received dividends of £3,000 and paid a dividend of £75,000 during the accounting period.

Corporation tax payable:

		£	£
Income: £70,000–£6,000=£64,000×30%			
(small company rate applicable to income)			19,200
Chargeable gain: 6,000 × 35%			2,100
			21,300
Less: ACT:			
Dividend paid		75,000	
Add: ACT at 1/3		25,000	
Franked payment		100,000	
	£		
Less: Dividend received	3,000		
Add: Tax credit	1,000		
FII	4,000	4,000	
Excess		96,000	

ACT paid: £96,000 × 25% = £24,000
Set-off restricted to income × 25%, i.e. £64,000 × 25%   16,000

Mainstream corporation tax		5,300

Note: Surplus advance corporation tax = £24,000 — £16,000 = £8,000.

3.6.3 Advance corporation tax rate change during accounting period

Where different rates of advance corporation tax apply in different parts of the accounting period of a company, it is necessary in calculating the restricted amount of advance corporation tax deductible, to apportion the company's income on a time basis to the different parts (S.103(4) FA 1972). The appropriate ACT percentage for each part is then applied to the apportioned income.

Example 20
Leapers Ltd has income of £100,000 for its accounting year ended 30 September 1999. The company paid a dividend of £83,750 on 1 July in that year.
Assume that advance corporation tax rates are as follows:
   Financial year 1998 35/65 (linked to a 35% basic rate of income tax)
   Financial year 1999 33/67 (linked to a 33% basic rate of income tax).

The maximum ACT that may be deducted from the corporation tax liability for the accounting period ended 30 September 1999 is calculated as follows:
Income apportioned to period 1 October 1998
to 31 March 1999

	£	ACT Restriction £
£100,000 × 6/12 =	50,000	
Amount of restriction:		
£50,000 × 35% =		17,500

Income apportioned to period 1 April 1999
to 30 September 1999

	£	£
£100,000 × 6/12 =	50,000	
Amount of restriction:		
£50,000 × 33%		16,500
Maximum ACT set off		34,000

The company paid a dividend of £83,750 on 1 July 1999 and had to account for advance corporation tax of £41,250. Although this amount was paid, only £34,000 may be deducted from the corporation tax liability and therefore the company has surplus advance corporation tax of £7,250. The methods whereby this surplus may be used are dealt with below.

3.7 SURPLUS ADVANCE CORPORATION TAX

We have seen that a surplus of advance corporation tax arises whenever more ACT has been paid in an accounting period than it is possible to set against the corporation tax liability for that accounting period.

There are three ways in which a company can use a surplus of ACT:

(a) In so far as the surplus arises in accounting periods ending on or after 1 April 1984 it may be carried back to accounting periods commencing in the six years preceding the accounting period in which the surplus arises (S.85(3) FA 1972).
(b) The surplus may be carried forward to future accounting periods (S.85(4) FA 1972).
(c) The company may surrender the surplus (or indeed any amount of ACT) to a 51% subsidiary of the company. The meaning of a 51% subsidiary and the nature and consequences of a surrender of advance corporation tax are considered in Chapter 5.

3.7.1 Carry back of surplus advance corporation tax

The surplus may be carried back and set off against the corporation tax liability on the company's income for accounting periods commencing in the six years preceding the accounting period in which the surplus arises (S.85(3) FA 1972 and S.52 FA 1984). The surplus is set, as far as possible, against corporation tax for a more recent accounting period before a more remote one. The claim to carry back the surplus must be made within two years after the end of the accounting period in which the surplus arose.

The six year period of carry back is only available in respect of a surplus of ACT attributable to an accounting period ending on or after 1 April 1984. For surpluses arising in accounting periods ending before 1 April 1984 the carry back period is two years.

A surplus of advance corporation tax which is carried back to an earlier accounting period will be applied after applying any ACT which actually was paid in respect of that earlier accounting period. The restriction on the set off of advance corporation tax applies not only in the accounting period in which a surplus arises but also in the application of ACT carried back to preceding years. See Example 19.

3.7.2 Carry forward of surplus advance corporation tax

If the company makes no claim to carry the surplus back, or if there remains some unrelieved advance corporation tax after it has claimed to carry back under S.85(3) FA 1972, the amount of the surplus, or the amount of the surplus unrelieved, will be carried forward and set off against corporation tax on income in the next accounting period. If it cannot be relieved or fully relieved in the next accounting period it will be carried forward as a surplus to the next accounting period again and so on (S.84(5) FA 1972).

Example 21

The following facts concern Trotters Ltd for the five years since trading commenced on 1 April 1980:

Years ended	31 March 1981	31 March 1982	31 March 1983	31 March 1984	31 March 1985
	£	£	£	£	£
Profits chargeable (all trading income)	80,000	70,000	60,000	30,000	10,000
Franked investment income	40,000	40,000	40,000	—	—
Franked payments	90,000	90,000	90,000	90,000	25,000
ACT paid	15,000	15,000	15,000	27,000	7,500
CT rate	50%	50%	50%	50%	50%
ACT rate	3/7	3/7	3/7	3/7	3/7

For simplicity a corporation tax rate of 50% has been applied for all years although the small company rate would apply in reality.

The first year in which a surplus of advance corporation tax arises is the year to 31 March 1984, therefore this is the first year that we shall consider.

	£	£
AP ended 31 March 1984		
Corporation tax payable £30,000 × 50% =		15,000
Less: Advance corporation tax:		
ACT paid year ended 31 March 1984	27,000	
Less: Maximum set-off permitted		
£30,000 × 30%	9,000	9,000
Surplus ACT	18,000	
Corporation tax payable		6,000

The surplus of ACT of £18,000 may be carried back and set off against the corporation tax liability for the *two* preceding accounting periods. (*Note:* carry back period is two years because accounting period ends before 1 April 1984).

	£	£
AP ended 31 March 1983		
Corporation tax payable £60,000 × 50% =		30,000
Less: ACT (maximum set off permitted,		
£60,000 × 30% = 18,000)		
ACT paid year ended 31 March 1983	15,000	
Add: Surplus ACT from year ended		
31 March 1984	3,000	18,000
Corporation tax payable		12,000

	£	£
AP ended 31 March 1982		
Corporation tax payable £70,000 × 50% =		35,000
Less: ACT (maximum set of permitted		
£70,000 × 30% = 21,000)		
ACT paid year ended 31 March 1982	15,000	
Add: Surplus ACT from 31 March 1984	6,000	21,000
Corporation tax payable		14,000

Summary of use of surplus ACT arising in year ended 31 March 1984

	£	£
Surplus ACT		18,000
Less: Utilized in year ended 31 March 1983	3,000	
Utilized in year ended 31 March 1982	6,000	9,000
Surplus ACT to carry forward		9,000

The surplus ACT arising in the year ended 31 March 1984 has been carried back as far as permitted, the balance of £9,000 will therefore be carried forward to future accounting periods (see section 3.7.2).

	£	£
AP ended 31 March 1985		
Corporation tax payable £10,000 × 50% =		5,000
Less: ACT:		
ACT paid year ended		
31 March 1984	7,500	
Less: Maximum set off permitted		
£10,000 × 30%	3,000	3,000
Surplus ACT	4,500	
Corporation tax payable		2,000

The surplus of advance corporation tax arising in the year ended 31 March 1985 may be carried back and set off against the corporation tax liability for accounting periods commencing in the preceding six years. In the years from 1 April 1981 to 31 March 1984 the maximum set off permitted has already been made, therefore this surplus may be carried back to the year ended 31 March 1981.

	£	£
AP ended 31 March 1981		
Corporation tax payable £80,000 × 50% =		40,000
Less: ACT (maximum set-off permitted,		
£80,000 × 30% = £24,000)		
ACT paid year ended 31 March 1981	15,000	
Add: Surplus ACT from year ended		
31 March 1985	4,500	
Total ACT deductible	19,500	19,500
Corporation tax liability		20,500

At the end of the accounting period ended 31 March 1985 the balance of the surplus arising in the year ended 31 March 1984, i.e. £9,000, is available for carry forward to the year ended 31 March 1986 and subsequent years.

3.8 USES OF SURPLUS ADVANCE CORPORATION TAX— ANTI-AVOIDANCE

A company which has a surplus of ACT, perhaps accumulated over some years, has an asset which in certain circumstances could be reflected in the value of the company's shares. Suppose company X has experienced many years of successful trading followed by several years of losses and ultimately by a decline in the company's business to the point where the business has become very small. In bad times as well as good the company has declared large dividends so that in the years when losses were made large surpluses of advance corporation tax arose. Company Y which is in the same line of business as company X considers that if it were to buy the shares of X from the present shareholders of that company, so that company X became the wholly owned subsidiary of company Y, it could divert sufficient business from its own activities to make company X profitable again. Against the subsequent corporation tax charge on the profits of company X, company X would be able to off-set the surplus of advance corporation tax which it is carrying forward from its loss-making years.

The existence of a surplus of ACT in company X in these circumstances effectively reduces the tax burden on company Y's profits. Accordingly, when company Y is considering the purchase price of X Ltd's shares it will pay a price which reflects the value to Y of X's surplus ACT.

To stop the buying and selling of 'surplus advance corporation tax companies', S.101 FA 1972 provides that in certain circumstances where there is a change of ownership (as for example when X Ltd above becomes a wholly owned subsidiary of Y Ltd), an accounting period is deemed to end on the date the change-over takes place. No ACT paid on distributions made in accounting periods preceding the change in ownership, including any paid in the deemed accounting period ending with the change of ownership, can be set off against the corporation tax liabilities of later accounting periods.

Section 101, Finance Act 1972 provides that where:

(a) within any period of three years there is:
    (i) a change in the ownership of a company, and
    (ii) a major change in the nature or conduct of the company's trade or business, *or*
(b) at any time after a company's business has become small or negligible and before any revival there is a change of ownership, surplus advance corporation tax from a period before the change of ownership can only be set against corporation tax liabilities up to the date of the change of ownership.

Alternative (b) above describes the position of companies X and Y. Alternative (a) arises where there is a change of ownership associated with a major change in the nature or conduct of a company's trade or business.

A major change in the nature or conduct of a trade or business includes:

(a) a major change in the kind of property dealt in or services or facilities provided,
(b) a major change in customers, outlets or markets (S.101(4) FA 1971).

The meaning of a 'major change' is not defined in the legislation.

The period of three years referred to in S.101 FA 1972 means that as long as the nature or conduct of the trade or business is not significantly changed until more than three years after a change of ownership, it should still be possible to carry forward pre-change advance corporation tax surpluses. Thus in many cases there will be a three-year quarantine. However, this possibility only arises in the case of alternative (a).

A change of ownership is determined in accordance with detailed rules contained in S.484 TA 1970. A change of ownership may be usefully thought of as occurring whenever a person acquires or persons acquire more than half of the ordinary shares of a company.

3.9 ACCOUNTING FOR ADVANCE CORPORATION TAX

We saw in section 1.8 that for the purposes of accounting for income tax each accounting period of a company is divided into quarterly return periods. The return of dividends and advance corporation tax payable is made by reference to the same return periods and is made on the same Revenue form CT61. As with income tax the return form and payment of advance corporation tax are due fourteen days from the end of the return period.

A return on form CT61 will give details of franked payments made during the return period and franked investment income received. As we have seen during this chapter advance corporation tax is payable in respect of the excess of franked payments over FII.

It may be that in some return periods the company makes distributions and therefore pays ACT, while in other return periods it receives FII but does not make franked payments. The general principle is that over the course of the whole accounting period the company should only pay ACT on the *excess* of franked payments over franked investment income. Thus the legislation specifies two sets of circumstances in which a return on form CT61 must be made:

(a) Any return period in which a franked payment is made, and
(b) Any return period in which the company receives franked investment income if in an earlier return period in the same accounting period the company made a distribution and paid ACT. (This is because by this means it will be repaid the ACT which has been paid earlier in the accounting period (Para.4, Sch.14 FA 1972).)

If neither of the two sets of circumstances outlined above applies, there is no requirement on the company to make a return.

Example 22
Runners Ltd provides details of the following transactions in its accounting period ended 31 March 1984:

FII received (inclusive of tax credit):

	£
12 April 1983	3,000
4 June 1983	900
10 October 1983	5,000

Franked payments made:

15 July 1983	50,000

Return period ended 30 June 1983
No return required because no franked payments made. FII received £3,900 is carried forward to next return period.

	£
Return period ended 30 September 1983	
Franked payment	50,000
Less: FII	3,900
	46,100

ACT payable by 14 October 1983	
£46,100 × 30%	13,830

Return period ended 31 December 1983
A repayment of £1,500 arises in this return period and a return which constitutes the claim to repayment, will be made on form CT61. The repayment arises because over the whole accounting period so far the advance corporation tax position is as follows:

	£	£
Franked payment		50,000
Less: FII		
13 April 1983	3,000	
4 June 1983	900	
10 October 1983	5,000	
	8,900	8,900
		41,100
ACT due so far: £41,100 × 30%		12,330
ACT already paid		13,830
Therefore repay		1,500

Return period ended 31 March 1984
No return required

3.10 SURPLUS FRANKED INVESTMENT INCOME

It has been seen above that franked investment income reduces the corporation tax that has to be paid in advance. It can happen that FII received in an accounting period exceeds the amount of franked payments. When this occurs we have what is called a *surplus of franked investment income*. A surplus of FII can be carried forward from one accounting period to the following accounting period and set off against franked payments in that accounting period. If the surplus plus any FII received in the following accounting period again exceeds franked payments the new surplus is carried forward to the next and succeeding accounting periods until the surplus is absorbed by franked payments. A trading loss may in certain circumstances be relieved by set-off against a surplus of franked investment income. This relief is dealt with in 4.6.

A surplus of franked investment income may not be carried back to earlier accounting periods.

Example 23
The following facts refer to Riders Ltd for the years stated:

Years ended	31 March 1984	31 March 1985
	£	£
Schedule D Case I (trading income)	60,000	80,000
FII	12,000	15,000
Dividends paid	—	18,000
Corporation tax rate assumed to be	50%	45%
ACT rate assumed to be	3/7	1/3

Note: Franked investment income *by definition* is the amount of dividends received plus tax credit. FII for both years is accordingly the 'gross amount' of such income which is found by applying the relevant ACT rate for each respective financial year.

Dividends by definition are qualifying distributions. Franked payments are qualifying distribution plus ACT. Thus dividends for the year ended 31 March 1985 are the 'net amounts' of those payments

	£	£
AP ended 31 March 1984		
Franked investment income		12,000
Franked payments		Nil
		———
Surplus of FII carried forward		12,000
		———
Corporation tax payable:		
£60,000 × 50% =		30,000

	£	£
AP ended 31 March 1985		
Surplus of FII brought		
forward		12,000
FII		15,000
		27,000
Franked payments:		
Dividends	18,000	
Add: ACT at 1/3 × £18,000	6,000	
Franked payment	24,000	24,000
Surplus of FII carried forward		3,000
Corporation tax payable:		
£80,000 × 45%		36,000

It will be observed that the tax credit that becomes available when a qualifying distribution is received by a company affords no ultimate relief from corporation tax. The benefit obtained by a company consists in not having to pay corporation tax in advance. Corporation tax is charged with reference to profits chargeable which are unaltered either by dividends received or dividends paid. You will remember that FII is not included in profits of a company for tax purposes.

3.11 CHANGE IN RATE OF ADVANCE CORPORATION TAX— GENERAL POINTS

The rate of advance corporation tax is fixed for each financial year, that is to say for each period starting on 1 April and ending on the following 31 March. Changes in the rate of ACT as between one financial year and the next give rise to a need for special rules about dividends paid in the period April 1 to 5 inclusive. The need for special rules is demonstrated by the following example.

Example 24
Walkers Ltd pays a dividend of £21,000 on 3 April 1984. Assume that the relative rates of ACT and basic rates of income tax are as follows:

	ACT	IT (basic rate)
FY 1983	3/7	1983/84 30%
FY 1984	1/3	1984/85 25%

The dividend paid on 3 April 1984 is paid in the financial year 1984 which begins on 1 April 1984. If there were no provisions to the contrary the ACT payable would be as follows:

£21,000 × 1/3 (rate for FY 1984) = £7,000

The amount taxable in the hands of shareholders is the total of the dividend and the tax credit:

	£
Dividend	21,000
Tax credit	7,000
Income	28,000

Basic rate tax on this amount of income for 1983/84 is 30%, i.e.
$$£28,000 \times 30\% = £8,400$$
The amount of the tax credit available to shareholders is £7,000 while the basic rate tax liability on the income is £8,400.

While there is no theoretical reason why the tax credit should not differ from the basic rate tax liability on the income, since the introduction of the imputation system of corporation tax the functional relationships between basic rate income tax, tax credit and advance corporation tax have always been maintained. Thus for dividends paid between 1 and 5 April inclusive S.103(5) FA 1972 provides that the advance corporation tax rate applicable is to be the rate in force in the *preceding* financial year, and not the rate in force in the financial year in which the dividend is paid. Thus in Example 24 above ACT paid in respect of the dividend on 3 April 1984 would be at the rate in force for financial year 1983, i.e. 3/7 and not the rate in force for FY 1984, 1/3. In this way the tax credit or ACT equals the basic rate of income tax of 30% on the amount of the 'shareholders' income.

Where the company prepares accounts to a date other than 31 March there are provisions in S.103(5)(b) FA 1972 which apply to years in which there is a change in the rate of advance corporation tax. Where a distribution is made on or before 5 April and later in the same accounting period the company makes another distribution or receives franked investment income, the period up to and including 5 April and the period after 5 April will be treated as separate accounting periods for the purposes of determining ACT liabilities and the amount of any FII surpluses.

Example 25
Dancers Ltd prepares accounts for the 12 months ended 30 September 1984. On 10 February 1984 the company pays a dividend of £7,000. On 17 July 1984 it receives a dividend of £6,000.

Assume that the rate of advance corporation tax is 3/7 for the financial year 1983 and 1/3 for the financial year 1984.

For the purposes of calculating ACT liability, Dancers Ltd will be treated as having two separate accounting periods:
(a) the period 1 October 1983 to 5 April 1984, and
(b) the period 6 April 1984 to 30 September 1984.

In the first accounting period, (a), the company pays a dividend of £7,000 and accounts for ACT of £7,000 × 3/7 = £3,000, giving a franked payment of £10,000.

In the second accounting period, (b), the company receives a dividend of

£6,000 which together with the tax credit of £2,000 (i.e. £6,000 × 1/3) amounts to franked investment income of £8,000.

Normally the company would set off the FII against the franked payment but that is not possible in this case because the franked investment income is deemed to have arisen in a separate, later accounting period.

It will be recalled that surplus FII may be carried forward to subsequent accounting periods but may not be carried back.

Assuming no further distributions are made nor FII received in the period ending 30 September 1984 the company will have paid ACT of £3,000 and at 30 September 1984 will have a surplus of franked investment income of £8,000.

The introduction of a notional accounting period ending on 5 April applies solely for the purposes of calculating the company's ACT liability and surplus FII amounts. All other corporation tax computations will be carried out with reference to the company's actual accounting period in accordance with the normal rules.

Question 3

Vibrations Ltd was incorporated in 1976 and trades as a supplier of musical instruments. It has no associated companies. During the accounting period ended 31 March 1984 the following transactions took place.

	£
10 April 1983: Dividend received on Beaters Ltd ordinary shares	700
1 July 1983: Paid half year's dividend on £70,000 15% preference shares	5,250
11 July 1983: Made fifth payment under deed of covenant to the Rock Musicians Charity	500 (net)
10 October 1983: Received dividend on Electric Bongos Ltd ordinary shares	4,200
1 January 1984: paid second half year's dividend on preference shares	5,250
22 February 1984: Paid dividend on ordinary shares for the year ended 31 March 1983	29,750

Required:
(1) Calculate the liability, if any, of Vibrations Ltd under Sch.14 FA 1972.
(2) You have been informed that the adjusted Case I profits of the company are £42,500 and there is a chargeable gain of £30,000. Compute the corporation tax payable for the year ended 31 March 1984.

CHAPTER 4

THE COMPUTATION AND USE
OF LOSSES

4.1 INTRODUCTION

This chapter will deal primarily with trading losses although there will also be reference to certain other kinds of losses and deficits.

A trading loss is computed for corporation tax purposes in the same way as a trading profit (S.177(6) TA 1970). This means that capital allowances which are deducted in arriving at a Schedule D Case I profit in the same way as any other trade expenses, may increase the amount of a trading loss or alternatively may turn a trading profit into a loss.

> **Example 1**
> Consider a simple example of a company which has a trading profit of £100,000 and capital allowances of £120,000.
> The trading loss available for relief will be:
>
> | | £ |
> |---|---|
> | Profit | 100,000 |
> | *Less:* Capital allowances | |
> | deducted as a trading expense | (120,000) |
> | Trading loss | (20,000) |

A trading loss for corporation tax may be relieved in a number of alternative ways. It is the existence of alternatives which sometimes gives the question of loss relief the appearance of being difficult. In practice, however, the appropriate route is often quite clear.

4.2 CARRY FORWARD OF TRADING LOSSES

Section 177(1) TA 1970 provides for the carry forward of the trading loss of an account period against *trading income* from the same trade in subsequent accounting periods. The carry forward must be claimed within six years of the accounting period in which the loss was incurred, however in practice a corporation tax computation showing a loss carried forward constitutes a claim.

Example 2

Allegro Ltd has the following results for the accounting periods ended on the dates indicated. The facts given below will be used to illustrate the three most common types of loss relief.

Year ended	31 March 1982	31 March 1983	31 March 1984
	£	£	£
Schedule D Case I			
profit/(loss)	20,000	(100,000)	65,000
Schedule A	16,000	20,000	22,000
Chargeable gain (abated)	4,000	5,000	1,000

Corporation tax computations:

Accounting period ended 31 March 1983	£
Schedule D Case I	NIL
Schedule A	20,000
Chargeable gain	5,000
	25,000
Trading loss carried forward S.177(1)	100,000

Accounting period ended 31 March 1984

	£	£
Schedule D Case I	65,000	
Less: Loss brought forward		
S.177(1)	65,000	
		NIL
Schedule A		22,000
Chargeable gain		1,000
Profits chargeable to corporation tax		23,000

There are a number of points which should be noted about this computation:

(a) At this stage we are only thinking in terms of the carry forward of the loss. Other types of loss relief have been ignored.

(b) Note that since the company has income from sources other than its trade there is still a liability to corporation tax for these two accounting periods.

(c) Lastly, and most important, note that a loss carried forward under S.177(1) TA 1970 may only be set against the *trading income*, that is to say the Schedule D Case I profits, of subsequent years. Thus the loss position for carry forward to 1985 and subsequent years is as follows:

	£
Loss incurred in year ended 31 March 1983	100,000
Less: utilized in year ended 31 March 1984	65,000
Loss to carry forward to 1985 and subsequent years	35,000

The carry forward of a trading loss is likely to be less attractive to a company than the loss reliefs that we will consider below. This is because the reliefs dealt with under headings 4.3 and 4.4 will either reduce the amount of corporation tax payable in respect of the accounting period in which the loss arises or will result in a repayment of corporation tax in respect of an earlier accounting period. However the possibility of the carry forward of a trading loss is still relevant to the extent that it is not possible to obtain relief in the accounting period of loss or in prior accounting periods.

4.3 LOSS SET OFF AGAINST OTHER PROFITS OF SAME ACCOUNTING PERIOD

We have seen in Example 2 that while the loss arising in the year ended 31 March 1983 was carried forward, the company's other income and chargeable gains remained liable to corporation tax.

S.177(2) TA 1970 gives a company the alternative possibility of claiming to set off a trading loss arising in an accounting period against the *total profits* of that same accounting period. You will recall that total profits comprise all the company's income *plus* its chargeable gains before deducting charges. Thus the company may set a trading loss against a profit arising on a capital asset. However, although it is possible in this way to set off a trading loss against a capital profit the reverse is not true; that is to say, it is not possible to set off a capital loss against a trading profit.

The time limit for making an election under S.177(2) is two years from the end of the accounting period in which the loss is incurred. In practice the Inspector of Taxes will accept the making of the appropriate deductions in a computation as constituting a claim.

Example 3
Assume the same figures for Allegro Ltd as were given in Example 2 but now apply S.177(2) relief as outlined above.
Corporation Tax Computations:

Accounting period ended 31 March 1983	£
Schedule D Case I	NIL
Schedule A	20,000
Chargeable gain	5,000
	25,000
Less: Loss relief S.177(2)	25,000
Profits chargeable to corporation tax	NIL

Summary:

	£
Loss incurred in year ended 31.3.83	100,000
Less: Utilized in current year	25,000
Balance of loss	75,000

Allegro Ltd at this stage can claim to carry forward the balance of the loss to the year ended 31 March 1984 under S.177(1) and if a claim is made the computation proceeds as follows:

	£	£
Accounting period ended		
31 March 1984		
Schedule D Case I	65,000	
Less: Loss brought forward		
(S.177(1))	65,000	
	———	NIL
Schedule A		22,000
Chargeable gain		1,000
Profits chargeable to corporation tax		23,000

Note that S.177(2) permits the loss to be set off against total profits but S.177(1) only permits the loss to be set off against Schedule D Case I profits in future years.

In this example the loss has been used as follows:

	£
Loss arising in year ended 31 March 1983	100,000
Less: Utilized in year ended 31 March 1983	25,000
	75,000
Less: Utilized in year ended 31 March 1984	65,000
Balance of loss available to carry forward to subsequent	
years S.177(1)	10,000

We have seen in the example above that the loss was used first of all in the accounting period in which it arose under S.177(2) and thereafter the balance was carried forward under S.177(1). There is one further important possibility open to the company. Instead of carrying the balance of the loss forward at this stage it may claim to carry the balance of the loss back and set it off against total profits of previous accounting periods. If after having done that there still remains a balance of loss unrelieved it can be carried forward under S.177(1).

4.4 LOSS SET OFF AGAINST PROFITS OF PREVIOUS ACCOUNTING PERIODS

The wording of S.177(2) TA 1970 offers the company a two-stage relief.

Here is what the section says:

'Where in any accounting period a company carrying on a trade incurs a loss in the trade, then . . . the company may make a claim requiring that the loss be set off for the purposes of corporation tax against profits (of whatever description) of that accounting period and, if the company was then carrying on the trade and the claim so requires, of preceding accounting periods ending within the time specified in Subsection (3)'. The 'claim so requires' means that the company makes such a claim.

The wording of this section makes it clear that relief is to be taken, *first* against the profits of the current accounting period, and *second* against the profits of the preceding accounting period.

A claim is competent for either the first stage of the relief only or for both the first and second stages of the relief.

Period of carry back

The period of time for which a loss may be carried back is specified in Ss.177(3) and (3A) TA 1970. In some cases the amount of the profits against which the loss may be set will be restricted by reference to the length of the accounting period in which the loss is incurred. Mot accounting periods are twelve months long and in such cases the loss will be carried back and set off against the company's total profits for the twelve months accounting period preceding the twelve month accounting period in which the loss arose.

Example 4

Again we will assume the same figures for Allegro Ltd as were given in Example 2.

Corporation Tax Computations:	
Accounting period ended 31 March 1983	£
Schedule D Case I	NIL
Schedule A	20,000
Chargeable gain	5,000
	25,000
Less: Loss relief S.177(2)	25,000
Profits chargeable to corporation tax	NIL
Summary:	
Loss available for relief	100,000
Less: Utilized in year to 31 March 1983	25,000
Balance of loss available to carry back if required	75,000

Accounting period ended 31 March 1982		£
Schedule D Case I		20,000
Schedule A		16,000
Chargeable gain		4,000
		40,000
Less: Loss carried back S.177(2)		40,000
Profits chargeable to corporation tax		NIL

	£	£
Summary of loss relief:		
Loss available		100,000
Less: Utilized in year to		
31 March 1983	25,000	
Utilized in year to		
31 March 1982	40,000	
		65,000
Balance of loss which will be		
carried forward S.177(1)		35,000

Summary

The three alternative loss reliefs provided in S.177 TA 1970 may be summarized as follows:

A trading loss for an accounting period may be:

(a) Carried forward and set off against future trading profits, with no part of the loss being set off against total profits of the accounting period, *or*

(b) Set-off against total profits of the accounting period, with any balance of loss then remaining being carried forward and set-off against future trading profits as in (a) above, *or*

(c) Set-off against total profits of the accounting period and then against total profits of the preceding accounting period, with any balance of loss then remaining being carried forward for set-off against future trading profits as in (a).

Of these alternatives (c) is the most common and in the case of a single company (not a member of a group of companies) such as Allegro Ltd, offers relief at the earliest possible time with repayment of corporation tax and the possibility of a repayment supplement. In practice the question of which relief or combination of reliefs is most advantageous for a given company will depend on the circumstances of that company.

There are two situations where the period of carry-back of a loss under S.177(2) TA 1970 differs from the general rule that we have so far considered.

4.4.1 Loss arising in accounting period of less than twelve months

When the loss arises in a twelve month accounting period the loss may be carried back and set off against the profits of the preceding twelve month accounting period. Where, however, the loss arises in an accounting period of less than twelve months the amount of the relief may be restricted. The profits of preceding accounting periods which are available for relief are those earned in a period of time equal in length to the AP in which the loss is experienced. Thus if a loss arises in an accounting period of nine months, the loss may only be set off against the profits for the nine months preceding the AP in which the loss arose. The total profits of a preceding nine month period will be arrived at by apportioning profits on a time basis.

Example 5

Poco Ltd prepares accounts to 31 March each year. On 1 April the whole of its ordinary share capital is acquired by Largo Ltd and it is decided to change the accounting date of Poco Ltd to 31 December each year.

The results of Poco Ltd are as given below:

	Year ended 31 March 1983 £	*9 months ended 31 December 1983* £	*Year ended 31 December 1984* £
Schedule D Case I profit/(loss)	32,000	(60,000)	80,000
Schedule A	6,000	2,000	8,000
Chargeable gain (abated)	2,000	14,000	—

The possibility of group relief for the trading loss (see Chapter 5) is ignored in this example.

Poco Ltd has claimed loss relief under S.177(2) TA 1970 against profits of both the nine month accounting period ended 31 December 1983 and part of the preceding accounting period of twelve months ended 31 March 1983.

Corporation Tax Computations:
Accounting period 1 April 1983–

	£
31 December 1983	
Schedule D Case I	NIL
Schedule A	2,000
Chargeable gain	14,000
	16,000
Less: Loss relief S.177(2)	16,000
	NIL

Summary:

Loss available for relief	60,000
Less: Utilized in current period	16,000
Loss available to carry back (but note that loss arises in nine month accounting period).	44,000

Accounting Period 1 April 1982–31 March 1983

The loss of £60,000 arose in a nine month accounting period. The balance of the loss, £44,000, may therefore only be set against computed profits for nine months of the preceding twelve month accounting period. The computation proceeds as follows:

	£
Schedule D Case I	32,000
Schedule A	6,000
Chargeable gain	2,000
Total profits	40,000

Less: S.177(2) relief:
Profits for 12 months = £40,000
∴ profit for 9 months = £40,000 × 9/12 = £30,000
∴ maximum loss relief that may be

claimed =	30,000
Profits chargeable to corporation tax	10,000

Summary:	£	£
Loss arising in nine months to 31 December 1983		60,000
Less: Utilized in current period S.177(2)	16,000	
Utilized against part of previous year's profits	30,000	46,000
Balance to carry forward S.177(1)		14,000

4.4.2 Loss attributable wholly or partly to first year allowances

Companies which incur capital expenditure before 1 April 1986 are entitled to *first year allowances* calculated at the following rates:

Date expenditure incurred on acquisition of asset	*% rate of FYA*
Prior to 14 March 1984	100
14 March 1984–31 March 1985	75
1 April 1985–31 March 1986	50

At the beginning of this chapter we saw that capital allowances are treated for corporation tax purposes in the same way as any trade expense. Thus if a company incurs substantial capital expenditure prior to 1 April 1986 the deduction of first year allowances may result in a trading loss of such a large amount that only a part can be used under the normal provisions of S.177(2) TA 1970. Without special relieving legislation the balance of the loss after S.177(2) relief could only be carried forward under S.177(1). The consequence of carrying forward losses arising out of FYAs would be to delay tax relief perhaps for a long time, and so defeat the economic purpose in granting high rates of FYA.

To meet these circumstances the legislation gives additional relief for losses which are wholly or partly attributable to first year allowances. S.177(3A) TA 1970 extends the period of carry back under S.177(2) from a maximum of twelve months to three years.

In this case there is no restriction on the carry back period if the loss arises in an accounting period shorter than twelve months in length. The loss is carried back and set off against the *latest* years profits in priority to earlier years.

If part of a loss is attributable to first year allowances and part is not, the amount of the loss should be split into two separate sums. The part of the loss that is not attributable to FYA's is set against other profits of the immediately preceding accounting period. In other words the normal provisions of S.177(2) are applied. Any balance of this part of the loss which has not been utilized in this way is carried forward under S.177(1). The part of the loss which *is* attributable to first year allowances is then dealt with under the extended carry-back provisions of S.177(3A) TA 1970.

Example 6

Largo Ltd makes up accounting to 31 March each year. The following are the results of the company for the years stated:

Years ended	31 March 1981 £	31 March 1982 £	31 March 1983 £	31 March 1984 £
Schedule D Case I profit/(loss)	30,000	24,000	3,000	(50,000)
Schedule A	1,200	1,500	1,800	—
Chargeable gain (abated)	500	1,000	1,500	—

The loss of £50,000 is made up as follows:	£
Trading loss	10,000
First year allowances	40,000
Loss for corporation tax	50,000

The company claims relief under S.177(2) as extended by S.177(3A).
Corporation Tax Computations

Accounting Period ended 31 March 1983	£
Schedule D Casc I	3,000
Schedule A	1,800
Chargeable gain	1,500
	6,300
Less: Loss carried back S.177(2)	6,300
Profits chargeable to corporation tax	NIL

Summary of loss relief:

	FYA loss £	*Trading loss* £
Loss available	40,000	10,000
Less: Used in year ended 31 March 1983		(6,300)
Balance of loss available	40,000	3,700

Note that the balance of the trading loss, i.e. £3,700, may only be carried forward under S.177(1) TA 1970. The remainder of the loss, namely that part attributable to first year allowances may be carried back to the year ending 31 March 1982 and then to the year ending 31 March 1981.

Accounting Period ended 31 March 1982	£
Schedule D Case I	24,000
Schedule A	1,500
Chargeable Gain	1,000
	26,500
Less: Loss S.177(2) and S.177(3A)	26,500
Profits chargeable to corporation tax	NIL

Summary of loss:	
Loss available S.177(3A)	40,000
Less: Utilized in year ended 31 March 1982	26,500
Available to carry back one further year	13,500

Accounting Period ended 31 March 1981	
Schedule D Case I	30,000
Schedule A	1,200
Chargeable gain	500
	31,700
Less: Loss S.177(2) and S.177(3A)	13,500
Profits chargeable to corporation tax	18,200

It may have been noted that in Example 6 the loss is shown as being carried back under S.177(2) *and* S.177(3A). The correct position is that a claim is made under S.177(2) to carry back the loss. S.177(3) and S.177(3A) are the sections which specify the period of time for which the loss may be carried back.

4.4.3 Inter-action between loss reliefs and charges

Loss relief claimed under S.177(2) is deducted from total profits and is deducted *before* charges. It is not possible to restict the amount of loss relief claimed so as to leave sufficient profits to relieve the charges available. If a claim is made under S.177(2) the loss will be set off to the *maximum extent possible*, so as to exhaust the relevant total profits.

The situation will therefore arise in practice where the claiming of S.177(2) relief results in an excess of charges. You will remember that an 'excess of charges' means the amount by which charges exceed total profits. We have already seen that in so far as the excess of charges are 'trade charges', then that excess may be carried forward to future years (note that the excess may not in any circumstances be carried back) (S.177(8) TA 1970). Where, however, the charges are *not* trade charges they may not be carried forward and the company does not obtain relief for them.

Example 7

Lento Ltd makes up its accounts to 31 August each year. The following are its results for the years stated:

Years ended	31 August 1982 £	31 August 1983 £	31 August 1984 £
Schedule D Case I profit/(loss)	20,000	(55,000)	35,000
Schedule A	6,000	3,000	15,000
Chargeable gain (abated)	10,500	—	—
Charges on income:			
trade	12,000	12,000	12,000
non-trade	200	200	200

Lento Ltd claims loss relief under S.177(2) TA 1970 for both the accounting period of loss and the preceding accounting period.

Corporation Tax Computations:

Accounting Period ended 31 August 1983	£
Schedule D Case I	NIL
Schedule A	3,000
	3,000
Less: Loss relief S.177(2)	3,000
	NIL

The charges are £12,200, and since after application of loss relief there are no profits against which they can be relieved there are excess charges of £12,200. The trade charges, £12,000, may be carried forward as a trading expense (S.177(8) TA 1970). The non-trade charges, £200, may not be carried forward.

Accounting Period ended 31 August 1982	£
Schedule D Case I	20,000
Schedule A	6,000
Chargeable gain	10,500
	36,500
Less: Loss relief S.177(2)	36,500
Profits chargeable to corporation tax	NIL

Excess charges available to carry forward from the accounting period ended 31 August 1982 are £12,000. Note again that the company will not obtain relief for the non-trade charges of £200.

Summary of loss relief:	£	£
Loss available for relief		55,000
Less: Loss utilized 1983	3,000	
1982	36,500	39,500
Loss available to carry forward S.177(1)		15,500

The loss carried forward of £15,500 is aggregated with the trade charges carried forward under S.177(8) so that the total amount of loss relief and trade charges available to deduct from the Schedule D Case I profit for the year ended 31 August 1984 is:

	£
Loss available to carry forward	15,000
Trade charges carried forward from the year ended 31 August 1982	12,000
Trade charges carried forward from the year ended 31 August 1983	12,000
Total	39,500

Accounting Period ended 31 August 1984

	£	£
Schedule D Case I	35,000	
Less: Loss and trade charges brought forward S.177(1) and S.177(8)	39,500	NIL
Schedule A		15,000
		15,000
Less: Charges (current accounting period)		12,200
Profits chargeable to corporation tax		2,800

Losses and trade charges brought forward under S.177(1) and S.177(8) may only be deducted from Schedule D Case I profits. Thus the amount to be carried forward to later years is as follows:

	£
Loss and trade charges brought forward	39,500
Less: Utilized year ended 31 August 1984	35,000
Carried forward to 1985 and subsequent years	4,500

It has been pointed out that as a result of claiming relief under S.177(2) for the year of loss and the preceding year, the company loses the benefit of relief for non-trade charges. Non-trade charges, as the name suggests, have about them the notion of 'gratuity', such as a four yer deed of covenant to a charity. It follows that in most companies they are unlikely to be so large in amount that they will be a determining factor in whether or not to claim S.177(2) relief. If, exceptionally, the loss of relief is significant a company would consider carrying forward a trading loss, or restricting a S.177(2) claim to the year of loss.

4.5 TERMINAL LOSS RELIEF

If a company experiences a trading loss in the last twelve months of carrying on its trade it can set off the loss against income from the trade arising in the three years preceding the final year of trading. To arrive at the trading loss of the final twelve months and the trading income of the preceding three years, apportionments are made, as necessary, on a time basis.

The terminal loss may also include an excess of charges over total profits in the final twelve month period of trading. In this case the excess charges will be restricted as for the carry forward of trading losses, to the amount of trade charges.

Terminal loss relief is an exception to the general principle that a trading loss carried back is set against total profits. Relief is restricted to set off against the Schedule D Case I profits of the three years preceding the final twelve months of trading, starting with the latest year first.

Terminal loss relief is given only after all other loss reliefs which may be available have been applied. Thus relief must be taken under S.177(2) *before* applying terminal loss relief.

The final point to be noted in connection with the application of terminal loss relief is that this relief may not interfere with relief for charges paid wholly and exclusively for the purposes of the trade (S.178(4) TA 1970). The effect of this rule is that trade charges must be relieved before terminal loss relief is given. In a simple computation where the company has no sources of income other than Schedule D Case I profits the trade charges will therefore be deducted from the trading profits first and then the terminal loss relief will be given. Where the company has other profits in addition to trading profits the trade charges will be dealt with as follows:

    (a) set off trade charges against profits other than trading profits,
    (b) set off balance of trade charges against Schedule D Case I profits, and
    (c) finally set off terminal loss relief against trading profits.

The rule which 'protects' trade charges is a common-sense approach to the juxtaposition of the two reliefs, for trade charges and for the terminal loss. It would not make sense to grant relief for a terminal loss if this gave rise to an equal loss of relief in respect of charges. Where there is a loss of relief for trade charges in the context of S.177(2) (set off of trading loss against total profits of current and preceding accounting periods) the excess trade charges are carried forward as trading expenses to future accounting periods. Such an option is not practicable in the case of a ceasing trade.

Example 8

Failure Ltd made up accounts to 31 March each year. The company ceased trading on 31 March 1984. The results for the four years prior to cessation are as follows:

Years ended 31 March	1981 £	1982 £	1983 £	1984 £
Schedule D Case I profit/(loss)	11,000	12,500	1,000	(23,000)
Unfranked investment income	400	500	500	500
Trade charges	1,300	1,300	1,400	1,000

The company claims terminal loss relief under S.178 TA 1970.

(1) *Application of S.177(2) TA 1970:*

Accounting Period ended 31 March 1984	£
Schedule D Case I	NIL
Unfranked investment income	500
	500
Less: Loss relief S.177(2)	500
Profits chargeable to corporation tax	NIL

Accounting Period ended 31 March 1983	£
Schedule D Case I profit	1,000
Unfranked investment income	500
	1,500
Less: Loss relief S.177(2)	1,500
Profits chargeable to corporation tax	NIL

Note that we are left with charges unutilized of £1,400 for the year ended 31 March 1983 and £1,000 for the year ended 31 March 1984. The charges for the final year will be included in the computation of the terminal loss since they are all trade charges. The charges of £1,400 for the year ended 31 March 1983 may not be included in the terminal loss computation (because they do not arise in the final twelve months of trading) and will thus not be relieved.

(2) *Calculation of terminal loss*:

	£	£
Loss for year ended 31 March 1984		23,000
Less: Utilized under S.177(2)		
Year ended 31 March 1984	500	
Year ended 31 March 1983	1,500	2,000
		21,000
Add: Trade charges for final twelve months		1,000
Terminal loss		22,000

(3) *Calculation of profits available for terminal loss relief*:

	£
Accounting Period ended 31 March 1983	
Profits available for terminal loss relief	NIL

Accounting Period ended 31 March 1982
Trade charges which must be protected:

Trade charges	1,300
Less: Set-off against UFII	500
Trade charges which are deducted from trading profits before application of terminal loss relief	800

Therefore profits available for terminal loss relief:

	£
Schedule D Case I	12,500
Less: Trade charges 'protected'	800
Profits available for terminal loss relief	11,700

	£
Accounting Period ended 31 March 1981	
Trade charges which must be protected:	
Trade charges	1,300
Less: Set-off against UFII	400
Trade charges which must be deducted from trading profits before application of terminal loss relief	900

Therefore profits available for terminal loss relief:

	£
Schedule D Case I	11000
Less: Trade charges protected	900
Profits available for terminal loss relief	10,100

(4) *Application of terminal loss relief*:
Accounting Period ended 31 March 1982

	£	£
Schedule D Case I	12,500	
Less: Terminal loss relief	11,700	
		800
Unfranked investment income		500
		1,300
Less: Charges		1,300
Profits chargeable to corporation tax		NIL

Accounting Period ended 31 March 1981

	£	£
Schedule D Case I	11,000	
Less: Terminal loss relief	10,100	
		900
Unfranked investment income		400
		1,300
Less: Charges		1,300
Profits chargeable to corporation tax		NIL

Summary	£	£
Terminal loss relief available		22,000
Less: Utilized:		
Year ended 31 March 1982	11,700	
Year ended 31 March 1981	10,100	21,800
Balance of terminal loss		
relief not utilized		200

In Example 8 the final accounting period was twelve months in length and therefore the computations were relatively simple. In the following Example the final accounting period is less than twelve months long. It will be seen that, in order to arrive at the terminal loss of the final twelve months and the trading income of the preceding three years, a number of apportionments are necessary.

Example 9

Complete Failure Ltd ceased trading on 31 March 1984. The following are the results for the years stated and for the final three months of trading:

Years ended *31 December*	*1980* £	*1981* £	*1982* £	*1983* £	*Three months* *ended* *31 March 1984* £
Schedule D Case I profit/(loss)	5,000	10,000	8,000	4,000	(50,000)
Schedule A	2,000	2,000	1,000	2,000	1,000
Charges: trade	1,500	1,500	1,500	1,500	375
non-trade	—	—	—	500	125

The company claims terminal loss relief under S.178 TA 1970.

(1) *Application of S.177(2):*

Accounting Period of three months ended 31 March 1984	£
Schedule D Case I	NIL
Schedule A	1,000
	1,000
Less: Loss relief S.177(2)	13,000
Profits chargeable to corporation tax	NIL

Year ended 31 December 1983		£
Schedule D Case I		4,000
Schedule A		2,000
		6,000
Less: Loss relief S.177(2) (*Note: Loss arose in a three month accounting period and can therefore only be set against profits of three months to 31 December 1983* ∴ relief restricted to £6,000 × 3/12 =		1,500
		4,500
Less: Charges		2,000
Profits chargeable to corporation tax (before terminal loss relief)		2,500

(2) *Calculation of terminal loss available for relief:*

	£	£
Trading loss for final three months		50,000
Trading loss for previous nine months—profit ∴		NIL
		50,000
Less: Relief given under S.177(2)		
AP ended 31 March 1984	1,000	
AP ended 31 December 1983	1,500	2,500
		47,500

Add: Excess charges for
AP of 3 months
ended 31 March
1984   375

Terminal loss   47,875

(3) *Calculation of trading profits available for terminal loss relief:*
Two points should be noted:
(a) The terminal loss relief may only be set against trading profits for the 3
    years preceding the final 12 months, i.e. profits for the period 1 April
    1980 to 31 March 1983.
(b) As in Example 8 you have to make sure that the giving of terminal loss
    relief does not interfere with relief for trade charges:

		Trading profits available for relief £	Period
(i)	Period of three months ended 31 March 1983 3/12 × £4,000	1,000	3 months
(ii)	Year ended 31 December 1982		
	Trading profits 8,000 *Less:* Trade charges 'protected' 500	7,500	1 Year
(iii)	Year ended 31 December 1981	10,000	1 Year
(iv)	Period of nine months from 1 April 1980 to 31 December 1980 9/12 × £5,000	3,750	9 months
		22,250	3 Years

(4) *Application of terminal loss relief:*
Accounting Period ended 31 December 1983

	£	
Schedule D Case I profit	4,000	
Less: Terminal loss relief	1,000	
		3,000
Schedule A		2,000
		5,000
Less: Loss relief S.177(2)		1,500
		3,500
Less: Charges		2,000
Profits chargeable to corporation tax		1,500

Accounting Period ended 31 December 1982

	£	£
Schedule D Case I profits	8,000	
Less: Terminal loss relief	7,500	
	———	500
Schedule A		1,000
		———
		1,500
Less: Charges		1,500
		———
Profits chargeable to corporation tax		NIL

Accounting Period ended 31 December 1981

	£	£
Schedule D Case I profits	10,000	
Less: Terminal loss relief	10,000	
	———	NIL
Schedule A		2,000
		———
		2,000
Less: Charges		1,500
		———
Profits chargeable to corporation tax		1,500

Accounting Period ended 31 December 1980

	£	£
Schedule D Case I profits	5,000	
Less: Terminal loss relief	3,750	
	———	1,250
Schedule A		2,000
		———
		3,250
Less: Charges		1,500
		———
Profits chargeable to corporation tax		1,750

Summary:

Terminal loss relief available	47,875
Less: Utilized	22,250
	———
Balance of terminal loss unrelieved	25,625

4.6 SET-OFF OF TRADING LOSSES AND OTHER ITEMS AGAINST SURPLUS FRANKED INVESTMENT INCOME

We have seen in Chapter 1 that franked investment income is not brought into the computation of profits chargeable to corporation tax. The main use of FII is the set-off against franked payments made during an accounting period since the company is only liable to pay advance corporation tax in respect of the excess of franked payments made over FII received. Full use of the company's franked investment income can only be made if the franked payments equal or exceed the amount of the dividends received plus the attached tax credit.

If, however, an investment or other company receives FII which exceeds in total the amount of its franked payments in the accounting period the company will have what is called a *surplus of franked investment income*. This will be carried forward to the next accounting period and will be regarded as franked investment income received by the company in that period (S.89(3) FA 1972). Where, however, the company makes a claim under S.254 TA 1970 the surplus FII of the accounting period, excluding surpluses brought forward will be treated as if it were an additional amount of profits chargeable to corporation tax. The company may then set off against these deemed 'profits' several types of losses and expenses including:

    (a) trading losses available for relief under S.177(2) TA 1970 but which cannot be relieved against total profits because profits are insufficient,

    (b) charges—both trade charges and other charges.

Before going on to look at the relief in detail we should perhaps explain that the relief, in the shape of a repayment of the tax credit inherent in franked investment income is unlike other loss reliefs in that some time after the repayment has been received it may become necessary in certain circumstances to repay the cash received back to the Inland Revenue. The more usual loss reliefs give a permanent reduction in profits with, perhaps, a repayment of tax, which one is never called upon to pay back. In contrast, this relief is a 'cash flow' relief which is to a greater or lesser extent, depending on circumstances, a temporary relief. When the amount of the relief is repaid to the Revenue the company is put back in the position in which it found itself before the claim for relief was made.

If in an accounting period a company has a surplus of franked investment income and, let us say, a trading loss, and relief for the whole of the trading loss has not proved possible under S.177(2) (set off against total profits) then the surplus of FII is treated as additional profits and the tax credit inherent in the income is repaid.

Example 10
Commotions Ltd has the following results for its accounting period ended 31 March 1984:

	£
Schedule D Case I Loss	(28,000)
Franked investment income	25,000
Franked payments made	15,000

The company claims relief under S.254 TA 1970.

S.254 Claim

Surplus franked investment income	
treated as profits	10,000
Less: Trading loss	28,000
Balance of loss carried forward S.177(1)	18,000

Tax credit repayment
£10,000 at 30% = £3,000

The trading losses which may be utilized in a S.254 claim are losses which are available for relief under S.177(2) TA 1970 but which have not been utilized because of an absence of normal profits chargeable to corporation tax. (S.254(3) TA 1970). It is significant that S.177(2) is referred to for you wll recollect that loss relief under that section is given in two stages, first againt other profits of the accounting period of loss and then against total profits of the preceding accounting period. Thus a loss arising for example in the twelve month accounting period ended 31 August 1984 may be set firstly against surplus franked investment income of that accounting period, and secondly against surplus franked investment income, if any, of the accounting period ending 31 August 1983.

We have seen in this chapter and in Chapter 3 that a surplus of franked investment income is, in the absence of a Section 254 claim, carried forward and treated as FII received in the subsequent period. It is important to note, however, that when considering Section 254 relief, any surplus of FII brought forward from earlier accounting periods is left out of account. It is only the surplus arising within the accounting period with which we are concerned.

Claims for relief under S.254 are made within two years of the accounting period of loss in the case of a claim for a trading loss. In the case of excess charges the time limit is six years from the end of the accounting period in which the charges were paid.

Example 11

Promotions Ltd has the following results for its twelve month accounting period ended 31 December 1983.

	£
Schedule D Case I Loss	(50,000)
Schedule A	6,500
Franked investment income received in year to 31 December 1983	81,000
Franked payments made	25,000
Surplus FII brought forward from year to 31 December 1982	10,000

Promotions Ltd claims relief under Section 177(2) and 254 TA 1970.

	£
(a) *Claim under S.177(2) TA 1970*	
Schedule D Case I	NIL
Schedule A	6,500
	6,500
Less: Loss relief S.177(2)	6,500
Profits chargeable to corporation tax	NIL

Summary:	
Loss available	50,000
Less: Loss relieved S.177(2)	6,500
Loss still available	43,500

	£
(b) *Claim under S.254 TA 1970*	
Surplus of FII in current year	56,000
Less: Loss relief S.254	43,500
Balance of surplus FII of current year	12,500
Add: Surplus FII of previous year	10,000
Surplus FII carried forward to year to 31 December 1984	22,500

Tax Credit Repayment
£43,500 × 30% = £13,050

Summary	£	£
Trading loss available		50,000
Less: Used S.177(2)	6,500	
Used S.254	43,500	
Balance of loss		NIL

Effect of S.254 claim in subsequent years

You will note in Example 11 that as a result of making a S.254 claim:
  (a) There is no loss relief available to carry forward to subsequent years.
  (b) The surplus FII available to carry forward to subsequent years is £22,500. (If no S.254 claim had been made the surplus franked investment income carried forward would have been £66,000.)

If, in a subsequent accounting period, the franked payments made by Promotions Ltd exceed the FII the company will have to account for a larger amount of ACT than would have been payable if no S.254 claim had previously been made. This is because the amount of surplus franked investment income available to set off against the franked payments is £22,500, whereas if no Section 254 claim had been made the amount available for set off would have been £66,000.

Example 12
In its accounting period ended 31 December 1984 Promotions Ltd receives franked investment income of £18,000 and makes franked payments of £90,000. The ACT payable is calculated as follows:
Advance Corporation Tax Accounting

	£	£
Franked payments		90,000
Less: Surplus FII brought forward	22,500	
FII received in year ended 31 December 1984	18,000	40,5000
Excess of franked payments over FII		49,500

ACT payable:
  £49,500 × 30% = £14,850

If the company had *not* made a S.254 claim in 1983, the ACT payable in respect of the year ended 31 December 1984 would have been calculated as follows:

	£	£
Franked payments		90,000
Less: Surplus FII brought forward	66,000	
FII of current year	18,000	84,000
Excess of franked payments over FII		6,000

ACT payable:
  £6,000 × 30% = £1,800

The difference between the amount of advance corporation tax payable in Example 12 and the ACT that would have been payable if

Promotions Ltd had *not* made a S.254 claim is £13,050. If you refer back to Example 11 you will see that this is equal to the amount of tax credit repayment obtained by the company after making the S.254 claim for 1983. Thus the whole of the tax credit repayment made by the Inland Revenue to Promotions Ltd in respect of the year to 31 December 1983 is in effect being paid back by the company to the Revenue in 1984, on payment of the ACT of £14,850.

The payment back to the Revenue of the tax credit places the company back in the position in which it would have been if a Section 254 claim had not been made. There is however one further step in this sequence. If the whole payment of £14,850 ACT were to be now allowed against the corporation tax payable to arrive at the mainstream corporation tax this would reduce the tax payable and the repayment to the Revenue on payment of advance corporation tax would be reversed.

To give effect of the repayment to the Revenue and otherwise to put the company back in the position it was in before it claimed S.254 relief, the two following steps are taken in the accounting period in which franked payments exceed franked investment income:

(a) The amount of ACT which may be deducted from the corporation tax liability is restricted to the amount actually paid less the amount of the tax credit repaid to the company previously on making a S.254 claim (S.90(3) FA 1972).

Example 13

In Example 11 Promotions Ltd paid advance corporation tax in the year ended 31 December 1984 of £14,850.

The advance corporation tax which may be deducted from corporation tax payable in respect of the year ended 31 December 1984 is:

	£
ACT paid	14,850
Less: Tax credit repayment in year ended 31 December 1983	13,050
Restricted ACT deductible from corporation tax liability	1,800

(b) The whole of the loss previously used against the surplus franked investment income is restored to the company in the form of a trading loss brought forward (as for S.177(1) TA 1970) to the accounting period in which franked payments exceed FII (S.254(5) TA 1970).

Example 14
Assume that Promotions Ltd had the following results for its accounting
period ended 31 December 1984.

	£
Schedule D Case I profit	120,000
Schedule A	1,200

The rate of CT is assumed to be 50%.

Corporation Tax Computation
Accounting Period ended 31 December 1984

	£	£
Schedule D Case I	120,000	
Less: Loss restored S.254(5)	43,500	
	———	76,500
Schedule A		1,200
Profits chargeable to corporation tax		77,700

Corporation tax payable:	
£77,700 × 50% =	38,850
Less: ACT (see Example 12)	1,800
Mainstream corporation tax	37,050

4.7 OTHER LOSSES AND DEFICITS

Throughout this chapter we have concentrated on relief available for
trading losses and we have seen how in certain circumstances it is
possible to set trading losses against profits other than trading profits.
Other kinds of deficits and allowable capital losses, may only be set off
against future surpluses or gains of the same nature.

Example 15
Mixed Emotions Ltd makes up accounts to 31 March each year, and has
the following results for the years stated:

Years ended	31 March 1983	31 March 1984
	£	£
Schedule D Case I profit/(loss)	50,000	(8,000)
Unfranked investment income	2,000	2,500
Schedule A (deficit)/surplus	(200)	3,000
Chargeable gain/(allowable loss)	(600)	6,000

The fraction for abatement of capital gains for financial year 1983 is 2/5.
The company claims relief under S.177(2) TA 1970.

Accounting Period ended 31 March 1984

	£	£
Schedule D Case I		NIL
Unfranked investment income		2,500
Schedule A	3,000	
Less: Deficit brought forward	200	
		2,800
Chargeable gain	6,000	
Less: Allowable loss brought forward	600	
	5,400	
Less: Abatement	2,160	
		3,240
Total profits		8,540
Less: Loss relief S.177(2)		8,000
Profits chargeable to corporation tax		540

4.8 CONSEQUENCES OF LOSS CLAIMS

A trading loss relief claim will normally result in a repayment of corporation tax or the reduction or the elimination of a liability to corporation tax. Among other possible consequences are the following:

(1) A repayment of income tax if the profits of the accounting period in which the loss arises include unfranked investment income and the income tax suffered has not been relieved elsewhere—see Chapter 1.

(2) A reduction in the rate of corporation tax as a result of a fall in the level of the company's profits to within the small companies rate band or the marginal small companies rate band—see Chapter 1.

(3) The payment by the Inland Revenue of a 'repayment supplement' in certain cases where corporation tax or income tax is repaid to the company—see Chapter 1.

(4) The creation of a surplus of ACT and consequential changes in ACT computations if the loss relief reduces the income of the company so that the maximum ACT that may be deducted from the corporation tax payable is reduced—see Chapter 3.

(5) The reduction or elimination of a 'shortfall' in the context of a family 'close' company—see Chapter 6.

Question 4

Machinations Ltd has the following results:

Years ended 31 March	1980 £	1981 £	1982 £	1983 £	1984 £
Trading profit (loss)	47,600	16,000	3,200	(15,000)	12,400
Capital Allowances:					
Writing down allowance	600	760	600	550	320
First year allowance	—	8,600	300	6,800	—
Debenture interest received (gross)	1,500	1,500	4,000	4,000	4,000
Rents received	720	720	720	720	720
Capital loss ⎱ before re-	—	(4,350)	—	—	—
Capital gain ⎰ duction	—	—	5,600	—	—
Royalties paid (gross)	1,100	1,100	3,100	3,100	3,100
Covenant to RSPCA	500	500	500	500	500

Required:

Show the corporation tax payable for the financial years 1979–1983 assuming that relief is taken for the loss at the earliest opportunity. Assume the following rates of tax:

Corporation tax	50%
Advance corporation tax	3/7
Abatement of chargeable gains	2/5
Income tax	30%

CHAPTER 5

GROUPS OF COMPANIES

5.1 THE NATURE OF A GROUP OF COMPANIES

The basic unit of charge to corporation tax is an individual company. For certain purposes, however, the corporation tax legislation looks beyond the separate company to companies associated with it in a group of companies. Sometimes taking account of companies in the group has the effect of restricting or limiting some relief or benefit, e.g. in the computation of the maximum relevant income of close companies (see Chapter 6) or in connection with the application of the small company rate of corporation tax (see Chapter 1). In other cases the existence of a group makes it possible to obtain special reliefs and advantages.

There are four common kinds of advantages enjoyed by companies which are members of groups. These are:

(1) The setting off of the trading losses of one group member against the profits of another (S.258 et seq, TA 1970) (see 5.2).
(2) The payment of dividends by a subsidiary to a parent company without accounting for advance corporation tax and payment of interest gross (ie, without payment of income tax) by a subsidiary to a parent company (S.256 et seq, TA 1970) (see 5.3).
(3) The surrendering of advance corporation tax paid by a parent company to a subsidiary and treating the advance corporation tax surrendered as paid by the subsidiary (S.92 FA 1972) (see 5.4).
(4) The transfer of assets between members of the same group of companies without giving rise to capital gains chargeable to corporation tax (S.272 et seq, TA 1970).

The relevant group structures in each of the four situations above are different one from the other but have many points of similarity.

Each group structure involves the notion of a parent and subsidiary company. The more important relationships are where one company is a 51% subsidiary of another and where one company is a 75% subsidiary of another.

To say one company is a 51% subsidiary of another means that more than 50% of the ordinary share capital is owned by the other. In the same way to describe a company as a 75% subsidiary means that at least 75% of the ordinary share capital is owned by the other (S.532(1) TA 1970). Ordinary share capital means all the issued share capital of a company other than capital entitled to a fixed rate of dividend only, e.g. preference shares (S.526(5) TA 1970).

When determining the extent of the share ownership by one company in another it is necessary to consider both direct and indirect ownership. Where company A owns shares in company B and company B owns shares in company C then company A is said to have indirect ownership of shares in company C through company B.

Example 1

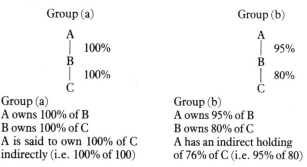

Group (a)	Group (b)
A owns 100% of B	A owns 95% of B
B owns 100% of C	B owns 80% of C
A is said to own 100% of C	A has an indirect holding
indirectly (i.e. 100% of 100)	of 76% of C (i.e. 95% of 80)

Both (a) and (b) are what are called 75% groups and are so described even if the actual share ownership, direct and indirect, is more than 75%. Relief for trading losses and 'tax free' transfers of assets arise in 75% structures (numbers (1) and (4) above); surrender of ACT and special group dividends and payments of interest (numbers (2) and (3) above) arise in 51% structures.

5.2 GROUP RELIEF

Group relief is available between a parent and its 75% subsidiary and between two or more 75% subsidiaries of the same parent. In addition to meeting the definition of 75% subsidiary referred to above, group relief is only available where the parent in relation to the subsidiary is entitled to not less than 75% of the profits available for distribution to equity holders, and to not less than 75% of the subsidiary's assets available to equity holders on a notional winding up (S.28 FA 1973). An equity holder is defined in Sch. 12 FA 1973 as a person holding ordinary shares or a loan creditor where the loan is not a normal commercial loan. The 1973 provisions comprise anti-avoidance legislation aimed at certain special share structures and arrangements which were developed in the years before 1973 to take advantage of features of the group structure for group relief purposes. In most straightforward commercial cases the parents of 75% subsidiaries, defined, as above, as companies whose ordinary share capital is held at least to the extent of 75% by their parents, will also be entitled to 75% of profits available to equity holders and to 75% of assets available on a winding-up to equity holders.

In what follows it will be assumed that when a company owns at least 75% of the ordinary share capital of another the group satifies all the requirements in order that group relief is available.

There are four different kinds of group relief:

(1) Group relief for trading losses.
(2) Group relief for excess charges.
(3) Group relief for certain special kinds of capital allowances, eg agricultural building allowances.
(4) Group relief for management expenses of an investment company (S.259 TA 1970).

The group company with the loss, charges, capital allowances or management expenses is said to surrender the loss or charge etc. and is called the *surrendering company*. The company against whose profits the loss or charge is set, is said to claim the loss and is called the *claimant company*.

In each case the items available in the surrendering company are set off against the claimant company's total profits for the *corresponding accounting period*. As between the group company surrendering the loss and a group claimant company the amount of the loss which may be surrendered is subject to a maximum. The maximum which may be surrendered is the amount of the loss or the amount of the claimant company's chargeable profits whichever is the less. In particular there is no question of a company surrendering a loss in excess of the claimants relevant profits and the claimant company then carrying forward or carrying back the excess of the losses surrendered. A claim for group relief must be made within two years of the end of the surrendering company's accounting period (S.264 TA 1970).

5.2.1 Group relief for trading losses

Group relief permits a company to set off a trading loss not only against its own profits in the ways we have seen in Chapter 4. but also against the total profits of companies in the same 75% group.

Example 2
Lord Ltd is a manufacturing company which makes up its accounts to 31 December in each year. Vassal Ltd is the wholly owned subsidiary of Lord Ltd and makes up its accounts to 31 December in each year also. The following are the results for the year ended 31 December 1983.

	Lord Ltd £	Vassall Ltd £
Schedule D Case I profit/(loss)	50,000	(270,000)
Schedule A surplus	7,500	
Chargeable gain (as abated)	60,000	
Unfranked investment income	12,000	10,000

The amount of trading loss available for group relief is £270,000. The amount which may be relieved is, however, limited to the profits available for relief as follows:

Total profits of Lord Ltd

	£
Schedule D Case I	50,000
Schedule A	7,500
Unfranked investment income	12,000
Chargeable gain	60,000
Profits available for relief	129,500

The relief is applied in the corporation tax computation of Lord Ltd with the effect of reducing the profits chargeable in Lord Ltd to nil.

Lord Ltd
Corporation Tax computation
Accounting Period ended 31 December 1983

	£
Schedule D Case I	50,000
Schedule A	7,500
Unfranked investment income	12,000
Chargeable gain	60,000
Total profits and profits	
chargeable	129,500
Less: Group relief	129,500
	NIL

As stated above, the amount of trading loss available for group relief is £270,000. However in some cases the surrendering company will take as much relief for its trading loss as is possible against its own profits before seeking relief against the profits of a group member. In this example Vassal Ltd might first set off £10,000 of its trading loss against its own profits of £10,000 (unfranked investment income) and, assuming chargeable profits for the year ended 31 December 1982 of £40,000, it could carry back £40,000 of loss under S.177(2). The loss available for group relief would then be £220,000, but since only £129,000 (ie the chargeable profits of the claimant company) may be surrendered, the balance of the loss (ie £90,500) will be carried forward and deducted from future trading profits of Vassal Ltd (S.177(1) TA 1970). The loss of Vassal Ltd would thus have been utilized as follows:

Vassal Ltd

	£	£
Schedule D Case I loss		270,000
Less: Utilized S.177(2):		
AP ended 31/12/83	10,000	
AP ended 31/12/82	40,000	
		50,000
		220,000
Less: Surrendered to Lord Ltd		129,500
Loss carried forward S.177(1)		90,500

5.2.2 Group relief for excess charges

A surrendering company may pass on to any other company in the same 75% group so much of its charges as exceed its profits. It should however, be particularly noted that in this context the term 'profits' has a specific meaning given to it in S.259(7) TA 1970. For these purposes the 'profits' are arrived at *before* deducting any losses or allowances which originated in some other accounting period. This means that, for example, losses brought forward under S.177(1) from an earlier accounting period must be *ignored* when deciding whether there are any excess charges available to surrender. Likewise a loss which could be carried back under S.177(2) TA 1970 to an earlier accounting period must also be ignored when calculating group relief for excess charges available for surrender in that earlier accounting period.

Example 3
Filius Ltd is the wholly owned subsidiary of Pater Ltd and has the following results for the year ended 31 March 1984.

	£
Schedule D Case I profit	6,000
Schedule A surplus	1,000
Chargeable gains (as abated)	500

In the year ended 31 March 1984 Filius Ltd paid debenture interest of £12,000.
An excess of charges arises as follows:

Accounting Period ended 31 March 1984

	£
Schedule D Case I	6,000
Schedule A	1,000
Chargeable gain	500
Total profits	7,500
Less: Charges	12,000
Excess charges	4,500

The excess of charges, £4,500 is available for surrender by way of group relief against the total profits arising in Pater Ltd for its accounting year ended 31 March 1984.

Example 4

Minor Ltd is a wholly owned subsidiary of Major Ltd and has a Schedule D Case I profit of £8,000 for the year ended 31 December 1983. Patent royalties of £10,000 were paid (gross) during this accounting period.

There are losses brought forward from earlier accounting periods under S.177(1) TA 1970 of £5,000.

The corporation tax computation will proceed as follows:

Accounting Period ended 31 December 1983

	£	£
Schedule D Case I profit		8,000
Less: Losses brought forward S.177(1)		5,000
		3,000
Less: Charges:		
Patent royalties paid	10,000	
Less: Used year end 31/12/83	3,000	3,000
Excess charges	7,000	
Profits chargeable to corporation tax		NIL

The excess charges of £7,000, being trade charges, may be carried forward (S.177(8)).

For group relief purposes, however, the excess charges will be calculated as follows:

	£
Schedule D Case I profit	8,000
Less: Charges	10,000
Excess charges for group relief	2,000

The excess of charges, £2,000 is available to surrender to Major Ltd under the group relief provisions for set-off against its total profits for the accounting year ended 31 December 1983.

One of the fundamental principles of group relief is that losses, excess charges, etc are only available to surrender from one group company to another in so far as they arise in a '*corresponding accounting period*'. A corresponding accounting period is defined by the legislation with reference to the company which has a loss, etc. to surrender. If an accounting period of a claimant company coincides with an accounting period of a surrendering company (in the sense of covering the same period of time) then the accounting period of the claimant company is said to 'correspond' with the accounting period of the surrendering company. Thus in Example 4, Major and Minor both have accounting periods of twelve months ended 31 December 1983 and the accounting periods are corresponding periods. The principle that only excess charges of corresponding accounting periods may be relieved is exemplified in Example 4 by the fact that if the S177(1) loss of Minor Ltd had been deducted from the trading profits before deducting royalties the excess charges for group relief would have been £7,000, i.e. £5,000 greater and the company would have effectively been able to use the group relief provisions to surrender a loss arising in an earlier accounting period.

5.2.3 Corresponding accounting periods

In the examples so far considered the accounting periods of the surrendering company and the claimant company have coincided. Thus the losses or excess charges have been available to deduct from the total profits of the claimant company subject only to the limit of the amount of the profits of the claimant company or the amount of the loss etc of the surrendering company, whichever is the less.

Where however, the claimant and the surrendering company do not have corresponding accounting periods it becomes necessary to apportion the profits of the claimant company, against which group relief may be set, and the loss or other type of relief available for surrender. This is done in order to ensure that relief is only given for that period of time which is common to the accounting periods of both the surrendering and claimant companies.

Example 5
C Ltd and S Ltd are members of a 75% group. S Ltd incurred a trading loss of £100,000 in the year ended 31 December 1983. The accounting periods and results of C Ltd are:

12 months to	*Profit*
31 March 1983	£80,000
31 March 1984	£120,000

Corresponding accounting periods are:
(a) Period 1 January 1983–31 March 1983
The loss which may be surrendered by S Ltd is £100,000 × 3/12 = £25,000
The profit of C Ltd against which the group relief may be set is
£80,000 × 3/12 = £20,000
S Ltd will surrender the smaller of these two figures, namely £20,000, and thus C Ltd may claim group relief of £20,000 to set against its profits of £80,000 for the period ended on 31 March 1983.

(b) Period 1 April 1983–31 December 1983
The loss which may be surrendered by S Ltd is £100,000 × 9/12 = £75,000

The profit of C Ltd against which the group relief may be set is £120,000 × 9/12 = £90,000.

S Ltd will surrender the smaller of these two figures, namely £75,000 and thus C Ltd may claim group relief of £75,000 against its profits for the year ended 31 March 1984.

It should be noted that the total loss surrendered by S Ltd is £95,000 (i.e. £20,000 + £75,000) thus there is a balance of loss of £5,000 which may not be surrendered under the group relief provisions. This must be dealt with under the normal loss relief provisions discussed in Chapter 4.

5.2.4 Companies joining or leaving group

The general rule is that group relief will not be available unless the surrendering company and claimant company are both members of the same group throughout the whole of their respective accounting periods (S.262(1) TA 1970). However to give effect to the intention to give relief for the time companies are members of the same group, an accounting period is deemed to end and a new accounting period to commence, whenever a company joins or leaves a group. The new accounting period then continues until the end of the actual accounting period. It should be stressed that this artificial splitting-up of the companies' true accounting periods is done solely for the purpose of ascertaining the amount of group relief available.

Example 6
A Ltd, a trading company, has two wholly owned subsidiaries, B Ltd and D Ltd. All three companies make up accounts to 31 December in each year. B Ltd has been a subsidiary of A Ltd for many years, but D Ltd became a subsidiary of A Ltd on 1 July 1983. The results of the three group members for the year ended 31 December 1983 are as follows:

	A Ltd £	B Ltd £	D Ltd £
Schedule D Case I profit/(loss)	280,000	50,000	(100,000)
Schedule A surplus	25,000		
Chargeable gain (as abated)	14,000		

Assume A Ltd is the claimant company in relation to the surrendering company D Ltd. For the purposes of group relief the accounting periods of A Ltd and D Ltd end on 30 June 1983 and a new accounting period is deemed to begin for both A Ltd and D Ltd on 1 July 1983. These deemed accounting periods will then end, as normal, on 31 December 1983. Profits and trading losses are apportioned to the deemed accounting periods thus created, on a time basis.

D Ltd

The amount of the trading loss of D Ltd available for group relief is thus:

	£
Trading loss for accounting period of twelve months	100,000

| Trading loss for deemed accounting period of 6 months beginning 1 July 1983 being loss available for group relief: 1/2 × £100,000 | 50,000 |

A Ltd

The amount of the profit of A. Ltd available for group relief is:
Total profits for accounting period of twelve months:

	£
Schedule D Case I	280,000
Schedule A	25,000
Chargeable gain	14,000
Total profits	319,000

| Total profits for deemed accounting period of 6 months beginning 1 July 1983 being profits available for group relief: 1/2 × £319,000 | 159,500 |

Since the loss available to surrender, £50,000, is smaller than the profits available for relief, £159,500, the relief is restricted to the amount of the loss, £50,000. The corporation tax computations of the companies concerned are then:

A Ltd

	£
Schedule D Case I	280,000
Schedule A	25,000
Chargeable gain	14,000
Total profits	319,000
Less: Group relief	50,000
Profits chargeable to corporation tax	269,000

B Ltd

	£
Schedule D Case I and profits chargeable	50,000

C Ltd

	£
Schedule D Case I loss	100,000
Less: Utilized by way of group relief	50,000
Balance of loss available for carry forward S.177(1)	50,000

In the above computation it was assumed that the whole of the loss available for relief £50,000 was surrendered to A Ltd. However, part of the loss could also have been surrendered to B Ltd. In the circumstances set out in Example 6 the maximum claim which B Ltd could make on D Ltd is restricted to £25,000, i.e. the profits of B Ltd for the deemed accounting period which began when D Ltd joined the group. Assuming B Ltd were to claim the maximum group relief possible, £25,000, the balance of the loss then available for surrender by D Ltd (also £25,000) could still be claimed by A Ltd. In short a loss available for group relief may be claimed by one or a number of group companies subject to the limit of the smaller of the profit to be relieved in the case of each claimant company and the loss available. There can, of course, be no question of having losses allowed twice (S.263 TA 1970).

It will be noted that in Example 6 where apportionments have been required as a result of D Ltd joining the group on 1 July 1983, these have been calculated on a time basis. As a general rule the Inland Revenue accepts that wherever a company enters a group apportionments of profits or losses should be carried out in this way. However, if time apportionment operates 'unreasonably or unjustly' some other 'just and reasonable' method can be used (S.47 FA 1984).

Although we have stressed the nature of the maximum group relief which may be obtained by a claimant company, the amount which is in fact claimed need not be the full amount which it is possible to claim (S.264(1) (a) TA 1970). This is in contrast to loss relief claims within a company itself, eg S.177(1) TA 1970 loss claims, where the maximum relief available has to be taken at the earliest moment.

5.2.5 Relation of group relief to other relief—the claimant company

We have talked so far of the right to set off group relief against the total profits of a claimant company. Examination of the corporation tax work form in Appendix 1 shows that group relief is the final deduction that is made in a corporation tax computation. That is to say, charges, trading losses brought forward under S.177(1) TA 1970 and trading losses of the current accounting period (S.177(2) TA 1970) are all deducted before group relief is given. There is however, one major exception to the general rule that group relief is the final deduction to be made in the computation of profits chargeable to corporation tax. This exception concerns trading losses carried back from a subsequent accounting period under the provisions of S.177(2). These must be deducted after group relief has been given.

Example 7
Province Ltd is the wholly owned subsidiary of Empire Ltd. Both companies are trading companies which make up their accounts annually to 30 June. The following are the summarised results of the two companies for the two years ended 30 June 1984.

Years ended 30 June	1983 £	1984 £
Empire Ltd		
Schedule D Case I (loss)	(172,000)	(50,000)
Province Ltd		
Schedule D Case I		
profit/(loss)	(26,000)	67,000
Chargeable gains		
(as abated)		1,000
Charges on income:		
Trade	2,000	2,000
Non-trade	500	500

In relation to the year to 30 June 1984, the parent company, Empire Ltd, is the surrendering company and Province Ltd, the subsidiary company, the claimant company. Since both companies made losses in the year ended 30 June 1983 there is no question of group relief in that year.
Group relief is available for the year ended 30 June 1984 as follows:

Empire Ltd
Trading loss accounting period
ended 30 June 1984, available for relief   £50,000
Note:
It may be assumed that Empire Ltd is carrying forward for set-off against future trading income (under S.177(1) TA 1970) the trading loss of £172,000 realised in the year ended 30 June 1983. A trading loss being carried forward like this is not available for group relief, ie the loss available for relief in the accounting period ended 30 June 1984 is *not* £50,000 + £172,000 = £222,000.

Province Ltd

Profit available for relief	£	£
Schedule D Case I		67,000
Less: Loss brought forward S.177(1)	26,000	
Trade charges brought forward S177(8) and 177(1)	2,000	
		28,000
		39,000
Chargeable gain		1,000
		40,000
Less: Charges (trade and non-trade)		2,500
		37,500

Since the profit available is smaller than the loss available, the amount of group relief which may be claimed is limited to the profit, £37,500.
The computations for the two companies for the year ended 30 June 1984 will be as follows:

Empire Ltd	£
Schedule D Case I (loss)	50,000
Less: Utilized Province Ltd	37,500
	12,500
Add: Brought forward S.177(1) TA 1970	172,000
Carried forward S.177(1) TA 1970	184,500

Province Ltd	£	£
Schedule D Case I		67,000
Less: Brought forward		
S.177(1) TA 1970	26,000	
Trade charges brought		
forward S.177(8) and		
S.177(1)	2,000	
		28,000
		39,000
Chargeable gain		1,000
Total profits		40,000
Less: Charges (trade		
and non-trade)		2,500
Profits chargeable		37,500
Less: Group relief		37,500
		NIL

5.2.6 Payment for group relief

In most cases where subsidiaries involved in a group relief claim are wholly owned by a parent holding company there will be no question of payment by the claimant company for the benefit of the losses made available by the surrendering company. In other cases however, particularly where a minority outside shareholder is involved the claimant company may make a payment to the surrendering company in respect of the group relief received. Such a payment is not taken into account in the corporation tax computation of either company involved, and will not be treated as a distribution made by the claimant company or as a charge on the claimant's income (S.258(4) TA 1970).

5.3 GROUP INCOME AND INTEREST

A 51% subsidiary of a United Kingdom company may elect under S.256 TA 1970 to pay dividends to its parent company or to a fellow 51% subsidiary without accounting for advance corporation tax. The dividends passing between them are not treated as franked payments made by the subsidiary, or as franked investment income of the recipient. Such dividends, paid under election, are called 'group income' of the recipient.

A 51% subsidiary is one in which more than 50% of the ordinary share capital is held by its parent. For the purposes of these provisions there are no further special requirements concerning the interests of equity holders in distributions or assets.

An election may also be made under S.256 for intra-group charges to be paid without deduction of income tax. This election may be applied both to payments by a 51% subsidiary up to its parent and also to payments by a parent down to its 51% subsidiaries, as well as to payments between fellow subsidiaries.

The consequences and disadvantages of not making a group election are illustrated in Example 8.

Example 8
Parent Ltd and Sub Ltd prepare accounts to 31 March each year. On 30 April 1984 Parent Ltd paid a dividend of £3,500. On 26 August 1984 Sub Ltd paid a dividend of £2,100 to Parent Ltd, of which it is a wholly owned subsidiary. If there is no S.256 election in force the procedure for dealing with the advance corporation tax will be as follows:

(a) Parent Ltd will account to the Collector of Taxes for ACT on the dividend paid on 30 April 1984. Assuming it has no franked investment income in this return period, Parent Ltd will pay ACT of £1,500 by 14 July 1984.
(b) Sub Ltd will account to the Collector for ACT on the dividend paid on 26 August 1984. A payment of £900 will be sent to the Collector by 14 October 1984.
(c) Parent Ltd will send to the Collector a form CT 61 in respect of the return period ending 30 September 1984, showing a dividend received on 26 August 1984. This franked investment income will be set against the franked payment made by Parent Ltd on 30 April 1984 and the tax credit of £900 will be repaid by the Collector of Taxes to Parent Ltd.

Had Parent Ltd and Sub Ltd made the group election the cumbersome roundabout of payment and repayment of advance corporation tax would have been avoided. In practice a group holding company will call up dividends from its wholly owned subsidiaries shortly before it pays its regular dividends. Having these paid under election maximizes the group's cash flow and minimizes the number of administrative procedures.

Example 9
Older Ltd owns 55% of the shares in Younger Ltd. Both companies prepare accounts to 31 December each year. On 13 January 1984 Younger Ltd paid a dividend of £35,000 to Older Ltd. On 6 June 1984 Older Ltd paid a dividend of £52,500. A S.256 election is in force.
The procedure for accounting for advance corporation tax can be stated simply:
(a) Younger Ltd pays a dividend to Older Ltd on 13 January 1984. A S.256 election is in force and therefore no ACT is payable.
(b) Older Ltd pays a dividend to the shareholders on 6 June 1984. The amount of the franked payment is £52,500 + (3/7 × £52,500) = £75,000. Since a S.256 election is in force, Older Ltd does not have any FII available

to set against the franked payment because group income is not franked investment income. Thus Older Ltd will pay to the Collector the ACT on the dividend which amounts to £22,500. This sum is payable by 14 July 1984.

In the above example where an election is in force Older Ltd is liable for advance corporation tax of £22,500 on paying a dividend on 6 June 1984. Had no election been made:

		£
Younger Ltd would have paid ACT on its dividend of 13 January to Older Ltd − 3/7 × £35,000		15,000
Older Ltd would have paid ACT on its dividend of £52,000 of 6 June to its shareholders as follows:		

	£	
Franked payment	75,000	
Franked investment income	50,000	
	25,000	
ACT at 30%		7,500
Total ACT payable		22,500

As you will observe, whether or not an election is in force the group pays the same amount of advance corporation tax. However, the dates of payment of tax differ in an important way.

With no election, tax of £15,000 is payable on 14 April 1984 and £7,500 on 14 July 1984. With an election, the whole tax of £22,500 is payable on 14 July 1984. The cash flow benefit of an election in this instance and on these facts is the postponement of payment of £15,000 tax for three months from 14 April 1984 to 14 July 1984.

The procedure for making group income and group interest elections is outlined in Sections 256(1) and 257 Taxes Act 1970. The election is made jointly by the paying company and the receiving company. The election is not effective until three months after it is made, or, if earlier, the date on which the Inspector of Taxes notifies the companies concerned that the conditions for the making of an election are satisfied.

From time to time a subsidiary company which has received some franked (or unfranked) investment income will find it more advantageous to pay a dividend (or a charge, eg debenture interest) outside of a group election. In these circumstances the company informs the Collector of Taxes that it does not wish the election to apply.

Let us assume that in Example 8, Sub Ltd had a surplus of franked investment income of £1,000 brought forward to the year ended 31 March 1985. The only way in which the group can obtain the benefit of the tax credit in Sub Ltd's FII is to set it off against franked payments. The benefit of the tax credit, which is to reduce or eliminate a payment of advance corporation tax in the first instance, is a cash flow benefit. This cannot be realized unless a way can be found of transferring the benefit of the tax credit in Sub Ltd's FII to Parent Ltd. This is achieved by Sub Ltd making a franked payment, ie a payment outside the election with notification to the Collector. Parent Ltd then receives £1,000 of franked investment income from Sub Ltd and this reduces its liability to pay advance corporation tax in respect of its franked payments.

The computation would then proceed along the following lines:

Sub Ltd
(a) Part of dividend to be dealt with under normal rules:

	£
Dividend paid	700
Add: ACT	300
Franked payment	1,000
Less: FII available	1,000
Excess	Nil

ACT payable nil
(b) Part of dividend to be dealt with under S.256 procedure:
Dividend paid £2,100 − £700 = £1,400

Parent Ltd
(a) FII received £1,000 (i.e. the amount of Sub Ltd's franked payment) Set FII against franked payment made (30 April 1984) and obtain repayment of tax credit of £300.
(b) Group income received   £1,400

Group income, which but for the S.256 election would be franked investment income, is *not* included in the profits of the recipient, ie the parent company, chargeable to corporation tax. By way of contrast group interest, which apart from the election would be unfranked investment income *is* included (as is UFII of course) in the corporation tax profits of the receipient company.

Example 10

Welshire Ltd has 3 subsidiaries: X Ltd, Y Ltd and Z Ltd. The following information is provided for the year ended 31 March 1984;

	£
Schedule D Case I profit	80,000
Schedule A	2,600
UFII	3,000
Group interest (representing loan interest payable by X Ltd under a S.256 election)	9,000
Group income (representing a dividend paid by Z Ltd under a S.256 election)	17,000

Corporation tax computation:

Schedule D Case I	80,000
Schedule A	2,600
UFII	3,000
Group interest	9,000
	———
Corporation tax profits	94,600
	———
Corporation tax payable:	
£94,600 × 30%	28,380
Less: Income tax suffered on UFII	900
	———
	27,480
	———

Notes:

(1) Group income is not taken into account when ascertaining whether or not the small companies rate of tax is applicable, see Chapter 1.

(2) No income tax was deducted from the group interest so it is only the income tax suffered in respect of the unfranked investment income that requires to be deducted from the corporation tax payable.

5.4 SURRENDER OF ADVANCE CORPORATION TAX

Advance corporation tax is set off against a corporation tax liability to arrive at corporation tax payable on the due date (mainstream corporation tax). ACT which is paid with respect to an AP can only be set off against corporation tax on income and is limited in amount, at the present time, to 30% of the company's income for the accounting period. Because of the restriction on the amount of ACT which can be deducted, more ACT may have been paid than it is possible to set-off against a parent company's corporation tax liability and in such circumstances it is possible within a 51% group for a parent to surrender the surplus ACT for the accounting period in which the surplus arises to a 51% subsidiary (S.92 FA 1972).

The need for, and advantages of, such a provision are most obviously evident in the case of wholly owned subsidiaries. As we have already seen it is likely that subsidiaries will have paid dividends under a group election up to the group holding company without payment of ACT. It follows that while a subsidiary may well have a corporation tax liability it has no ACT to set against this liability (because of the group election), while a parent company may have a surplus of ACT which it cannot deduct from its corporation liability because of the 30% of income restriction referred to above. From the group point of view this is an unsatisfactory state of affairs which the provision for surrender of ACT seeks to remedy.

Section 92 Finance Act 1972 allows a company which has paid advance corporation tax in respect of dividends paid by it, to surrender the ACT in whole or in part to its 51% subsidiary. Although a surrender will most often arise when there is a surplus of advance corporation tax in the parent company as described above, in theory there is no need for a surplus of ACT to exist; the parent could, if desired, surrender ACT rather than setting it off against its own corporation tax liability.

As we have seen a 51% subsidiary is one in which more than 50% of the ordinary share capital is held by its parent. In addition, the parent company must be beneficially entitled to more than 50% of profits available to equity holders and more than 50% of assets of the subsidiary available for distribution to equity holders were the subsidiary to be wound up (S.92(9) FA 1972). These and other anti-avoidance provisions in subsection 9 of S.92 will not usually be of relevance to normal commercial groups of companies.

Advance corporation tax which is surrendered by a parent to its 51% subsidiary is treated by the subsidiary as having been paid by it in respect of a distribution made by that subsidiary on the date when the actual dividend was paid by the parent company (S.92(2) and (3) FA 1972).

Surrendered ACT is available for set off against the corporation tax charged on the subsidiary. If the subsidiary is unable to utilise the full amount of the surrendered ACT in the current accounting period the surplus surrendered advance corporation tax may be carried forward by the subsidiary and set off against its corporation tax liability on income in future accounting periods.

Example 11
Minnow Ltd is the 51% subsidiary of Whale Ltd. Both companies prepare accounts to 31 March each year.
The following are the results for the year ended 31 March 1984:

Whale Ltd	£
Schedule D Case I	280,000
Chargeable gain (as abated)	40,000
Ordinary dividend paid in March 1984	210,000
Related ACT	90,000

Minnow Ltd	£
Schedule D Case I	15,000
Assume a rate of corporation tax of 50%	

Whale Ltd	£
Corporation tax computation	
Schedule D Case I	280,000
Chargeable gain (as abated)	40,000
Profits chargeable to corporation tax	320,000
Corporation tax at 50%	160,000
Less: ACT (maximum) 30% × £280,000	84,000
Mainstream corporation tax	76,000

Surplus ACT	£
ACT paid	90,000
Maximum ACT deductible,	
30% × £280,000	84,000
Surplus ACT	6,000

The surplus ACT of £6,000 (being part of ACT paid by Whale Ltd) may be surrendered to Minnow Ltd.

Minnow Ltd	£
Corporation tax computation	
Profits chargeable	15,000
Corporation tax at 50%	7,500
Less: ACT surrendered by Whale Ltd	
(maximum) 30% × £15,000	4,500
Mainstream corporation tax	3,000

Surplus ACT	£
Advance corporation tax surrendered	
by Whale Ltd	6,000
Less: Utilized in year ending	
31 March 1984	4,500
Surplus ACT available to Minnow Ltd to	
carry forward	1,500

We have seen above that surrendered advance corporation tax may be carried forward by the subsidiary and utilized in subsequent years in the same way as if the subsidiary had paid the dividend and the resulting ACT itself. A company which has surplus ACT on its own account may also claim to have that surplus carried back for up to six years. A subsidiary which has a surplus of *surrendered* advance corporation tax may *not* however, make a claim to have that surplus carried back.

Thus a subsidiary may carry back its own surplus ACT but may not carry back surrendered ACT. In these circumstances, if we are dealing with a subsidiary which has both surrendered advance corporation tax and advance corporation tax paid on its own account, we need to know which of the two amounts will be utilized in priority to set off against the corporation tax liability for the current accounting period. Section 92(3A) FA 1972 provides that a surrendered amount of advance corporation tax will be set off against the subsidiary's liability to corporation tax for the current accounting period *before* ACT paid on a dividend actually paid by the subsidiary itself.

Example 12
Sub-Editor Ltd is the only 51% subsidiary of Editor Ltd. Both companies make up accounts annually to 31 December.
The following are the results for Sub-Editor Ltd for the years ended 31 December 1983 and 1984:

Years ended 31 December	*1983*	*1984*
	£	£
Schedule D Case I profit	20,000	40,000
Dividend paid	—	14,000
ACT surrendered by Editor Ltd		10,000
A single corporation tax rate of 50% will be assumed		

Sub-Editor Ltd
Corporation tax computation
Year ended 31 December 1984

Schedule D Case I profit		40,000
Corporation tax payable £40,000 × 50%		20,000
Advance corporation tax		
ACT on dividend paid £14,000 × 3/7	6,000	
Add: ACT surrendered by Editor Ltd	10,000	
Total ACT available	16,000	
Deduct: ACT set off, restricted to £40,000 × 30%	12,000	12,000
Surplus ACT	4,000	
Mainstream corporation tax		8,000

The advance corporation tax that has been set off in the year ending 31 December 1984 is £12,000. This is treated as being made up as follows:

		£
(a)	ACT surrendered	10,000
(b)	ACT paid by Sub-Editor Ltd £6,000 was available but only £2,000 was utilized in 1984	2,000
	(And therefore the balance may be carried back to 1983)	
		12,000

Since Sub-Editor Ltd is treated as using the surrendered advance corporation tax first, there is a surplus of the company's *own* advance corporation tax and since it was actually paid by Sub-Editor Ltd it can be carried back.

Corporation tax computation

Year ended 31 December 1983	£
Schedule D Case I profit	20,000
CT £20,000 × 50%	10,000
Less: ACT brought back from 1984	4,000
Mainstream corporation tax	6,000

5.5 TRANSFER OF CHARGEABLE ASSETS WITHIN GROUPS

Transfers of chargeable assets may be made within 75% groups without giving rise to any corporation tax charge on capital gains. A 75% group is defined with reference to ordinary share capital only and the 1973 'equity holder' legislation does *not* apply.

A group for this purpose is defined in S.272(1) TA 1970 and means a company called a 'principal company' and all its 75% subsidiaries. If the subsidiaries themselves have 75% subsidiaries the definition of group member embraces these further subsidiaries and so on. A principal company means a company of which another is a 75% subsidiary.

Example 13
The following is the diagramatic representation of a group of companies. The percentages indicated are the percentage holdings of ordinary share capital owned by the parent in the relevant subsidiary:

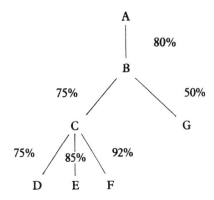

Since companies A, B and C each have 75% subsidiaries, A, B and C are principal companies, as defined. Each principal company and its 75% subsidiaries forms a group for the purposes of the rules regarding the transfer of chargeable assets within 75% groups. Thus A and B are a group; B and C are a group; C and D E and F are a group; moreover since B, a 75% subsidiary of A, has itself a 75% subsidiary, C, which in turn has three 75% subsidiaries, D, E and F, the group of A and B is extended to include C, D, E and F. This means that company F for example, can transfer a chargeable asset to company A without any tax charge on a capital gain.

The intention of the legislation regarding capital gains and groups of companies is that all the companies within the same 75% group should be treated as if they were a single entity. Transfers of chargeable assets between companies within the group do not give rise to chargeable gains or allowable losses.

Example 14
Alpha Ltd and Beta Ltd prepare accounts to 31 March each year.
On 10 January 1968 Alpha Ltd acquire a small office block at a cost of £110,000.
On 4 June 1982 Alpha Ltd transfers the office block to Beta Ltd, one of its wholly owned subsidiaries. The market value of the office block at that time is £175,000.
On 6 September 1984 Beta Ltd sells the office block to Mr Roger—an individual unconnected with the group. The sale proceeds are £250,000.
Beta Ltd has sold a chargeable asset and is treated as having acquired that asset in January 1968, the date of acquisition by Alpha Ltd, at a cost of £110,000. Thus the full amount of the gain arising during the whole of the period of ownership by the group is charged to tax on Beta Ltd.

If a group company to which an asset has been transferred under the above provisions subsequently leaves the group within six years of the date of the transfer, the transferee company is deemed to have disposed of the asset on the date on which it acquired it. Thus a chargeable gain may arise covering the period from the original date of acquisition by the group to the date of transfer although the chargeable asset has not at the time the subsidiary leaves the group, been sold (S.278 TA 1970).

Example 15

Assume the same facts as in Example 14 except that we are now told that Alpha Ltd sold its 100% holding in Beta Ltd in February 1983, i.e. Beta left the Alpha group.

The corporation tax computation of Beta Ltd for the year ended 31 March 1983 will include a chargeable gain calculated under S.278 TA 1970 as follows:

	£
Market value at date of transfer from Alpha Ltd to Beta Ltd	175,000
Less: Cost 10 January 1968	110,000
Chargeable gain	65,000
Chargeable gain	65,000
Less: Abatement S.93 FA 1972 £65,000 × 11/26	27,500
Chargeable gain included in computation	37,500

It should be noted that a computation under S.278 TA 1970 is not required if a company ceases to be a member of a group as a result of being wound-up or dissolved.

5.6 CONSORTIA

We have seen above that the reliefs available to groups of companies apply where there is a parent company or holding company with a number of subsidiaries.

Two of the reliefs that we have considered are extended to consortia of companies, namely:

(a) Group relief for trading losses and charges etc. (S.258 TA 1970) and
(b) Payments of dividends and charges gross under a S.256 TA 1970 election.

A feature of modern commercial transactions has been the coming together of a number of previously unconnected companies to carry out an activity. The companies form a *consortium* and the activity is carried out by a trading company owned by the consortium or by a trading company owned by a holding company which in turn is owned by the consortium members.

An example of a consortium for consortium reliefs is as follows:

Consortium member companies:

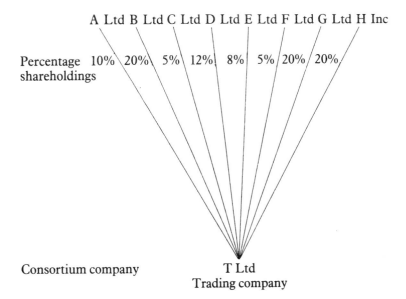

A Ltd B Ltd C Ltd D Ltd E Ltd F Ltd G Ltd H Inc

Percentage 10% 20% 5% 12% 8% 5% 20% 20%
shareholdings

Consortium company   T Ltd
                              Trading company

A consortium company is commonly a trading company etc whose ordinary share capital is owned to the extent of 75% or more by UK resident companies; each UK company must own at least 5%. Although overseas resident companies may be members of a consortium they do not obtain consortium reliefs which are reserved to UK resident companies (S.46(3) FA 1984).

5.6.1 Surrender of trading losses

Consortium relief for trading losses is available between a consortium trading company and a consortium member or vice versa (S.258 TA 1970).

Example 16

T Ltd is a consortium company which makes up accounts annually to 31 March. In the year ended 31 March 1985 T Ltd makes a loss for group relief purposes (consortium relief) of £100,000. The percentage ordinary shareholdings of T Ltd owned by the companies indicated are as follows:

	%
F Ltd	10
G Ltd	5
H Ltd	20
I Ltd	12
J Ltd	15
K Ltd	10
L Ltd	8
M Inc	20

M Inc is a US resident company. All the other consortium members are UK resident companies.

Subject to the matter of corresponding accounting periods each UK company will be entitled to claim its percentage share of the loss of T Ltd by way of group relief, e.g. F Ltd is able to claim up to 10% of £100,000, £10,000, and so on for the other companies assuming they have sufficient profits available for relief. The US company cannot claim group relief since this is restricted to UK resident companies.

It should be noted that if, in another year, J Ltd incurred a loss, a proportion of that loss could be surrendered to T Ltd. In this case, since J Ltd owns 15% of the shares in T Ltd, the maximum amount of loss which could be surrendered is 15% of the profits of T Ltd.

5.6.2 Payment of dividends and charges under S.256 election

The group income and group interest provisions of S.256 TA 1970 are extended to consortia of companies. This means that:

(a) A trading or holding company owned by a consortium may pay dividends to any consortium member without accounting for advance corporation tax, and

(b) Any company within the consortium may pay charges to any other consortium member or any company owned by the consortium without deducting income tax.

All the points discussed in relation to S.256 in a 51% group context apply equally to a consortium of companies.

Question 5

T Ltd owns 100% of the ordinary share capital of H Ltd, 80% of that of M Ltd and 60% of that of D Ltd. The companies have the following results for the twelve month chargeable accounting period ended 31 December 1984:

	T Ltd £	H Ltd £	M Ltd £	D Ltd £
Case I income	100,000	(15,000)	20,000	10,000
Capital gains before abatement	30,000	(5,000)	3,000	3,000
Case I losses brought forward	125,000	—	—	—
Dividends paid	70,000	10,000	—	—
Group income	10,000	—	—	—
Franked investment income —inclusive of tax credit	5,000	—	—	—
Charges on income paid (gross)	20,000	10,000	—	—

The following additional points of information have been obtained:
(1) All the shareholdings in the four companies, other than those referred to above as being owned by T Ltd, are held by individuals.
(2) The group income of £10,000 of T Ltd is the receipt of the dividend paid by H Ltd.
(3) Advance corporation tax on the dividend paid by T Ltd has been duly accounted for after taking account of the franked investment income received by that company.
(4) Income tax on the two amounts of charges on income paid has been duly accounted for.

Assume the following:

Corporation tax	50%
Advance corporation tax	3/7
Abatement of chargeable gains	2/5
Income tax	30%

Required:
(1) Explain, in the context of corporation tax the meaning of the terms 'group income' and 'group relief'.
(2) Calculate the outstanding corporation tax liabilities, if any, of each of the four companies on the assumption that the desired aim is for the group as a whole to pay the minimum of taxation.
(3) State what utilized losses, if any, are available for carry forward at 31 December 1984.

Institute of Chartered Accountants of Scotland
Question 1, Part I Examination
September 1981 (amended)

CHAPTER 6

CLOSE COMPANIES

6.1 THE NATURE OF CLOSE COMPANIES

Many family companies are what the Taxes Act calls close companies. A close company, broadly, is one which is under the control of five or fewer of its shareholders or is under the control of those shareholders who are its directors, even if there are more than five of them (S.282(1) TA 1970).

This is not the place to trace the history and development of the joint stock company, nor of the concept of the 'one man' company. It is sufficient to observe that legally a single individual (with another perhaps nominee shareholder) can incorporate his business, and thereby create a legal person distinct from himself, with separate powers, rights and liabilities. This fact has important implications for taxation. What it means is that an individual who conducts a business as an individual is subject to the income tax code involving progressive rates of income tax, while the same individual who forms a company may conduct the same business through the agency of the company subject to the corporation tax code with a single proportional rate of corporation tax. At higher rates of income tax it will, other things being equal, be advantageous for a business to be carried on by a company rather than by a sole trader or partnership. The exact point at which the advantage lies with trading as a company depends on the facts of each case.

Because of the opportunities for tax avoidance using companies in this way, and so as to maintain horizontal equity (equality of the tax burden between taxpayers in similar positions) there is a substantial body of legislation concerning the special class of company controlled by a few persons which we have identified above. The purpose of this anti-avoidance legislation was broadly to ensure that cash received by shareholders in an otherwise tax advantageous way, e.g. by way of a loan, should suffer a tax charge and that a company should adopt an adequate dividend policy so that income should reach shareholders and be subject to higher rate income tax in their hands. In pursuit of the latter object the legislators imposed distribution standards which if they were not attained could result in income being apportioned (for tax purposes only) among the company's shareholders. Prior to 1980 these dividend standards were a consideration for a very large number of trading companies. Since 1980 for reasons inherent in the calculation of the distribution standard, family trading companies, while remaining close companies by definition, have been removed from what most would regard as the major effect of the legislation (although remaining subject to other minor rules); however for trading companies accumulating and investing cash surpluses, and investment companies, including property investment companies, the whole body of legislation retains something of its earlier significance.

It is necessary to establish at the outset what is and what is not a close company. Our consideration of the definition will require us to look at further special meanings given to words in the definitions and other special features of the legislation. In later sections of this chapter we shall consider the consequences for a company and its shareholders of being found to be close.

6.1.1 Close company—definition

The words of S.282(1) TA 1970 define a close company as follows: '. . . *a close company is one which is under the control of five or fewer participators or of participators who are directors . . .*'. Another definition of a close company is discussed in 6.8.

6.1.2 Participator

A participator can for many practical purposes be thought of as a shareholder, but the definition in S.303(1) is much wider and embraces not only those who at present possess shares but also those who are or will be entitled to acquire shares, e.g. by means of a present option or a right to a future option to buy shares. A participator is '*a person having a share or interest in the capital or income of the company*'. This definition includes an important class of persons described as loan creditors. A loan creditor is defined in S.303(7) and includes someone having loan capital of the company, e.g. a debenture holder, as well as someone who simply advances money to a company on a loan account. It may be wondered how a lender of money to a company can be said to 'control' the company (see definition of close company above). However, 'control' has a technical meaning in the context of the legislation and means, in addition to more obvious meanings like voting control, an entitlement to receive more than half the assets of the company on a winding up (see 6.1.3). In this way, loan creditors, who are participators by definition can control a company.

A bank lending money to a company in the ordinary course of business is not a loan creditor for the purposes of the definition or a participator.

6.1.3 Control

A person or persons have control of a company if they exercise control or are able to exercise control, or are entitled to acquire control, direct or indirect over the company's affairs (S.302(2) TA 1970). Control may be 'exercised' for this purpose in the following ways:

(1) The possession of, or the right to acquire:
     (a) the greater part of the share capital, or
     (b) the greater part of the issued share capital, or
     (c) the greater part of the voting power in the company, or
(2) The possession of, or the right to acquire such part of the issued share capital as would result in an entitlement to more than half the income of the company if the whole of the company's income were distributed among the participators of the company. For this purpose a loan creditor is not to be regarded as a participator; or
(3) The right to receive more than half the company's assets on a winding up or in any other circumstances.

An entitlement to acquire control means not only a present entitlement but also a future entitlement (S.302(4) TA 1970).

6.1.4 Associate

For the purpose of determining what person or persons have control, as defined, of a company, you must ascribe to a participator the powers and rights of his nominees and of any associate of that participator. An associate is defined in S.303(3) TA 1970, and means:

(a) a 'relative', that is husband or wife, parent or remoter direct ascendant, e.g. grandfather, grandmother, child or remoter direct descendant, or brother or sister,
(b) a partner,
(c) the trustees of any settlement set up by the participator or by one of the participator's relatives (as defined in (a) above),
(d) any person interested in shares of the company which are held in trust or as part of a deceased's estate if the participator also has an interest in the shares.

A participator may also have attributed to him the powers of a company which he, or he and his associates, control.

Attributions of power have to be made in such a way as will result in the company being under the control of five or fewer participators if this is possible.

Example 1
A company has the following share capital which is authorized, issued and fully paid:

  10,000 ordinary shares of £1 each   £10,000

The shareholders and their respective shareholdings are as follows:

A	1,000
B (Wife of A)	500
C	1,500
D (Brother of A)	1,000
E	500
Z Ltd	900

and twenty other shareholders each holding 230 shares.

The share capital of Z Ltd is owned by A, B, C, D and E equally.
Who has control?
All the shareholders are participators as defined. Control for the purpose of
the legislation is exercised by those who possess the greater part of the share
capital of the company. Without regard to the question of associates and
attribution of powers, control is exercised by the following persons (taking
the holdings in descending order of magnitude):

C	1,500
A	1,000
D	1,000
Z Ltd	900
B	500
E	500
	5,400

Since the share capital (authorized and issued) is 10,000 shares the six
persons listed above, on this basis, have control.
Attributing to shareholder A the shareholdings of associates has the
following results:

Attribution to A	
From wife B	500
From brother D	1,000
From Z Ltd, controlled by A and associates (60% 'owned' by A, B and D)	900
	2,400

Control is then exercised by the following:	
A—own holding	1,000
—attribution	2,400
	3,400
C	1,500
E	500
	5,400

Thus the company for the purposes of close company legislation is under
the control of three participators and is accordingly close.[1]

---

[1]For a reason which is discussed later (see 6.8) even if no shareholder were associated with
another, the company would still be close.

Even if a company falls within the primary definition of a close company (control by five or fewer participators etc.) it may not be a close company for the purposes of the legislation. The exceptions are as follows:

(a) Companies not resident in the United Kingdom.

(b) A registered industrial and provident society or a building society.

(c) A company controlled by or on behalf of the Crown, and not otherwise a close company (S.282(1) TA 1970).

(d) A company where not less than 35% of the shares are held by the public and the shares have been quoted in the previous twelve months, and there have been dealings in the shares on a recognized stock exchange in the previous twelve months (S.283(1) TA 1970). Companies of this sort are subject to further conditions which are discussed below.

(e) A company which is controlled by one or more non-close companies and the company cannot be considered as being controlled by five or fewer participators except by taking as one of the participators a non-close company (S.282(4) TA 1970).

Example 2

(a) An unquoted company has the following share capital:

Authorized	£50,000
Issued and full paid:	
42,000 ordinary shares of £1 each	£42,000

The shareholders are as follows:

A Ltd—a non-close company	22,000
M	14,000
N	4,000
O, sister of M	2,000
	42,000

A non-close company owns more than half of the issued share capital of the company, and accordingly a non-close company controls the company. There is no way in which the company may be considered close except by taking A Ltd, a non-close company, as one of the participators. Accordingly the company is not close.

(b) Suppose in the case of the company above that M has an option to subscribe for the 8,000 unissued shares of £1 each at £1.25 per share. As we have seen when we were considering who has control of a company, we must consider not only those who possess shares but also those who are entitled to acquire them; moreover, the possession of more than half of a company's share capital as well as the possession of more than half of a company's issued share capital will give control. As regards the *issued* share capital of the company, the position is as in (a) above. The company is controlled by a non-close company and is itself non-close.

As regards the share capital of the company, which we may regard as the authorized share capital, a part of which is issued and a part of which M is entitled to have issued to him, the position is as follows:

M own holding (issued)	14,000
M own holding (option)	8,000
Ascribed holding (sister)	2,000
	24,000
N	4,000
	28,000

M and N accordingly control the company and the company is close. Note that with regard to the non-close company A, its holding of 22,000 shares does not give it control when we are considering the authorized capital of the company.

We see here that more than one person or group of persons can be said to control a company depending on what test you apply. Although A Ltd controls the company from the point of view of issued share capital, M and N also control it if you apply the authorized share capital test. Since the company on one of these tests can be found to be close, without taking account of A Ltd's shareholding, the company that we are considering is close.

6.1.5 Companies with a public interest

We have referred above to the fact that where at least 35% of the shares of a company are quoted and held by the public the company will not be close. The conditions of S.283 TA 1970, where the legislation is contained, are quite stringent. They are as follows:

(a) Shares carrying not less than 35% of the voting power of the company must be held by 'the public' (see below).
(b) The shares must not be shares entitled to a fixed rate of dividend, e.g. preference shares.
(c) The shares must have been dealt in on a recognized stock exchange within the preceding twelve months and the shares in that time must have been included in the official list of a recognized stock exchange.
(d) The voting power possessed by the company's 'principal members' must not exceed 85% (see below).

Shares are held by 'the public' if they are held by:

(a) A non-close company or a non-resident company which would not be close if it were resident, or
(b) Trustees for approved superannuation and retirement schemes, or
(c) Someone other than a 'principal member'.

A person is a 'principal member' if he possesses more than 5% of the voting power of the company and he is one of the five persons who possess the greatest percentage of the voting power of the company (see below).

The following shareholdings are not to be considered as held by 'the public' (even if they fall into one of the categories above):

    (a) Shares held by a director or associate of a director,
    (b) Shares held by a company which is controlled by such a director or associate,
    (c) Shares held by an associated company of the company. A company is another's associated company at a given time if, at that time or at any time within one year previously, one of the two has control of the other, or both are under the control of the same person or persons (S.302(1) TA 1970),
    (d) Shares held by a fund the capital or income of which is applicable for the benefit of employees or directors of the company, or the employees or directors of a company controlled by a director (see (b) above) or those of an associated company.

A 'principal member' is a person who possesses more than 5% of the voting power of a company including for this purpose any attribution of powers from nominees, associates, and controlled companies. In addition, where there are more than five members holding more than 5% of the voting power, a 'principal member' is one of five persons possessing the greatest percentage of the voting power of the company. There can be more than five principal members if two or more such members hold equal percentages. Thus if there are two who hold equal percentages the number of principal members is increased to six, if there are three, the number of principal members is seven and so on.

Example 3

A quoted company has the following share capital which is authorised, issued and fully paid: 500,000 ordinary shares of £1 each.

Each ordinary share is entitled to one vote and thus the voting power of shareholders is determined by the number of shares held. There have been dealings in the shares in the last year and the company has been quoted in the last year.

The shareholders, the directors, and their percentage holdings of shares are as follows:

	%	
A	5	(Director)
B (Wife of A)	5	
C (Son of A)	5	(Director)
D Ltd (Controlled by A)	15	
E (Cousin of A)	20	
F	5	(Director)
G	5	
Other shareholders holding less than 5% of share capital:		
Directors	3	
Others	37	40
		100

Company is controlled by:	%
A own holding	5
wife's holding	5
sons's holding	5
D Ltd's holding	15
	——
	30
E (a cousin, therefore not an associate of A)	20
F	5
	——
	55 per cent
	——

The greater part of the company's share capital is held by three persons and the company is prima facie close.

The 'principal members' are as follows:	%
A (including attributions)	30
E	20

There are only two persons, namely A and E, holding more than 5% of the voting power of the company and therefore only two principal members.

The percentage of shares held by 'the public' is as follows (excluding the percentage held by principal members, directors, companies controlled by directors and associates of directors).

	%
A director or principal member	—
B associate of director	—
C associate of director	—
D Ltd controlled by A, a director	—
E principal member	—
F director	—
G	5
Other shareholders, excluding directors	37
	——
	42
	——

Since more than 35% of the voting power of the company is held by the public, and the voting power of its principal members does not exceed 85% and the other conditions of S.283 TA 1970 are satisfied or assumed to be satisfied, the company is non-close.

6.2 THE EXTENDED MEANING OF DISTRIBUTIONS

In Chapter 3 we considered the general nature of distributions. Because of the special character of close companies many payments and benefits, not within the general definitions of a distribution, were at one time treated as distributions when made by a close company. The purpose was to prevent cash or other benefits being received by a shareholder in a way which gave tax advantages to the shareholder. Of these many instances happily only one now remains—benefits for participators.

Any 'benefit' which is provided by the company to a participator, e.g. a house to live in, domestic services, etc., is a distribution (S.284(2) TA 1970). A very important exclusion from this special category of distribution is expenses and other benefits taxed in the hands of employees or directors under the Schedule E rules contained in Sections 60–72, FA 1976. In practice most benefits afforded shareholders of a close company are enjoyed by them as employees or directors and not as simply participators.

There is a further exclusion for pensions, gratuities etc. paid to the wife or children or a former director or employee.

> **Example 4**
> Waverley Ltd, a close company, employs a painter for general maintenance of the company's factory. He is instructed to paint the exterior of the house of Mrs Jeanie Deans who is a shareholder. She is not an employee. The cost to the company of the painter's wages while painting the house and the cost of other materials used is a distribution to Mrs Deans. Since it is a qualifying distribution advance corporation tax is payable. The distribution plus the tax credit is included in Mrs Deans' income.

Where the shareholder receiving the benefit is a resident United Kingdom company, and both the shareholder and the close company are fellow subsidiaries of a third resident company or one is the subsidiary of the other, no distribution arises when an asset is transferred from one to the other (S.284(4) TA 1970).

There is anti-avoidance legislation dealing with mutual arrangements between two or more close companies for each to benefit shareholders of the other or others (S.284(6) TA 1970).

6.3 LOANS TO PARTICIPATORS

A loan by a company to a shareholder or an associate of a shareholder, e.g. wife of a shareholder, is one way by which a close company could make cash available without the tax consequences of making a distribution. However, S.286 TA 1970 provides for the payment of an amount of tax calculated by applying to the amount of the loan the rate of advance corporation tax for the financial year in which the loan is made. Although the amount payable is calculated as ACT would be calculated, it is not in fact advance corporation tax, and is not deductible from corporation tax liabilities or otherwise treated as ACT.

The provisions extend to debts incurred by the shareholder to the close company, but debts for goods supplied in the ordinary course of business are excluded unless the credit given is exceptional or exceeds six months. If the borrower is a full time employee of the company and does not hold more than 5% of the ordinary share capital (that is he does not have a 'material interest'), a loan which, together with previous loans, does not exceed £15,000 is exempt from payment of tax. If the loan was made before 31 March 1971, the exemption will apply if the loan was made for the purchase of the borrower's main residence and did not exceed £10,000 in amount (S.286(3) TA 1970).

Where a loan which has been charged to tax is repaid in whole or in part the relative tax will be repaid. A claim has to be made to the Inland Revenue within six years from the end of the year of assessment in which the repayment of the loan occurs.

All the above applies to an individual who is a participator; the charge to tax also arises on the making of loans by a close company in certain other exceptional circumstances, in particular to a shareholder which is a non-resident company.

The making of a loan as such has no consequences for an individual's income tax liability. That is to say, the individual is not treated as having received a distribution or indeed any other type of income.

Tax consequences for an individual shareholder do however arise when a loan to the shareholder is written off or forgiven. When this happens the shareholder is treated as having received an amount equal to the amount written off, grossed up. In other words the written off amount is treated as if it were a net sum corresponding to a gross amount from which income tax had been deducted (S.287 TA 1970).

Example 5

Mannering Ltd is a close company. On 30 June 1982 it advanced £7,000 on loan to Walter Guy, an ordinary shareholder. Walter Guy holds 20% of the ordinary share capital of the company, and is not a director of the company. On 30 June 1983, Walter Guy repaid £2,000 and on 30 June 1984 the company wrote off the balance of the loan, £5,000, and have informed Mr Guy that he is released from his debt.

The relevant tax consequences of these transactions are as follows:

(1) The advance of £7,000 to Walter Guy will give rise to a tax payment by the company of $3/7 \times £7,000 = £3,000$.

(2) The repayment of £2,000 by Walter Guy will result in a claim by the company for a repayment of tax of $3/7 \times £2,000 = £857$.

(3) The writing off of £5,000 by the company will result in £5,000 $\times \frac{100}{70}$,

£7,142 (see below) being included in Walter Guy's total income for 1984/85, viz.

	£
Gross amount	7,142
Less: Basic rate income tax 1984/85, 30%	2,142
Net amount	5,000

6.4 RELEVANT INCOME

We have seen how the legislation ensures that benefits and loans involving participators of close companies are adequately taxed. This and the following sections describe and illustrate the legislation which tries to make sure that if certain close companies (non-trading or trading companies with investment etc. income) make no distributions to shareholders or make what is thought to be too small distributions, income tax may be charged on shareholders as if adequate distributions had in fact been made. There are rules which the Revenue apply for deciding what amount of a company's income for an accounting period should be distributed and this amount which is called the company's relevant income cannot exceed a certain maximum. The legislation in Sch. 16 FA 1972 uses the computation of chargeable profit for corporation tax as the basis for the relevant income computation adding qualifying dividends in franked investment income (not included in the computation of chargeable profits) and deducting any capital gains.

In the case of a trading company (or a member of a trading group) the relevant income is defined as 'so much of its distributable income, (the product of the computation outlined above) other than trading income . . . as can be distributed without prejudice to the requirements of the company's business' (Para. 8(1)(a) Sch. 16 FA 1972).

A *trading company* is:

(a) a company which exists wholly or mainly to carry on a trade, or
(b) a company whose income does not consist wholly or mainly of investment income, i.e. income which would be unearned income in an individual's hands.

Because the above definition excludes trading income arising to trading companies from relevant income, most trading companies in practice are effectively removed from the worst effects of being a close company.

Let us suppose however that a long established trading company with a successful profitable business begins to accumulate profits and invest these profits in shares or interest bearing securities or rented properties. If this investment income is large enough then a trading company may have to introduce the notion of the 'requirements of the business' to show that it is unable to distribute the investment income.

In the case of a non-trading company whose income includes estate or trading income relevant income is:

(a) so much of the estate or trading income as can be distributed without prejudice to the requirements of the company's business so far as concerned with the activities or assets giving rise to estate or trading income,
(b) as far as the rest of the company's income is concerned, e.g. interest and dividends, the whole of that income (Para. 8(1)(b) Sch. 16 FA 1972).

It often happens that an investment company may have both estate income (income from land chargeable under Schedules A, B and D) and some trding income. In respect of both types of income 'business requirements' can be called in aid. You will note that unlike the position with trading companies, trading income of an investment company cannot be ignored.

Finally if an investment company has no estate or trading income the relevant income is the distributable income.

In all the cases above relevant income is subject to an arithmetical maximum which is discussed below.

6.4.1 Distributable income

The distributable income of a company is the amount of the distributable profits less chargeable gains net of corporation tax. The amount of distributable profits is the total of the following:

(a) The amount of any profits on which corporation tax falls finally to be borne, less the amount of that tax. The amount of any profits on which corporation tax falls finally to be borne is the familiar amount of chargeable profits in a corporation tax computation. The corporation tax chargeable on these profits is deducted.

(b) An amount equal to the qualifying distributions comprised in any franked investment income. You will remember that franked investment income is inclusive of relative tax credits. The amount to be included in the total making up distributable profits is 'net' franked investment income.

(c) An amount equal to group income; group income is a distribution from a 51% subsidiary in respect of which an election has been made such that no ACT is paid by the subsidiary and no tax credit is received by the parent (see 5.3).

Distributable income and distributable profits may be set out diagrammatically as follows:

	£	£
Chargeable profits		X
Less: corporation tax		X
		X
'Net' franked investment income		X
Group income		X
Distributable profits		X
Less: Chargeable gains	X	
Less: Corporation tax	X	
	—	X
Distributable income		X

6.4.2 Business requirements

In the above discussion you will have found more than one reference to '*business requirements*'. Business requirements are not defined. However not only current requirements are relevant. Regard is had 'to such other requirements as may be necessary or advisable for the maintenance and development of that business; (Para.8(2) Sch.16 FA 1972); in addition 'requirements necessary or advisable for the acquisition of a trade or of a controlling interest in a trading company' also fall within the category of a 'business requirement' of a trading company (Para.8(3) Sch.16 FA 1972). The latter requirement is hedged about with anti-avoidance legislation concerning acquisitions of associated companies (Para.12A, Sch.16 FA 1972).

Business requirements are the normal short and long term financial and commercial needs of the company. These might include:

(a) The company's need for working capital,
(b) A need to repay share or loan capital by a trading company. Statutory provision is specifically made for this need in Para.8(3–5) Sch.16 FA 1972,
(c) The need to finance expansion of the company,
(d) The need to be able to meet the known and contingent liabilities of the company,
(e) The need to provide for depreciation and obsolescence of plant and machinery.

Non-trading companies with no estate or trading income cannot reduce relevant income by arguing that the company has business requirements.

A non-trading company with estate or trading company can claim business requirements with respect to that income. However such a company, for example a property investment company with a rental income (estate income) must regard as income available for distribution, sums applied or to be applied out of income in repayment of any loan capital or debt, e.g. bank loan, or in the purchase of land or on the construction or extension of a building (Para.12(1)(c) and (d) Sch.16 FA 1972). Thus it is not possible to regard these payments or purchases as business requirements. This is very significant for property companies. Non-trading companies with estate or trading income claiming business requirements must also consider the legislation concerning repayment of what are called 'first business loans', e.g. loans towards payment for the business undertaking or property which the company was formed to acquire (Para.12 Sch.16 FA 1972).

6.5 EXCESS OF RELEVANT INCOME OVER DISTRIBUTIONS

Having arrived at the amount of a company's relevant income for an accounting period (the amount which may be distributed without prejudice to the business), the rules require us to compare this amount of income with the distributions for the accounting period which have been made within the accounting period or within a reasonable time afterwards (Para.10 Sch.16 FA 1972). If relevant income for the accounting period is more than the distributions for the accounting period there is what is called 'an excess of relevant income over distributions' or simply 'an excess of relevant income'. The term 'shortfall' which derives from earlier legislation is still used.

The excess of relevant income for an accounting period is apportioned among the participators of the company in accordance with their respective interests. This apportionment is not a payment of cash but a computation of the amount which, in a straightforward case, a shareholder might have received as a dividend, had there been a distribution of an amount equal to the excess of relevant income. Each shareholder is then deemed to have received as income, as at the end of the accounting period in which the shortfall arises, the apportioned amount plus a proportion corresponding to advance corporation tax on that amount. Further details of apportionments and the consequences as regards the close company itself of an excess of relevant income are to be found in Section 6.7.

Relevant income on cessation or liquidation
When a close company ceases to carry on a trade, or is wound up, relevant income will take no account of business requirements. The interests of creditors (other than creditors who are participators or associates of participators) will however, be safeguarded (Para.13 Sch.16 FA 1972).

6.6 MAXIMUM RELEVANT INCOME

We have referred from time to time to the fact that a close company's relevant income is limited to an arithmetical maximum. The method of computation of this amount is described in Para.9 Sch.16 FA 1972. The computation produces the maximum amount which may be regarded as relevant income. The details of the computation refer from time to time to kinds of income and other matters some of which we have already mentioned. The principles underlying the computation are as follows:

(a) For trading companies the maximum relevant income is 50% of the company's estate income and 100% of the company's distributable investment income (Para.9 Sch.16 FA 1972).

(b) For non-trading companies the maximum relevant income is 50% of estate or trading income and 100% of the company's distributable investment income (Para.9 Sch.16 FA 1972).

It follows from the above that for the purposes of the computation, a company's income has to be analysed between estate, trading and investment income. Because of other features of the computation it is necessary to extend the analysis of income.

Example 6

Lammermuir Limited is a close property company which has the following results for the accounting period of twelve months ended 31 March 1984:

	£
Schedule D Case I	20,000
Schedule A	500,000
Franked investment income	30,000
Unfranked investment income	1,000
Chargeable gains (as abated)	40,000
Debenture interest paid (gross)	10,000

The computations of the company's relevant income and maximum relevant income are as follows:

Relevant income	£
Schedule D Case I	20,000
Schedule A	500,000
Unfranked investment income	1,000
	521,000
Less: Charges	10,000
	511,000
Less: Corporation tax at 50%	255,500
	255,500
'Net' FII £30,000 — (30% × 30,000)	21,000
Distributable income	276,500

Distributable income is arrived at in a manner similar to that discussed in 6.4.1. Instead of deducting chargeable gains net of corporation tax from distributable profits, chargeable gains have been excluded from the computation above which gives the same result. As to charges these are deducted from different kinds of income in a certain order (see below and Para.10(8) and (9) Sch.16 FA 1972); the effect of the rules is that in the above computation no part of the charges of £10,000 is deductible from the chargeable gain since this is excluded.

Relevant income is distributable income £276,500 less whatever amounts require to be retained for business requirements; if these requirements were £40,000 with respect to say, estate income, relevant income would be £236,500. Note that this latter figure cannot exceed the maximum figure of relevant income as follows:

Maximum relevant income

	Total £	Estate or trading £	Investment income FII (net) £	UFII £	Chargeable gain £
Schedule D Case I		20,000			
Schedule D		500,000			
FII			21,000		
UFII				1,000	
Chargeable gain					40,000
	582,000	520,000	21,000	1,000	40,000
Charges	10,000	9,000		1,000	
	572,000	511,000	21,000		40,000
CT at 50%	275,500	255,500	—		20,000
Distributable profits	296,500	255,500	21,000		20,000
Less: Chargeable gain	20,000				20,000
Distributable income	276,500	255,500	21,000		
Less: Lesser of £1,000 and 10% of estate or trading income			1,000		
Distributable investment income			20,000		
Estate or trading income		255,500			

Maximum is:

	£
50% of estate or trading income, 50% × £255,500	127,750
100% of distributable investment income, 100% × £20,000	20,000
	147,750

The computation of maximum relevant income contained in the above example flows directly from the requirements of the legislation. As we have seen, in the case of a non-trading company relevant income cannot exceed 50% of the estate or trading income and 100% of the company's distributable investment income. For this purpose both kinds of income are after tax and in the above case after an abatement in respect of investment income in distributable profits of 10% of estate or trading income or £1,000 whichever is smaller (Para.10(3) Sch.16 FA 1972 and S.35(3) and (4) FA 1978).

In the case of a *trading* company there is also an abatement in respect of investment income in the same form as above but the figure of £1,000 in the non-trading case is increased to £3,000 (Para.10(3) Sch.16 FA 1972 and S.44(2) and (3) FA 1980).

A trading company enjoys a further important abatement with respect to estate income. It will be remembered that for a trading company trading income as such is deducted from distributable income and is not part of relevant income (and it follows is not part of maximum relevant income). However in the computation of the abatement of estate incoem referred to above we have, for calculation purposes only, to take account of trading income.

Let us assume that a trading company has trading income of £45,000 and estate income of £15,000 after deduction of corporation tax, etc. We first have to compute a fraction called in the legislation 'the appropriate fraction', which is:

$$\frac{\text{Estate income}}{\text{estate income} \ + \ \text{trading income}}$$

$$= \quad \frac{£15,000}{£15,000 \ + \ £45,000}$$

$$= \quad 1/4$$

The factor of 1/4 is then applied to a maximum and minimum amount specified in the legislation, the latter being £25,000 and the former £75,000, that is:

$$1/4 \times £75,000 \ (\text{maximum amount}) \ £18,750$$
$$1/4 \times £25,000 \ (\text{minimum amount}) \quad £6,250$$

If the estate income of the company is less than the appropriate fraction of the minimum amount the estate income is disregarded, i.e. 'abated' by the whole amount of it. If the estate income is less than the appropriate fraction of the maximum amount it is abated by half the difference between the fractional part of the maximum amount and the amount of the estate income. Thus in the above example estate income is £15,000. This is more than $1/4 \times £25,000$, £6,250 and less than $1/4 \times £75,000$, £18,750. Accordingly the abatement is $1/2 \ (18,750–15,000) = £1,875$.

All of the above is an expression by way of a figure example of the legislation contained in Para.9(2) and (3) Sch.16 FA 1972.

It may be more simply expressed as follows:

(1) If the aggregate trading and estate income is less than £25,000, the whole of the estate income is excluded.
(2) If the aggregate trading income (T) and estate income (E) is between £25,000 and £75,000 the estate income is abated by:
$$1/2 \times \left(\left(\frac{E}{E + T} \times £75,000\right) - E\right)$$

The above maximum and minimum amounts (£75,000 and £25,000) may be reduced if a company has associated companies (Para.9(3)(4) and (5) Sch.16 FA 1972).

In Example 6 a division is made of investment income between unfranked and franked investment income. This division is between investment income chargeable to corporation tax (unfranked investment income) and franked investment income which is not chargeable to CT. The necessity to distinguish between these two kinds of investment income arises from the treatment of charges in the computation of maximum relevant income.

Charges are deductible from total profits in a corporation tax computation. If we now divide these total profits between different kinds of income we need to have rules which will guide us in deducting charges from the different sorts of income. Para. 10(8) and (9) Sch. 16 FA 1972 contains two sets of rules, one for trading companies and one for non-trading companies. As regard non-trading companies the order is as follows:

(a) *First* from the company's income charged to corporation tax other than estate or trading income, e.g. unfranked investment income,
(b) *Second* from the company's estate or trading income,
(c) *third* from development gains,
(d) *Fourth* from chargeable gains.

For trading companies the order is slightly amended, the first and fourth remain as before; the second deduction is from estate income and the third deduction from trading income.

6.6.1 Cessations and liquidations

Where a close company ceases to trade or is wound up, the computation of the amount of the company's relevant income and maximum relevant income proceeds without reference to the requirements of the company's business and there is no limitation to 50% of estate or trading income (Para. 13(1) Sch. 16 FA 1972). These rules apply to the accounting period in which the trade ceases or which ends with the cessation of the trade or the winding up of the company. In addition they apply to all accounting periods of the company ending within twelve months of the cessation or winding up, and in the latter case with any subsequent accounting period of the company (Para. 13(1) and (5) Sch. 16 FA 1972).

6.6.2 Inspector's clearance

A close company may prompt a review of its position for any year by submitting its accounts and directors report and other information to the Inland Revenue and seeking a statement from the Inspector of Taxes as to whether or not he intends to make an apportionment (Para. 18 Sch. 16 FA 1972).

6.7 APPORTIONMENT OF EXCESS

Example 7
In Example 6 above we computed that the maximum relevant income of Lammermuir Ltd for the year ended 31 March 1984 was £147,750.

The share capital authorized issued and fully paid of Lammermuir Ltd is as follows:

200,000 ordinary shares of £1 each

The shareholders and their respective shareholdings are:

A	40,000
B (wife of A)	40,000
C (son of A)	40,000
D	20,000
E	8,000
F	52,000
	200,000

The dividend paid by Lammermuir Ltd in the year ended 31 March 1984 was:

Final dividend in respect of year ended 31 March 1983   £80,000

Since no dividend in respect of the year ended 31 March 1984 was paid in that year (and on the assumption that no such dividend is paid within a reasonable time after 31 March 1984) the excess of relevant income over distributions is:

	£
Maximum relevant income	147,750
Less: Distributions	NIL
Excess of relevant income over distributions	147,750

The above excess is apportioned among participators in accordance with the respective interests of participators as follows:

	£
A 1/5	29,550
B 1/5	29,550
C 1/5	29,550
D 1/10	14,775
E 2/50	5,910
F 13/50	38,415
	147,750

The apportioned amounts are treated as income received by the shareholders at the end of the accounting period concerned, i.e. 31 March 1984. Furthermore, the amounts assessable are the same as if the company had paid a dividend, i.e. a proportion has to be added for 'advance corporation tax' at the rate which is in force at the year end (Para.5(7) Sch.16 FA 1972).

A shareholder will only be assessed to income tax on an apportionment if the amount which has been apportioned to him (inclusive of ACT) is at least £1,000 or 5% of the total amount (plus advance corporation tax) to be apportioned amount participators, whichever is the less.

Amounts which are apportioned to shareholders are assessable and charged to higher rate tax. No assessment is made at basic rate (Para.5(2)(b) Sch.16 FA 1972). If the individual shareholders do not pay the tax within certain time limits the company can be required to pay the tax. Since no actual cash income is received by shareholders companies usually pay the tax arising on apportionments (Para.6 Sch.16 FA 1972).

The apportionment of an excess of relevant income among participators of a company has no effect on the corporation tax liability of the company. However there are provisions in Paragraph 7 of Schedule 16 which try to ensure that a close company does not obtain any cash flow advantage from waiting for a shortfall assessment rather than paying a dividend.

6.7.1 Excess of £1,000 or less

No apportionment is made where the excess of relevant income over distributions of a trading company is £1,000 or less. (Para.1(3) Sch.16 FA 1972).

6.7.2 Apportionment of charitable deeds of covenant

Whether or not there is an excess of relevant income over distributions, Para.3 Sch.16 FA 1972 provides for the apportionment among shareholders of the gross amount of payments to charities under deeds of covenant. These payments will have been deducted as charges on income in the company's corporation tax computation. Such apportionments, since they are made in respect of a gross sum, are not grossed up in the hands of the shareholders, nor is a proportion added for ACT (Para.5(7) Sch.16 FA 1972). If there is any excess of relevant income over distributions, the apportionment of these payments is in addition to the apportionment of the excess.

Four year deeds of covenant up to a maximum of £5,000 are deductible for higher rate tax purposes in arriving at an individual's total income (S.457(1A) TA 1970).

In a case where charitable deeds of covenant paid by a close company are apportioned to an individual, there may be deducted from his total income the lesser of (a) the apportioned amount and (b) the balance of the £5,000 'allowance' referred to above (Para.5(5A) Sch.16 FA 1972).

6.7.3 Apportionment of interest

Payments of interest which are annual payments, e.g. debenture interest made by a non-trading company may be apportioned to shareholders whether or not there is an excess of relevant income over distributions.

There will be no apportionment if the interest would be allowed to an individual (S.75 FA 1972) or more than 75% of the company's income is estate or trading income as is the case in Example 6 above (Lammermuir

Ltd) (Para.3A Sch.16 FA 1972). This provision does not apply to trading companies.

6.7.4 Dividend restriction

Where a company is subject to dividend restriction by law, e.g. company law, no apportionment will be made of any excess of relevant income over distributions, to the extent that the company could not make distributions except by breaking the law (Para.14 Sch.16 FA 1972).

6.8 ANOTHER DEFINITION OF CLOSE COMPANY

A close company is usually a company under the control of five or fewer participators or of its directors. A further definition is contained in S.282(2) TA 1970. This provides that if on the assumption that the company is close (and any other company which is a participator is also close) more than half of any excess of relevant income could be apportioned among five or fewer participators or among participators who are directors, the company will be close.

In terms of this definition the company in Example 1 above is close, even if no one shareholder were associated with any other.

Question 6

Mortality Ltd is an old established trading company with a successful profit record. The company, which is a close company, has been managed by the majority shareholders, a bachelor and his brother, for more than forty years. The company has no plans for expansion and cash surpluses have accumulated and continue to accumulate in the company. Apart from debentures held by an aged sister the company has no indebtedness. The following is the company's corporation tax computation for the year ended 31 March 1986:

	£
Schedule D Case I	200,000
Schedule A	44,000
Unfranked investment income	30,000
Schedule D Case III	12,000
Total profits	286,000
Charges	10,000
Profits chargeable	276,000

In addition the company received £100,000 of franked investment income.

The brothers are in receipt of substantial salaries and other private income and wish to receive as dividends as little as possible from Mortality Ltd. They have asked you to advise on the minimum dividend which they might receive from Mortality Ltd to avoid any question of an apportionment.

As a first step in your considerations you are required to prepare a maximum relvant income computation for Mortality Ltd for the year ended 31 March 1986.

CHAPTER 7

FOREIGN ELEMENT

7.1 INTRODUCTION

The tax jurisdiction of the British State extends to the land mass of Scotland, England, Wales, Northern Ireland and the UK territorial waters within the so-called three mile limit. Some extension of jurisdiction has been made to the continental shelf. The rest of the world (including the Channel Islands and the Isle of Man) lies beyond its authority.

Limits to taxing power imply that in any case it will be possible to say what income or profits are taxable by the authority and what items are not taxable by it. Wholly domestic companies naturally pose no problems but issues will arise wherever there is a foreign element, for example, a trade conducted abroad by a domestic company, or a trade conducted here by an overseas company. The general principle is that the UK seeks to tax the worldwide profits of UK resident companies and in addition profits which arise from a UK source, e.g. the UK branch of an overseas company. The questions of residence and source are thus key issues in the consideration of the foreign element which are considered later in this chapter.

In the context of international trade and investment it will often happen that two or more states will charge the same profits to taxation. For example the profits of an overseas branch operated by a UK resident company will invariably be assessed under Schedule D Case I in the same way as a trade in the UK. In addition to being charged to UK corporation tax the profits of the overseas branch will usually be charged to tax in the overseas country. Without a means of relief the profits would be doubly and excessively taxed. To provide relief the UK has entered into numerous double tax conventions with other states, which override the effect of domestic legislation and which are an important aspect of the foreign element.

Although the vast majority of overseas investments undertaken by UK companies have a straightforward commercial motive it would be unrealistic to suppose that low rates of tax and other benefits may not be either the dominant or a secondary concern of the companies involved. The ending of exchange control and the growth of international movements of capital and other resources have caused the Treasury and the

Inland Revenue to become concerned about the loss of tax revenue which has occurred. The UK authorities are not alone in their concern about the ways in which companies may walk out of a state's territorial jurisdiction and aspects of modern UK legislation dealing with this problem mirror the legislation enacted in Japan and elsewhere. This concern is not new and anti-avoidance legislation, in part unused in practice, has been on the statute book for some time. The more recent legislation concerns controlled foreign companies, described as CFC's where the companies are controlled by UK residents and are resident in low tax areas. This aspect of the legislation and its effect is of significance to tax havens and tax avoidance activities.

7.2 RESIDENCE

Corporation tax is charged on United Kingdom resident companies, and on the chargeable profits of a non-resident company which carries on a trade in the UK through a branch or agency. (Ss.238(2) and S.246(2) TA 1970).

Prior to the Finance Act 1984, when an attempt was made to define residence for the purposes of CFCs (but not for other purposes or other companies) UK domestic legislation contained no definition of residence. Over the years since the end of the last century there has been built up a substantial body of case law concerning a company's place of residence. The distillation of the decisions in these cases is the assertion that a company is resident where its central management and control resides. In practice the country in which the board of directors meets is considered as prima facie evidence that such central management and control is exercised in that country. It has long been established that the country of incorporation is no more than a factor in deciding where a company is resident. Thus a company incorporated in Scotland with UK shareholders would be resident in France if its whole business and trade was conducted in France and its directors met there. By the same token a French incorporated company would be resident in Scotland if the whole business and central management were in Scotland.

The significance of these matters is of course that while the whole trade of an English incorporated company may be conducted abroad, if the directors of the company meet in London and exercise central management and control from there, the whole profits computed in acordance with UK legislation will be assessed to UK corporation tax.

Where it is desired that UK corporation tax is avoided with respect to an overseas trade or activity the appropriate action would be to form an overseas subsidiary company and transfer the trade to the overseas company. On the assumption that central management and control of the subsidiary company is overseas and that the board of directors also meets overseas then the overseas subsidiary will be resident outside the UK.

It will be clear from the above that it is entirely possible for a UK resident company to become non-resident with respect to the whole or part of its trade, e.g. the transfer of the trade of an overseas branch (a UK trade for tax purposes) to a non-resident subsidiary company. Since this has important economic and fiscal consequences and in the face of the behaviour of certain companies the Finance Act 1951 introduced the legislation now contained in S.482 TA 1970, dealing with 'Migration, etc., of companies'.

7.3 MIGRATION AND TREASURY CONSENTS

Certain actions taken without the consent of the Treasury are unlawful. These are:

(a) for a resident UK company to become non-resident, i.e. for the company to emigrate;

(b) for the trade or business (or part of the trade or business) of a UK resident company to be transferred to a non-resident person;

(c) for a non-resident company which is controlled by a resident UK company, e.g. an overseas subsidiary of a UK parent, to create or issue shares or debentures;

(d) for a UK resident company to transfer to any person any shares or debentures which it owns in a non-resident company which it controls, e.g. sale by a UK parent of its shares in an overseas subsidiary (S.482(1) TA 1970).

The penalties for an offence under these provisions are heavy and uniquely in UK tax legislation provide specifically for the possibility of imprisonment for up to two years (or fines up to £10,000). As a matter of fact however no prosecutions have taken place since 1951, and although the Inland Revenue has aired the possibility of repealing the legislation it remains on the statute book.

The above actions (a) to (d) will not be unlawful if the Treasury gives consent and the Treasury may give consents generally or specifically. The general consents have been published and are summarized below. Special consents will apply only to a particular transaction or a particular company and the information which the Treasury requires to make a decision is published. In the case of the general consents referred to above no application to the Treasury for further consent is necessary.

In respect of the unlawful actions referred to in (a) and (b), emigration of a company or trade, consent is given if the resident UK company in question is a company incorporated to carry on a new trade or business and more than 50% of the issued share capital is owned by persons not ordinarily resident in the UK.

In respect of action (b) above, i.e. emigration of a trade, a general consent is given if the transfer is an outright sale for less than £50,000 and if other conditions concerning the buyer are satisfied (not controlled by

UK residents and not associated with seller). The sale must not be associated with other operations whereby the business may revert to the seller.

In the case of action (c) above, i.e. issue of shares by a controlled non-resident company, consent is given if the shares are issued for cash or in purchase of a business. The shares issued must not be redeemable preference shares or such that the UK resident company loses control; nor must they be issued to a non-resident company over which a UK resident company has control.

Consent is also given in relation to action (c) if the non-resident company was incorporated in a Commonwealth country to start and carry on a new industrial activity in that country.

Finally consent is generally available in respect of an action within (d), i.e. transfer of shares by a controlled non-resident company, if the transfer is to another UK company unless the effect of the transfer is that the transferor UK company loses control.

7.4 INWARD INVESTMENT

In considering the foreign element it is common to consider the position under two aspects, that of the foreign resident company investing in the UK, so called 'inward investment', and that of the UK resident company investing overseas, that is to say 'outward investment'. Many of the reflections which apply to inward investment will apply to outward investment and vice versa. We shall look at inward investment first.

Corporation tax applies to the chargeable profits of a non-resident company which carries on a trade in the UK through a branch or agency. A branch or agency means any factorship, agency, receivership, branch or management (S.527(1) TA 1970). So if Zavok Inc., an overseas manufacturer of cars, were to set up a factory in the UK to assemble cars, this would be a branch of Zavok Inc. and the profits of the branch would be liable to corporation tax; so also if Zavok Inc. instead of acquiring a factory etc. were to appoint a resident UK individual as the company's full-time agent for the sale and importation of cars, concluding sales contracts in the UK, then Zavok Inc. would be liable to corporation tax on the profits of the agency. The profits of the branch or agency wherever arising are chargeable. Thus if the Zavok factory above were to sell cars assembled in the UK to say Scandinavia, the branch would be liable to corporation tax on the profits of the sales to Scandinavia.

It follows that a non-resident company which does not trade through a branch or agency is not charged to corporation tax; if it does in fact trade in the UK (but *not* through a branch or agency) e.g. by reason of a visiting employee of the overseas resident company concluding contracts in the UK, the profits of this trade, earned by the overseas resident company, will be liable to *income tax* (Ss.238(2) and 246(1) TA 1970). This is one of the rare circumstances in which a company can be liable to income tax on its profits.

As to a trade being conducted in the UK early cases established that if sales contracts were made *outside* the UK between a UK resident purchaser and a non-resident company then this was trading *with* the UK and no liability to UK tax arose. A trade conducted *in* the UK, liable to corporation tax if conducted through a branch or agency and otherwise to income tax, was a trade where contracts were completed *in* the UK, for example by an agent (profits resulting would be liable to corporation tax) or a visiting employee (profits resulting would be liable to income tax).

The above are the rules of the domestic law. These are superseded by the rules of any double tax convention in any particular case (S.497 TA 1970). In most cases in practice a double tax convention will apply and will require study. Generally the provisions of the double tax agreement will have a thrust which is similar in its overall effect to the domestic law.

In the context of the chargeability to corporation tax of profits of a 'branch or agency', the words 'branch or agency' have been superseded by the term 'permanent establishment' in double tax treaties. The general notion is that the profits of a non-resident company will only be chargeable to the extent that they arise to a 'permanent establishment'.

In 1963 the organization for Economic Co-operation and Development (OECD) adopted a draft double tax convention which has formed the framework of modern UK double tax agreements. In this moden agreement a 'permanent establishment' is defined as follows:

(a) a place of management
(b) a branch
(c) an office
(d) a factory
(e) a workshop
(f) a mine, quarry or other place of extraction of natural resources
(g) a building site or construction or assembly project which exists for more than twelve months.

A permanent establishment also includes an agent (not of independent status) if he has, and habitually exercises, an authority to conclude contracts in the name of the overseas company (but not if his activities are limited to the purchase of goods or merchandise for the enterprise). Various operations are excluded however from the definition of a permanent establishment including facilities for storage, display, advertising, purchasing and gathering information.

If the non-resident company intends to establish itself in the UK the most common choice lies between a branch of the overseas company or a subsidiary of the overseas company. The profits arising to both entities are subject to corporation tax. As to the choice between a branch or corporate structure this will depend on a range of factors including the domestic tax laws of the non-resident investor, and whether or not the non-resident company has other UK subsidiaries.

The conventional widsom is that a new UK activity is begun in a branch which is subsequently incorporated as a UK subsidiary of the non-resident parent. In this way any start-up losses experienced by the branch, other things being equal, may be allowed against the profits of the overseas company under the tax rules of the overseas country and also carried forward for set off against the profits of the UK subsidiary (see below). Subsequently any profits of the UK subsidiary will only be taxed in the country of the overseas parent to the extent that dividends are paid.

Any losses in the UK branch are available for carry forward into the UK subsidiary company since the overseas company is ceasing to carry on a trade and another company which it controls begins to carry it on. These are circumstances which bring S.252 TA 1970 (Company reconstructions without change of ownership) into play.

There are not only tax but commercial and financial considerations to be considered when deciding whether a branch or subsidiary company is the appropriate medium for investment. For example the liability of an overseas company for the debts of a branch will be unlimited whereas the liability of an overseas parent for the debts of its UK subsidiary are strictly limited. A branch can be set up with fewer administrative and legal requirements than can a limited company. Again it may be more commercially successful to market a product or activity through a local UK company rather than through what is perceived by the public as a foreign operation. Confidentiality about the operation is best maintained through a branch which only discloses details of its operations and profits to a few persons, including the Inland Revenue, while a UK subsidiary makes public disclosure of its accounts in the normal way. If a non-resident company has other UK subsidiaries it will only obtain group relief for any losses if the new activity is incorporated and the new company is a member of the UK group with a UK holding company; group relief in relation to an overseas company as such, e.g. in relation to a branch, is not possible since the provisions for group relief only apply to companies resident in the United Kingdom (S.258(7) TA 1970).

Finally whereas there are no obstacles as far as tax is concerned in remitting branch profits to its overseas head office tax issues arise in remitting profits of a UK subsidiary to its overseas parent. Payments of dividends involve payments of advance corporation tax in the UK. Certain double tax agreements (but by no means all) provide for a repayment to the overseas company of a part (calculated in accordance with the treaty) of the ACT (or what is the same thing, the tax credit). Payment of a management charge to the overseas parent may be made gross as can payments for know-how. However payments of patent royalties and interest generally have to be made under deduction of basic rate tax unless a double tax treaty permits payment gross and the Inspector of Foreign Dividends has granted permission.

7.5 OUTWARD INVESTMENT

Outward investment is the mirror image of inward investment and many of the considerations discussed above apply to outward investment.

The double tax treaty with the country in which it is proposed to operate will form the framework of reliefs and charges. In all cases whether or not a treaty is in existence the commercial, legal and fiscal position overseas will need to be considered.

The profits of an overseas branch of a UK resident company are chargeable to corporation tax under the UK schedules appropriate to each source which in the case of a trading branch will be principally Schedule D Case I. The computation of profits, relief for capital allowances, etc., will proceed in the normal way and the profits or losses of the branch being part of a UK company's results will be available for group relief purposes to other UK group members and for deduction of charges. Corporation tax arises on chargeable gains realized on overseas assets of an overseas branch but roll-over relief is available (S.115 CGTA 1979). Roll-over relief is a postponement of tax on capital gains when the proceeds of disposal of most business assets are re-invested in other business assets.

As in the case of investments in the UK it is often suggested that a UK company should begin with a branch overseas and obtain any loss relief which may be available. It will then, subsequently, incorporate.

On the incorporation of an overseas branch capital gains which would otherwise accrue (on the transfer of chargeable assets from the UK company, a legal person to an overseas subsidiary, a separate legal person) may be postponed in the way set out in S.268A TA 1970.

When sales of certain assets including industrial buildings which have obtained capital allowances are made between, for example a UK parent company and a UK subsidiary, a number of special rules apply including the application of open market value as the sale price. This can have the result of creating a substantial balancing charge in the hands of the seller and provision is made in respect of UK companies to elect that the special rules do not apply and that, generally, the subsidiary company stands in the shoes of the parent as regards e.g. industrial buildings allowances and balancing adjustments (Paras.1 and 4 Sch.7 CAA 1968). The elective procedure will not apply where a non-resident company is involved and as a result balancing charges particularly in respect of industrial buildings may arise where a branch is incorporated.

The profits of a foreign subsidiary of a UK company will not, it may be assumed, be subject to corporation tax because it will be possible to show that the board of the subsidiary meets overseas and that central management and control is overseas. Dividends from the subsidiary will be assessed under Schedule D Case V and treaty relief or unilateral relief will be available in respect of so-called withholding and underlying taxes (see below).

7.6 DOUBLE TAX RELIEF

As we have seen above where a UK company trades through a branch overseas the profits of the branch trade will be taxed both in the state of its operations and in the UK. Furthermore when a dividend is paid to a UK parent by an overseas subsidiary a withholding tax may be deducted from the dividend and the gross amount of this dividend taxed under Schedule D Case V in the UK. To provide relief from the effects of profit and income being taxed twice in this way double tax conventions provide for relief in a variety of ways. A common relief is called *credit relief* where foreign tax charged on the income is deducted from the UK corporation tax charged on the same income.

The amount of the double tax credit relief is limited to the amount of the corporation tax charged on the foreign income (S.505 TA 1970). In arriving at the amount of the foreign income, charges and expenses of management may be set off as the company sees fit (and is most advantageous to it) (S.100(5) FA 1972). The corporation tax charge on the foreign income is before deduction of any ACT paid in the accounting period (S.100(6) FA 1972).

Example 1

Northern Gate Limited in its accounting period ended 31 December 1984 has total profits of £800,000. The company paid no charges or dividends in the year ended 31 December 1984 and total profits of £800,000 are made up of UK profits £600,000, foreign profits £200,000. Foreign profits suffered foreign tax of £104,000.

Double tax relief is limited as follows:

	United Kingdom £	Foreign source £	Total £
Profits	600,000	200,000	800,000
Corporation tax chargeable:			
¼ × £600,000 at 50%	75,000		75,000
¼ × £200,000 at 50%		25,000	25,000
¾ × £600,000 at 45%	202,500		202,500
¾ × £200,000 at 45%		67,500	67,500
	277,500	92,500	370,000
Double tax relief restricted to		92,500	92,500
	277,500		277,500

Foreign tax unrelieved is:

	£
Foreign tax paid	104,000
Relieved	92,500
Unrelieved	11,500

Note particularly that unrelieved foreign tax is not available for carry forward for relief in subsequent years.

In the above case the amount of unrelieved tax is the difference between the higher overseas rate of tax and the lower UK rate. It represents the 'premium' for operating in the overseas country and there would seem to be no self-evident reason why it should be relieved. On the other hand circumstances may arise where by reason, for example, of first year allowances, no UK tax is payable on overseas profits but foreign tax arises because the overseas country does not operate the same system of accelerated capital allowances. Since no UK tax is payable there is no tax against which credit relief can be taken and credit relief is not available in later years when perhaps first year allowances are not available and consequently UK tax becomes payable. In such circumstances the appropriate action will be to disclaim first year allowances in order that profits suffer UK tax in the same year as that in which foreign tax is payable.

In other situations where UK losses arise and it is not possible to obtain treaty credit relief for foreign tax paid on overseas profits the foreign tax may be regarded as an expense and increase the amount of UK tax losses. This method of proceeding (treating foreign taxes paid as an expense) antedates treaty credit relief or unilateral credit relief and gives substantially less relief than does credit relief (tax against tax), which will be taken wherever possible.

The amount of foreign income to be included in total profits for corporation tax is the amount received plus the amount of the foreign tax. The foreign tax on overseas dividends in certain circumstances may include underlying tax on the profits out of which the dividends were paid. Underlying tax is the foreign tax paid by the overseas company on the company profits out of which it has paid dividends. Underlying tax will be included in foreign dividend income where convention relief or unilateral relief (see immediately below) is available in respect of underlying tax.

Where convention relief is not available S.498 TA 1970, provides what is known as unilateral relief, generally, and in the context of underlying taxes and dividends provides relief for underlying taxes where the UK company controls at least 10% of the voting power of the overseas company paying the dividend. S.506 TA 1970 sets out the statutory provisions concerning the computation of underlying tax.

Example 2

Globo Ltd is a company resident in the United Kingdom. In addition to the trade which Globo Ltd conducts in the United Kingdom, the company conducts a trade through a branch in an overseas country. Globo Ltd also has a wholly owned overseas subsidiary from which it receives dividends. The double tax convention provides relief for underlying as well as withholding taxes. The results of Globo Ltd for the year ended 31 March 1985 are as follows:

	£	£
Schedule D Case I, UK		500,000
Schedule D Case I, foreign branch		100,000
Foreign tax payable £40,000		
Schedule D Case V, dividend received		
from subsidiary	50,000	
Less: Withholding tax at 15%	7,500	
		42,500

Underlying tax with respect to the dividend computed to be 35%

In June 1984 Globo Ltd paid a dividend of £140,000. The surplus of ACT brought forward from the year ended 31 March 1984 is £200,000. Double tax relief is available as follows:

	UK Trade £	Foreign Dividend £	Foreign Branch Trade £	Total £
Trading income	500,000		100,000	600,000
Dividend income £50,000 × 100				
——		76,923		76,923
65				
(grossed up for underlying tax)				
	500,000	76,923	100,000	676,923
Corporation tax at 45%	225,000	34,615	45,000	304,615
Double tax relief	—	34,423	40,000	74,423
	225,000	192	5,000	230,192
ACT restricted to	150,000	192	5,000	155,192
Mainstream corporation tax	75,000	—	—	75,000

	£
Surplus ACT at 31 March 1985	
Surplus at 31 March 1984	200,000
Paid on dividend June 1984	60,000
	260,000
Applied year ended	
31 March 1985	155,192
Surplus at 31 March 1985	104,808

As you see above, the ACT deduction from the corporation tax liability on the foreign income is restricted to the corporation tax which remains payable after deduction of double tax relief, £192 and £5,000 in the above example. The amount of the ACT deduction from the corporation tax chargeable on the UK income is still restricted to 30% of the UK taxable income, 30% of £500,000 in the above example, £150,000.

7.7 CONTROLLED FOREIGN COMPANIES

At the start of the 1980s the Board of the Inland Revenue issued a consultative document entitled 'Tax Havens and the Corporate Sector'. In this document it was stated 'The use of tax havens for tax avoidance companies has shown a marked growth in recent years, and the Government is particularly concerned to counter avoidance of United Kingdom tax by the accumulation of profits and investment income of United Kingdom groups in tax haven subsidiaries'. The paper proposed two things, first that the terms on which a company is regarded as resident should be recast (a consultative paper on residence was issued at the same time) and that legislation should be introduced which would impose a UK charge to tax on the income and gains of defined companies resident in tax havens. The proposal was that such a UK charge would be apportioned to the overseas companies' corporate shareholder or shareholders, i.e. the UK parent of a tax haven subsidiary.

The legislation to give effect to these proposals is contained in Ss.82–91 FA 1984 embracing 42 pages of legislation. All of this is highly detailed anti-avoidance legislation much of which is out of place here.

The legislation applies to UK companies with at least a 10% interest (including the interests of associated or connected persons) in a controlled foreign company and apportions the 'chargeable profits' and 'creditable tax' of the controlled foreign company to any UK resident company which is a shareholder. The effect of this is to charge the profits, other than capital gains, of the CFC as if it had been resident in the UK. The apportioned sum is charged to UK corporation tax in the hands of the UK shareholder company subject to relief for double tax (S.82(4) FA 1984).

A controlled foreign company is

(a) resident outside the UK,
(b) controlled by persons resident in the UK, and
(c) subject to a lower level of taxation in the territory in which it is resident (S.82(1) FA 1984).

A 'lower level of taxation' is defined as less than one-half of the corresponding UK tax (S.85 FA 1984).

The legislation is not mandatory and only applies where the Board of Inland Revenue directs (S.82(1) FA 1984).

The government has gone to some lengths to detail the circumstances in which a direction will *not* be given, the object being in a general way to exclude from the effects of the legislation, trivial cases, where chargeable profits are less than £20,000; cases where the CFC pursues an 'acceptable' distribution policy (e.g. 50% of available profits of a CFC which is a trading company); cases where the activity of the CFC is exempt, i.e. the CFC has a business establishment and its business affairs are effectively managed in the overseas territory and where other very detailed conditions are satisfied; cases where the CFC has a public quotation, i.e. 35% of the voting power is held by the public and shares are quoted and dealt in on a local stock exchange, and cases where the motive for setting up the CFC or transactions giving rise to a reduction in UK tax was not to reduce UK tax or to divert profits (S.83 and Sch.17 FA 1984).

The intentional effect of these conclusions will be that bona fide commercial investments in tax havens will not be subject to a statutory apportionment.

Question 7

Xan Ltd a UK resident company manufacturing specialized tools and drills for the mining and oil industries sells annually £200,000 worth of plant to Norway. In order to meet an increased demand from Norwegian customers it is proposed that Xan Ltd set up a factory in Norway. It is believed that a suitable factory can be purchased for £100,000 and that equipment for the factory will cost a further £90,000. In the first year to 30 September 1986 it is anticipated that the Norwegian operation will make a trading loss of £50,000. It is anticipated that the UK operations of Xan Ltd will also make a loss in that year. However Zax Ltd a wholly owned UK subsidiary of Xan is expected to make substantial profits in the same year.

After a time it is expected that Xan Ltd will incorporate its Norwegian operations when they become profitable.

You are required to prepare notes for a preliminary meeting with the managing director of Xan Ltd setting out the likely taxation consequences of the course of action proposed. What further information might you require?

APPENDIX 1

CORPORATION TAX WORK FORM

Accounting period from . . . . 19 . . . . . to . . . . 19 . . . . .

	£	£
Schedule D Cases I and II (If a loss, enter 'NIL')	. . . .	. . . .
Less: Losses or charges treated as losses (S.177(1), S.177(8), S.254(5))	. . . .	. . . .
Schedule D Case III		. . . .
Schedule D Cases IV and V		. . . .
Schedule D Case IV	. . . .	. . . .
Less: Losses (S.179)	. . . .	. . . .
Unfranked Investment Income		. . . .
Group interest		. . . .
Building Society interest		. . . .
Schedule A		
Chargeable gains	. . . .	
Less: Losses	. . . .	
Less: Abatement (S.93 FA 1972)	. . . .	
	. . . .	. . . .
		. . . .
Less: Trading losses set against profits S.177(2)	. . . .	
Management expenses		
Less: Charges paid	. . . .	
Less: Group relief	. . . .	
Profits chargeable to corporation tax		£

179

TAX CHARGEABLE	£
Relevant Financial year(s):	
19 . . . . . at . . . . .% on £	. . . .
19 . . . . . at . . . . .% on £	. . . .
19 . . . . . at . . . . .% on £	. . . .
19 . . . . . at . . . . .% on £	
Less: Marginal Small Companies Relief	
(S.95(2) FA 1972) (restricted if necessary)	. . . .
Less: Double Taxation Relief (for AP	
ending on or after 1 April 1984)	
(S.100(6) FA 1972)	. . . .
Less: ACT (restricted if necessary)	. . . .
. . . .	
	. . . .
Less: IT set-off	
CT PAYABLE	
IT REPAYABLE	

APPENDIX 2

INDUSTRIAL BUILDINGS: TABLE OF RATES, INITIAL AND ANNUAL ALLOWANCE

Date of expenditure		Rates of allowance	
		Initial	Annual
From	To	%	%
6/4/44	5/4/52	10	2
6/4/52	14/4/53	—	2
15/4/53	6/4/54	10	2
7/4/54	17/2/56	—	2
18/2/56	14/4/58	10	2
15/4/58	7/4/59	15	2
8/4/59	5/11/62	5	2
6/11/62	16/1/66	5	4
17/1/66	5/4/70	15	4
6/4/70	21/3/72	*40	4
22/3/72	12/11/74	40	4
13/11/74	10/3/81	50	4
11/3/81	13/3/84	75	4
14/3/84	31/3/85	50	4
1/4/85	31/3/86	25	4
1/4/86	onwards	—	4

[1]30% if not in Development or Intermediate Area, for expenditure between 6/4/70 and 21/3/72.

APPENDIX 3

Question 8

Micro Chip Ltd is a non-close company involved in the distribution of micro-processors. It has an issued share capital of 100,000 ordinary shares of £1 each. The accounts to 31 March 1984 show a profit of £175,000 before tax and appropriations. The profit was arrived at after charging:

	£
Depreciation	27,875
Directors' remuneration	14,000
Legal expenses re sale of field	1,500
Loan interest—gross	2,400
Auditors' remuneration	2,500
Loss on realization of motor vehicle	500

and after crediting:

	£
Rental income	1,500
Gain on sale of field	12,000
Bad debts recovered	4,000
Dividend received	7,000
Interest on tax repayment	1,000

The fixed asset note to the accounts is as follows:

	Warehouse and land £	Plant and machinery £	Motor vehicles £
Cost at 1 April 1983	150,000	100,000	25,000
Additions 1983	—	25,000	10,000
Disposals	(20,000)	—	(2,500)
Cost at 31 March 1984	130,000	125,000	32,500
Accumulated depreciation at 1 April 1983	15,000	45,000	15,000
Eliminated in respect of disposals	—	—	(1,093)
Charge for year	7,500	16,000	4,375
Accumulated depreciation at 31 March 1984	22,500	61,000	18,282
Net book value at 31 March 1984	107,500	64,000	14,218

Notes:

1. The tax written down value of the car pool brought forward at 1 April 1983 was £10,000. The motor vehicle disposed of was the managing director's Rover bought second-hand two years ago and replaced in October 1983 with a new one costing £10,000.

2. The loan interest was unpaid at the year end although outstanding loan interest at 31 March 1983 of £2,100 net was paid during the year on 15 November 1983.

3. A field adjoining the warehouse which was acquired in December 1972 was sold in September 1983 for £32,000 (ignore indexation and Development Land Tax).

4. A general provision for bad debts of £10,000 has been made in the accounts.

5. Miscellaneous expenses include:

	£
Staff party	1,250
Entertaining—foreign	500
—home	750
Interest on overdue tax	70

6. The dividend of £7,000 exclusive of tax credit was received on 4 June 1983.

7. Micro Chip Ltd paid a dividend for 1983 of 14p per share on 30 April 1983. Assume the following:

Corporation tax—normal	50%
Corporation tax—small company	30%
Marginal small company relief— profits between £100,000 and £500,000	
Fraction	1/20
Abatement of chargeable gains	2/5
Advance corporation tax	3/7
Income tax	30%

Required:

1. Set out the information which requires to be included in the returns under Schedule 14 and Schedule 20 (Forms CT61) for the year, detailing the return periods and the amount and date of payment of tax.

2. Calculate the corporation tax payable for the accounting period ended 31 March 1984.

(*The Institute of Chartered Accountants of Scotland*).

Question 9

The undernoted are the agreed results of five companies for the year ended 31 December 1984:

	One Ltd £	Two Ltd £	Three Ltd £	Four Ltd £	Five Ltd £
Case I profit/(loss)	30,000	(60,000)	(82,000)	660,000	100,000
Case III	10,000	—	2,000	10,000	—
Schedule A surplus/ (deficit)	5,000	—	—	1,000	—
Chargeable gain/(loss)	(100,000)	—	—	60,000	—
Non-trading charges paid (gross)	—	—	30,000	20,000	—

The five companies are connected as follows:
   (1)   One Ltd owns 100% of Two Ltd and 60% of Three Ltd.
   (2)   Two Ltd owns 80% of Four Ltd.
   (3)   Three Ltd owns 100% of Five Ltd.
The following additional information has been ascertained:
   (1)   The 100% shareholding in Five Ltd was acquired by Three Ltd on 1 July 1984.
   (2)   One Ltd paid a dividend of £56,000 on 1 November 1984 and remitted the appropriate advance corporation tax on 14 January 1985.
   (3)   The chargeable gain of Four Ltd is stated before abatement.
Assume the following:

Corporation tax rate	50%
Advance corporation tax	3/7
Abatement of chargeable gains	2/5
Income tax rate	30%

Required:
1.   Determine which of the above companies form a group for the purposes of group relief in the context of corporation tax.
2.   Compute the corporation tax liabilities, if any, for each of the five companies for the year to 31 December 1984 on the basis that the desired aim is for the five companies in aggregate to pay the minimum amount of taxation.
3.   State what unutilized losses and other reliefs are available for carry forward at 31 December 1984.

(*The Institute of Chartered Accountants of Scotland*).

Question 10

Tugela Ltd, which is not a close company, was incorporated and commenced a manufacturing business in rented premises on 1 April 1981. The company issued 200,000 ordinary shares of £1 at par on that date, and on 1 July 1981 it issued £80,000 12% debenture stock, on which interest is payable half yearly at 30 June and 31 December.

On 1 August 1981 Tugela Ltd acquired 30,000 ordinary shares of £1 in Modder Ltd, which has an issued capital of 50,000 such shares, at a price of £44,000.

On 1 October 1981 Tugela Ltd acquired 12,000 ordinary shares of £1 in Klip Ltd, which has an issued capital of 40,000 such shares, at a price of £35,000. The business of Klip Ltd deteriorated during 1982 and heavy losses were suffered, following which Tugela Ltd sold its holding for £8,500 on 15 March 1983.

On 15 October 1982 Tugela Ltd brought £60,000 British Gas 3% Stock 1990/95, which is included in Schedule 2 Capital Gains Tax Act 1979 as being exempt from capital gains tax in certain circumstances, at a price of £30,200. The company sold this holding for £36,350 on 18 July 1983.

The profits of Tugela Ltd chargeable to corporation tax for the first two accounting periods have been agreed as follows:

	Year ended 31 March	
	1982	1983
	£	£
Schedule D Case I profit	25,450	108,500

	£	£
Bank deposit interest	—	3,100
		111,600
Less: Debenture interest	4,800	9,600
	20,650	102,000

Tugela Ltd did not receive any dividends during either of these years.

The next accounts were made up for the 8 months ended 30 November 1983 and showed the following figures:

	£	£
Trading loss (after charging depreciation £17,700)		(91,050)
Surplus on sale of government stock	6,150	
Interest on government stock (gross)	900	
Dividend from Modder Ltd (paid under a group election to pay dividends without accounting for advance corporation tax)	3,000	
Dividends from other United Kingdom companies (including tax credit)	5,800	
Bank deposit interest	2,550	
		18,400
		(72,650)
Debenture interest (gross)		6,400
Net loss		(79,050)

The only capital allowances available for the 8 months ended 30 November 1983 relate to a factory which was constructed for Tugela Ltd at a cost of £78,000, paid on 1 July 1983 when the building was put into use; the land had been bought by Tugela Ltd in 1982. Stock relief for the period is £5,170.

Tugela Ltd paid a dividend of 26.25% in January 1983, but has paid no other dividend.

The Schedule D Case I profits of Modder Ltd for corporation tax purposes have been agreed as follows:

	£
Year ended 31 March 1982	14,300
Year ended 31 March 1983	18,400
8 months ended 30 November 1983	17,150

Modder Ltd has no other source of income and pays no charges. The company paid a dividend of 10% in July 1983.

Tugela Ltd wishes to claim all relief as soon as possible.

The following matters are currently under consideration by the directors of both companies:
(1) A member of Modder Ltd, holding 20% of the issued capital, is prepared to sell his shares to Tugela Ltd at a reasonable price.
(2) Modder Ltd has recently completed a profitable contract and the customer wishes to place a further contract. This could be undertaken by Tugela Ltd or Modder Ltd.

The directors ask for your advice in connection with the taxation implications of these matters.

You are required to:

(b) calculate the relief which may be claimed for the trading loss suffered by Tugela Ltd in the 8 months ended 30 November 1983, showing the total amount of tax repayable as a result of the claims (**18 marks**),

(b) list the amounts carried forward for future relief, indicating how relief may be obtained (**5 marks**), and

(c) state briefly the advice you would give in response to the request by the directors (**4 marks**).

Note: The rate of advance corporation tax has been unchanged since 6 April 1979.

(**27 marks**)

Further Notes:

1. The relevant corporation tax rates are as follows:

Financial years	*1981*	*1982*	*1983*
Ordinary rate	52%	52%	50%
Small companies rate (if profits do not exceed £90,000 1981 or £100,000 1982 and 1983)	40%	38%	30%
Fraction for marginal relief (if profits do not exceed £225,000 1981 or £500,000 1982 and 1983)	2/25	7/200	1/20
Fraction for reduction of chargeable gains of companies	11/26	11/26	2/5

2. Stock relief of £5,170 should be treated as a trading expense of Tugela Ltd for the accounting period ended 30 November 1983.

(*The Institute of Chartered Accountants in England and Wales*).

Question 11

Lindsay Ltd is a trading company with an issued capital of £200,000 in ordinary shares of £1. Since 1972 the company has owned 50,000 ordinary shares of £1 in Cropper Ltd, which has an issued capital of 60,000 such shares.

On 1 July 1982 Lindsay Ltd acquired the whole issued capital of Bigley Ltd, which has been trading at a loss since 1978. It is hoped that the management changes instituted by Lindsay Ltd will lead to Bigley Ltd becoming profitable in 1985.

The profit and loss account of Lindsay Ltd for the year ended 31 December 1982 showed a profit before taxation of £184,142. The following items were included in the accounts:

INCOME	£
Dividend from Cropper Ltd (paid under a group election to pay dividends without accounting for advance corporation tax)	4,000
Dividends from other United Kingdom companies (including tax credit)	2,860
Surplus on sale of freehold factory	65,000
Profit on sale of quoted investments	3,770

EXPENDITURE	
Depreciation	48,600
Directors' remuneration	59,500

	£
Legal expenses: staff service agreements	195
advice on acquisition of Bigley Ltd	650
Debenture interest (gross)	10,800

The surplus on sale of the freehold factory is made up as follows:

	Land £	Buildings £	Total £
Proceeds in Febraury 1982	28,000	107,000	135,000
Cost in 1968	10,000	60,000	70,000
	18,000	47,000	65,000

The factory had been built for Lindsay Ltd in 1968 and had been used continuously, the residual value for industrial buildings allowance purposes being £17,400 on 1 January 1982. The sale proceeds did not reflect any development value.

On 1 February 1982 Lindsay Ltd occupied a new factory built on land which had been bought for £25,000 in 1980. The cost of construction was £139,000: a progress payment of £55,000 was made in July 1981 and the final payment of £84,000 was made on the due date in January 1982.

All possible allowances and relief are claimed in respect of both factories.

Capital allowances on plant and machinery have been calculated at £71,640 for the year ended 31 December 1982.

The profit on sale of quoted investments relates to shares in United Kingdom companies bought for £25,400 in August 1981 and sold for £29,170 in June 1982.

Lindsay Ltd issued £90,000 12% debenture stock in 1978; interest has been paid regularly on 31 March and 30 September.

The trading stock of Lindsay Ltd was £83,240 on 31 December 1981 and £96,280 on 31 December 1982. The All Stocks Index was 214.5 for December 1981 and 227.1 for December 1982.

The trading profit of Cropper Ltd for corporation tax purposes, including the deduction for capital allowances and stock relief, has been agreed at £26,760 for the year ended 31 December 1982. The company has no other source of income.

Bigley Ltd had made up accounts to 28 February 1982 prior to the acquisition of shares by Lindsay Ltd, and the next accounts were made up for ten months ended 31 December 1982. For this period the trading loss for corporation tax purposes, including the deductions for capital allowances and stock relief, has been agreed at £63,500. Bigley Ltd has no other source of income.

Dividends paid by group companies during the year ended 31 December 1982 were 14% by Lindsay Ltd and 8% by Cropper Ltd.

You are required to:
(a) calculate the mainstream corporation tax payable by Lindsay Ltd and Cropper Ltd for the year ended 31 December 1982 (**17 marks**), and
(b) list the ways in which relief can be obtained for the loss of Bigley Ltd for the ten months ended 31 December 1982, including the advantages and disadvantages of each method and suggesting which method should be adopted (**5 marks**).

Assume that the rates of corporation tax for the financial year 1981 apply throughout. (**22 marks**)

Notes:
1.   The relevant corporation tax rates for 1981 are as follows:

Financial year	*1981*
Ordinary rate	52%
Small companies rate (if profits do not exceed £90,000)	40%
Fraction for marginal relief (if profits do not exceed £225,000)	2/25
Fraction for reduction of chargeable gains of companies	11/26

2.   The amount of stock relief in the above question is computed as follows:

$$\frac{227.1 - 214.5}{214.5} \times (£83,240 - £2,000) = £4,772$$

Stock relief should be treated as a trading expense of Lindsay Ltd in the same manner as capital allowances. Stock relief was ended for accounts beginning after 12 March 1984 by Section 48 Finance Act 1984.

(*The Institute of Chartered Accountants in England and Wales*).

Question 12

The following information has been extracted from the records of these companies:

Turret Ltd

Ordinary £1 shares isued £40,000, of which Castle Ltd owns £22,500.

Years ended 31 March	*1982*	*1983*
	£	£
Schedule D Case I	80,000	120,000
Dividends paid—to Castle Ltd under group election	49,218	63,000
—to others	38,282	49,000

Castle Ltd

	£	£
Schedule D Case I	220,000	300,000
Bank interest: Bank of Cornwall (received 1 March)	1,000	1,200
Dividends received—from Turret Ltd	49,218	63,000
—other UK companies	10,500	10,500
Dividends paid	175,000	252,000
Loan interest payable (1981—nil)	35,000	33,000
Capital gains	13,000	—
Accrued liabilities—loan interest	5,000	7,000

All ACT of Castle Ltd prior to 1982 has been utilized. For Turret Ltd for the years to 31 March 1980 and 1981 Case I, Schedule D, profits were £62,000 (CT thereon £29,200) and £48,000 (CT thereon £19,800) respectively. ACT paid was £16,200 in 1980 and £9,750 in 1981. Relief for Advance Corporation Tax is required as early as possible.

Required:

Compute Mainstream Corporation Tax for each company for 1982 and 1983 and for Turret Ltd for 1980 and 1981: show the amount of any unrelieved ACT.

The following Finance Act 1982 tax rates are to be used in answering this question:

Corporation tax	52%

Advance corporation tax	3/7
Chargeable gains abatement	11/26
Corporation tax—small companies rate	40% (lower limit, £90,000)

Marginal relief

$$2/25 \, (M-P) \times \frac{I}{P}$$

$$(\text{where } M = £225,000)$$

Notes:

1. For accounting periods ended after 31 March 1984 a surplus of ACT can be carried back and set off against the corporation tax of accounting periods beginning six years prior to the AP in which the surplus arises. In your solution to the question the carry back should be restricted to two years which was the position prior to the Finance Act 1984.

2. Loan interest paid by Castle Ltd in the year ended 31 March 1983 was £31,000.

(Chartered Association of Certified Accountants).

Question 13

(a) Q Ltd which commenced to trade on 1 December 1982, is a wholly owned subsidiary of T Ltd. Trading results are as follows:

	Q Ltd £	T Ltd £
Year to 30 November 1982		
Trading profit/(loss)	—	(5,000)
Year to 30 November 1983		
Trading profit/(loss)	(12,000)	10,000
Bank Interest received	—	5,000
Debenture interest (gross) paid	—	2,000
Year to 30 November 1984		
Trading profit/(loss)	(5,000)	(10,000)
Bank Interest received	—	5,000
Debenture Interest (gross) paid	—	2,000

Required:

Illustrate how loss relief is claimed and why you make your particular form of claim in these circumstances. Explain how unrelieved losses and charges may be dealt with.

(b) The issued share capital of Z Ltd is 80,000 £1 ordinary shares. 48,000 are owned by A Ltd, 24,000 by B Ltd and 8,000 by C Ltd. Trading results of all companies, which are resident in the United Kingdom for the year to 30 June 1984 are:

		£
Z Ltd	profit	50,000
A Ltd	profit	40,000
B Ltd	loss	(60,000)
C Ltd	profit	10,000

Explain fully how and in what conditions B Ltd's loss may be relieved.

(Chartered Association of Certified Accountants).

APPENDIX 4

SOLUTIONS TO QUESTIONS 1–13

Question 1

Exer Sighs Ltd
Corporation Tax Computation
Year ended 31 March 1984

1. *Schedule D Case I computation*

	£	£
Profit before tax		77,075
Add: Depreciation		11,625
Loss on sale of machine		650
Charges		7,000
		96,350
Deduct: Franked investment income	2,000	
Deposit account interest	300	
Debenture interest	6,200	
Building Society interest	500	9,000
		87,350
Deduct: Capital allowances		26,350
Schedule D Case I profit		61,000

2. *Corporation Tax computation*

	£	£
Schedule D Case I profit		61,000
Schedule D Case III		300
Unfranked Investment Income		6,200
Building Society interest $£500 \times \dfrac{100}{70}$		714
Chargeable gain	56,000	
Less: Abatement: £56,000 × 2/5	22,400	
		33,600
c/f		£101,814

		£	£
	b/f		101,814
Less: Charges: Deed of covenant		2,000	
Loan interest		2,500	
			4,500
Profits chargeable to corporation tax			97,314

	£		£
Corporation Tax payable:			
Income	97,314		
Less: Chargeable gains	33,600		
	63,714	× 30%	19,114.20
Chargeable gains £33,600 × 50%			16,800.00
			35,914.20
Deduct: Income Tax suffered £2,074 — £1,350			724.00
Corporation Tax payable by 1 January 1985			35,190.20

Notes to Computation

1. The total of the 'other income', £9,000, is deducted in arriving at the Schedule D Case I profit since this is not trading income. Items (b), (c) and (d) are then included in the Corporation Tax computation under the relevant headings. Franked investment income is not included in the computation of profits chargeable to CT.

2. Charges of £7,000 are included in the profit and loss account and are added back in arriving at the Schedule D Case I profit. Note that only £4,500 may be deducted in the corporation tax computation. The payment of £2,500 due on 31 March was not paid until after the end of the accounting period.

3. For small company relief purposes (S.95 FA 1972) the 'profits' of Exer Sighs Ltd are calculated as follows:

		£
Profits chargeable to CT		97,314
Add: FII		2,000
'Profits'		99,314

Since the profits are les than £100,000 the 'income' will be charged to tax at the small company rate of 30%.

4. The company has suffered income tax of £1,860 by deduction at source from the debenture interest. During the year the company deducted income tax of £1,350 from the charges paid. The income tax deducted will have been set-off against the income tax suffered and this will be shown on the forms CT 61 submitted during the twelve months to 31 March 1984. The balance of income tax suffered on the UFII, for which the company has not obtained relief is £510. In addition the company is deemed to have suffered income tax of £214 by deduction at source from the Building Society interest. Thus there will be a deduction of £724 from the corporation tax liability.

Question 2

Davy Jones Ltd

1. *Industrial Buildings Allowance*
   AP ended 31 March 1984

				£
Qualifying expenditure:				
Total cost				142,000
Less: Cost of land and relevant legal fees				21,000
Qualifying expenditure				121,000

Years ended	Residue 31/3/83 £	Expenditure AP 31/3/84 £	Initial allowance £	Writing down allowance £	Residue 31/3/84 £
1984		121,000	90,750	4,840	25,410
1981	798			84	714
1976	2,304			512	1,792
1970	2,494			344	2,150
1959	5,920			296	5,624
			90,750	6,076	
Writing down allowance			6,076		
Industrial buildings allowance			96,826		

Notes:
(i) All the expenditure qualifies for industrial buildings allowance (other than the cost of land, etc.) by reason of being a factory used in a qualifying trade or welfare premises (canteen and kitchen, etc.) or offices directly related to production (drawing office and works manager's office). A storeroom in the context of a manufacturing company qualifies where the store is of raw materials or of finished goods.

(ii) The writing down allowance in respect of expenditure from 6 April 1946 to 5 November 1962 (inclusive dates) is at 2%. Thereafter it is 4%.

2. *Notes for meeting with accountant*
   (a) The estimated £400,000 will require to be analysed between the sale price of the industrial buildings and the sale price of the land.
   (b) Since it seems likely that both land and buildings will be sold for more than cost a chargeable gain will arise.
   (c) The possibility of rolling-over the chargeable gain into group acquisitions of replacement and other business assets will require to be considered. In this regard acquisitions one year before disposal and three years after disposal are in point. What acquisitions have been made or projected?
   (d) The allocation between land and buildings should be agreed in due course between Davy Jones Ltd and the purchaser.
   (e) The sale price of the buldings only will require to be apportioned between the different expenditures in each accounting period. This

might be done in proportion to cost but some other manner of apportionment might be appropriate. In particular are the costs and residues the only expenditure on this factory. There may be expenditures many years ago which do not enter into the industrial buildings allowance computations which are relevant to the calculation of balancing adjustments.

(f) Balancing adjustments will arise in respect of each year's expenditure. These are likely to be balancing charges (limited to allowances given) treated as trading income in the accounting period of sale.

(g) No allowances (i.e. writing down allowances) will be granted in the accounting period of sale.

(h) No balancing adjustment is necessary fifty years after a building (or part of a buiding) came into use if expenditure was incurred before 6 November 1962 (twenty-five years if the expenditure is after 5 November 1962).

(i) Has the factory been used as an industrial building throughout its ownership by Davy Jones Ltd; in particular were there periods of time during which it was in use otherwise than as an industrial building? In the latter case notional allowances will be deducted in arriving at the residue of expenditure before sale. Any balancing charge will be restricted to allowances actually granted against profits.

Question 3

Vibrations Ltd
1. *Liability under Schedule 14 FA 1972*
    Return Period ended 30 June 1983

		£
10/4/83	Dividend received	700
	Add: Tax credit at 3/7	300
	FII carried forward	1,000

Return Period ended 30 September 1983

		£
1/7/83	Dividend paid	5,250
	Add: ACT	2,250
	Franked payment	7,500
	Less: FII	1,000
		6,500

ACT payable (by 14/10/83)
£6,500 × 30% = £1,950.

Return period ended 31 December 1983

			£
10/10/83	Dividend received		4,200
	Add: Tax credit at 3/7		1,800
	FII		6,000
	Total franked payments to date		7,500
	Less: Total FII to date:		
	10/4/83	1,000	
	10/10/83	6,000	7,000
	Excess of franked payments over FII		500

		£
ACT paid to date		1,950
Less: ACT due		150
Repayment to be made by Collector of Taxes		1,800

Return period ended 31 March 1984

			£
1/1/84	Dividend paid		5,250
22/2/84	Dividend paid		29,750
			35,000
	Add: ACT at 3/7		15,000
	Franked payments		50,000

ACT payable: £50,000 × 30% = £15,000

2. *Corporation Tax computation*
   Year ended 31 March 1984

	£	£
Schedule D Case I profit		42,500
Chargeable gain	30,000	
Less: Abatement: £30,000 × 2/5	12,000	
		18,000
		60,500
Less: Charge: Deed of covenant payment 11/7/83		500
Profits chargeable to corporation tax		60,000

Corporation tax payable:			£
Income (£60,000 — £18,000 = £42,000) × 30%			12,600
Chargeable gain £18,000 × 50%			9,000
			21,600
Less: ACT:			
Dividends paid		40,250	
Add: ACT		17,250	
		57,500	
Less: Dividends received	4,900		
Add: Tax credit	2,100	7,000	
		50,500	
ACT paid: £50,500 × 30% =		£15,150	
ACT set-off restricted to income			
(i.e. £42,000) at 30%			12,600
Corporation tax payable 1 January 1985			9,000

Note:

The amount of ACT paid in respect of the accounting period ended 31 March 1984 amounts to £15,150. Advance corporation tax may only be set against the company's CT liability on its income and so only £12,600 ACT may be deducted in arriving at the mainstream corporation tax payable.

The definition of income both for the purposes of restriction of ACT set-off and for the calculation of the small company rate is given at S.85(6) FA 1972. The application of this definition means that the charges are in effect set off against the Schedule D Case I profits in priority to the chargeable gains.

Question 4

Machinations Ltd

(1) *Corporation Tax Computations*

Years ended	31/3/80 £	31/3/81 £	31/3/82 £	31/3/83 £	31/3/84 £	
Schedule D Case I	47,000	6,640	2,300	—	12,080	
Less: Losses and charges b/f S.177(1) and (8)					9,260	(Note 2)
					2,820	
UFII	1,500	1,500	4,000	4,000	4,000	
Schedule A	720	720	720	720	720	
Chargeable gain	—	—	750	—	—	
	49,220	8,860	7,770	4,720	7,540	
Less: Loss relief S.177(2) and (3A)	—	(6,800)	(7,770)	(4,720)	—	
	49,220	2,060	Nil	Nil	7,540	
Less: Charges	1,600	1,600	—	—	3,600	
Profits chargeable	47,620	460	—	—	3,940	
CT (assumed at 50%)	23,810	230	Nil	Nil	1,970	
Less: IT suffered	—	—	—	—	120	
	23,810	230	—	—	1,850	
IT repayable	—	—	120	120	—	
Trade charges b/f	—	—	—	3,100	6,200	
Trade charges unused/(used)	—	—	3,100	3,100	(6,200)	
Trade charges c/f (S.177(8))	—	—	3,100	6,200	Nil	

Notes:

1. The total loss available for relief in the year to 31/3/83 is:

	£
Trading loss	15,000
Writing Down Allowance	550
	15,550
First Year Allowance	6,800
	22,350

This loss is utilized as follows:

(a) Non-First Year Allowance loss—£15,550

	£
LOSS	15,550
Less: Used in year ended 31/3/83	(4,720)
Less: Carried back to year ended 31/3/82	(7,770)
Balance of non-FYA loss to be carried forward S.177(1)	3,060

(b) First Year Allowance loss—£6,800—can be carried back under S.177(3A) to the year ended 31/3/81.

2. Note that trade charges unutilized in 1982 and 1983, £6,200, are carried forward to 1984 and are set off together with the loss carried forward of £3,060 against the Schedule D Case I profit in 1984.

3. Note that in 1982 and 1983 UFII received by the company (under deduction of tax) exceeds the charges paid. There is therefore an excess of income tax suffered on the UFII over income tax deducted from charges. This excess is repayable by the Inland Revenue to the company.

Question 5

1. *Group Income*
S.256 TA 1970 provides that in certain circumstances dividends may be paid by one company within a group to another company within the same group, without accounting for ACT. In the hands of the company receiving the dividend this income is classified as group income. A joint election must be made by the company receiving the dividend and the company paying the dividend and will apply where:
(i) the company paying the dividend is a 51% subsidiary of the recipient company (i.e. the parent company owns more than 51% of the ordinary share capital of the other); or
(ii) the company paying the dividend is a 51% subsidiary of another UK resident company of which the recipient company is also a 51% subsidiary.
Group income is not included in the profits of the recipient company chargeable to Corporation Tax.

Group Relief
The provisions relating to Group Relief (Ss.258–264) enable a company which is a member of a 75% group to surrender trading losses, excess charges, management expenses and certain capital allowances to other companies within the same group. For these purposes, a 75% group consists of a parent company and any company of which the parent owns 75% or more of the ordinary share capital. In addition the parent must be entitled to not less than 75% of the profits available for distribution to equity holders and to not less than 75% of the subsidiary's assets available to equity holders on a notional winding up.

A company which has incurred trading losses or excess charges etc. may surrender the whole of the amount available to one company or it may apportion the relief between a number of claimant companies.

Where, however, the accounting period of the surrendering company does not coincide with that of the claimant company it is necessary to apportion the profits of the claimant company and the losses of the surrendering company in order to ensure that relief is only given for the period common to both the surrendering and the claimant companies' accounting periods. Likewise where a company joins or leaves a group, apportionment of profits and losses will be necessary in order that relief should only be given for the period during which both companies are members of the same group.

2. *Corporation Tax Liabilities*

(a) H Ltd

	£	£
Year ended 31 December 1984		
Case I loss	15,000	
Charges	10,000	
Total available for surrender	25,000	25,000

CGT loss carried forward £5,000

(b) M Ltd

	£		
Year ended 31 December 1984			
Case I profit		20,000	
Chargeable gains	3,000		
Less: Abatement 2/5	1,200		
	1,800	1,800	
Total profits		21,800	
Less: Group relief from H Ltd		21,800	21,800
Profits chargeable		Nil	
			3,200

(c) T Ltd

Year ended 31 December 1984			
Case I profit		100,000	
Less: Loss brought forward S.177(1)		100,000	
		Nil	
Chargeable gains	30,000		
Less: Abatement	12,000		
	1,800	18,000	
		18,000	
Less: Charges		18,000	
Profits chargeable		Nil	

Loss carried forward S.177(1) £25,000

Charges available to carry forward £2,000 (assuming charges are incurred wholly and exclusively for the purposes of the trade).

Note: (i) The balance of charges of £2,000 is not available for surrender under the provisions of S.259(6). This section permits relief only for charges which exceed the profits for an accounting period *before* deducting losses or allowances brought forward or carried back from any other accounting period.

(ii) T Ltd has paid ACT of £28,500 calculated as follows:

	£
Dividend paid	70,000
Add: ACT	30,000
Franked payment	100,000
Less: FII	5,000
	95,000

ACT payable: £95,000 × 30% = £28,500

All or part of this ACT may be surrendered to D Ltd. The balance then left in T Ltd may be carried forward, or carried back and set against the CT payable in respect of income of accounting periods commencing within the previous six years.

(d) *D Ltd*

Year ended 31 December 1984	£	£
Case I profit		10,000
Chargeable gains	3,000	
Less: Abatement	1,200	1,800
Profits chargeable		11,800
Corporation tax payable: £11,800 × 50%		5,900
Less: ACT surrendered by T Ltd		3,000
Mainstream CT payable		2,900

3. *Unutilized losses available for carry forward*

		£
(a)	*H Ltd*	
	S.177(1) loss = £25,000 — £21,800	3,200
	Loss	5,000
(b)	*M Ltd*	Nil
(c)	*T Ltd*	
	S.177(1) loss .	25,000
	Charges (assumed to be trade charges)	2,000
	ACT £28,500 — £3,000	25,500

Note that D Ltd is not entitled to claim group relief for the losses of H Ltd because the former is not within the 75% group comprising T Ltd, H Ltd and M Ltd.

Question 6

Mortality Limited
Maximum Relevant Income Computation
Year ended 31 March 1986

	Trading income £	Estate income £	FII £	UFII £	Schedule D Case III £	Total £
				Investment Income		
Income	200,000	44,000	70,000	30,000	12,000	356,000
Charges				10,000		10,000
	200,000	44,000	70,000	20,000	12,000	346,000
CT at 39.1754% (see note)	78,351	17,237	—	7,835	4,701	108,124
Distributable income	121,649	26,763	70,000	12,165	7,299	237,876
Less:						
Trading income	121,649					(121,649)
Abatement 10% of estate or trading or £3,000 if less				3,000		(3,000)
No abatement of estate income since aggregate of estate and trading income in excess of £75,000						
Total						113,227
Estate income		26,763				26,763
Distributable investment income			70,000	9,165	7,299	86,464
Total						113,227

Maximum relevant income:	£
50% Estate income (50% × £26,763)	13,382
100% Distributable investment income	86,464
	99,846

Note:
Small company rate

	£
Profits:	
Profits chargeable	276,000
Add: FII	100,000
Profits for small company rate	376,000

	£
Corporation tax payable £276,000 at 40%	110,400

Less: Marginal relief

$$\frac{1}{40} \quad (M - P) \times \frac{I}{P}$$

$$\frac{1}{40} \quad (£500,000 - £376,000) \times \frac{£276,000}{£376,000} \qquad 2,276$$

108,124

Equivalent to 39.1754% of profits chargeable

Question 7

Notes for preliminary meeting with MD of Xan Ltd

1. Setting up a factory in Norway will be to set up a branch of Xan Ltd in Norway and the results of the branch will be governed by the rules of corporation tax.
2. Industrial buildings allowance will be available in respect of the Norwegian factory. An initial allowance of 25% will be granted for expenditure incurred before 1 April 1986, together with a writing down allowance of 4%. After 31 March 1986, only a WDA of 4% is available. Otherwise the normal rules about IBA apply.
3. Normal rules about plant or machinery allowances also apply to expenditure on plant for the Norwegian factory. No first year allowance is available for expenditure after 31 March 1986 and if it is suitable the branch will wish to make its acquisitions prior to that date.
4. The amount of the loss will be computed in accordance with corporation tax provisions. Together with the anticipated loss of Xan Ltd in the UK the loss may be surrendered by way of group relief to Zax Ltd.
5. On incorporation of the Norwegian branch the capital allowances previously granted to Xan Ltd may be clawed back by way of balancing charges because the disposal value will be market value.
6. If shares are exchanged by the Norwegian company for the branch trade any capital gains arising on the disposal of buildings and goodwill from Xan Ltd to the Norwegian company can be postponed in terms of Section 268A TA 1970.
7. Incorporation of the Norwegian branch will require Treasury consent in terms of Section 482 TA 1970.
8. It is assumed that the directors of the proposed Norwegian company will meet in Norway and that central control and management on a day to day basis will be there, and that accordingly it will be resident in Norway.
9. The Norwegian company will be subject to Norwegian tax on the basis of the assumption in (8). The UK company Xan Ltd will be liable under Schedule D Case V and Schedule D Case IV on dividends and interest received from the Norwegian company.
10. Double tax convention relief will be available on dividends etc. from the Norwegian company. There is a limit on the amount of this relief which is the UK corporation tax on the foreign income.

11. No group relief will be possible for any losses the Norwegian company may make nor can the Norwegian company set-off losses of its UK parent or UK fellow subsidiaries against any profits it makes.

12. Further matters to be considered include:
   (a) How is the Norwegian company to be financed, locally or from the UK?
   (b) Will there be a management charge from Xan Ltd to the Norwegian company?
   (c) What are the terms of the UK-Norway double tax treaty?
   (d) What sources of local information are available to the company and yourself?

Question 8

Micro Chip Ltd

1. *Schedule 14*

Return Period 1 April 1983–30 June 1983	£	£
30/4/83 Distribution made		14,000
Add: ACT at 3/7		6,000
Franked payment		20,000
Less: FII		
Dividend received	7,000	
Plus Tax credit	3,000	
Excess of franked payment over FII		10,000
		10,000
ACT payable by 14/7/83		
10,000 × 30% =		3,000

Schedule 20

Return Period 1 October 1983–31 December 1983	£
15/11/83 Loan interest payable	3,000
Less: income tax deducted	900
Net payment	2,100

Tax payable to Collector of Taxes:
£900 by 14/1/84

2.   *Micro Chip Ltd*
                         Year ended 31 March 1984

(a) *Case I Computation*	£	£
Profit per profit and loss account		175,000
Add: Depreciation		27,875
Legal expenses		1,500
Loan interest		2,400
Loss on car		500
General provision for bad debts		10,000
Miscellaneous expenses—		
Entertaining, home		750
Interest on overdue tax		70
c/f		218,095

		£	£
	b/f		218,095
Deduct: Rental income		1,500	
Gain on sale of field		12,000	
Dividend received		7,000	
Interest on tax repayment		1,000	21,500
			196,595
Deduct: Capital allowances			29,273
Case I Profit			167,322

(b) *Capital Allowance Computation*

	£	£	Car pool £	Car £	Total £
WDV b/f			10,000		
Less: Sale of car:					
Cost		2,500			
Less: Depreciation	1,093				
Loss	500	1,593			
Sale proceeds		907	907		
			9,093		
Cost of plant and maintenance		25,000		10,000	
Less: FYA		25,000			25,000
WDA on pool (25%)			2,273		2,273
WDA on car restricted to				2,000	2,000
			6,820	8,000	
					29,273

(c) *Corporation Tax Computation*

Year ended 31/3/84	£	£	£
Schedule D Case I			167,322
Schedule A			1,500
Chargeable gain: Proceeds		32,000	
Less: Cost	20,000		
Expenses	1,500	21,500	
		10,500	
Less: Abatement 2/5		4,200	6,300
			175,122
Less: Charges paid during year:			
$£2,100 \times \dfrac{100}{70}$			3,000
Profits chargeable to corporation tax			172,122

	£	£
Corporation tax payable:		
£172,122 × 50%		£86,061

Less: Marginal small companies relief:

$$\frac{1}{20} \times [(500,000 - 182,122) \times \frac{165,822}{182,122}] = \quad 14,471$$

Advance Corporation Tax:	£		
Dividend paid 30/4/83	14,000		
Add: ACT	6,000		
	20,000		
Less: FII (7,000 + 3,000)	10,000		
	10,000		
£10,000 × 30%		3,000	17,471
Corporation tax payable			68,590

Question 9

1. For the purposes of group relief given under the provisions of S.258 TA 1970 a group of companies comprises a parent company and all subsidiaries in which that parent owns, either directly or indrectly, 75% or more of the ordinary share capital.

   There are thus two groups of companies in this question, namely:
   (a) a group comprising One Ltd, Two Ltd and Four Ltd; and
   (b) a group comprising Three Ltd and Five Ltd (with effect from 1 July 1984).

2. *Corporation Tax Liabilities*
   (a) *Two Ltd*
       Corporation Tax Computation

	£
Year ended 31 December 1984	
Schedule D Case I profit	Nil
Loss available for surrender (S.259 TA 1970)	60,000

   (b) *One Ltd*
       Corporation Tax Computation

	£
Year ended 31 December 1984	
Schedule D Case I	30,000
Schedule D Case III	10,000
Schedule A	5,000
Profits chargeable to corporation tax	45,000
Corporation tax payable: £45,000 × 50%	22,500
Less: ACT:	
£56,000 × 3/7 =£24,000	
ACT set-off restricted to £45,000 × 30% =	13,500
Mainstream corporation tax payable	£9,000

	£
ACT available to surrender to Four Ltd (S.92 FA 1972):	
ACT payable	24,000
Less: ACT set-off	13,500
Available to surrender	10,500

   (c) *Four Ltd*
       Corporation Tax Computation

	£
Year ended 31 December 1984	
Schedule D Case I	660,000
Schedule D Case III	10,000
Chargeable gain £60,000 × 3/5	36,000
	706,000
Less: Charges	20,000
	686,000
Less: Group relief surrendered by Two Ltd	60,000
	626,000
Corporation tax payable: £626,000 × 50%	313,000
Less: ACT surrendered by One Ltd	10,500
Mainstream Corporation Tax	302,500

(d) *Three Ltd*
     Corporation Tax Computation

	£
Year ended 31 December 1984	
Schedule D Case I	Nil
Schedule D Case III	2,000
	2,000
Less: Charges	2,000
	Nil

Group relief available for surrender:	£
Trading loss	82,000
Charges unutilized (S.259(6)): £30,000 — £2,000	28,000
Available to surrender	110,000

(e) *Five Ltd*
     Corporation Tax Computation

Year ended 31 December 1984	£
Schedule D Case I profit	100,000
Less: Group relief surrendered (S.262(2))	50,000
Profits chargeable to Corporation Tax	50,000
Corporation tax payable: £50,000 × 50%	25,000

Note:

Five Ltd did not become a subsidiary of Three Ltd until 1 July 1984 and therefore the provisions of S.262 apply:

S.262(2)(a) The maximum loss that can be surrendered by Three Ltd is £82,000 × 6/12 = £41,000

S.262(2)(b) The maximum profits of Five Ltd against which group relief may be allowed is £100,000 × 6/12 = £50,000

The group relief surrendered to Five Ltd will be taken to comprise:

	£
Charges	14,000
Loss	36,000
	50,000

3. *Unutilized losses and reliefs*

One Ltd—Allowable capital loss of £100,000 available to carry forward.

Three Ltd—Trading loss available for carry forward:

	£
Trading loss	82,000
Less: Surrendered to Five Ltd	36,000
Loss to carry forward S.177(1)	46,000

Note the balance of non-trade charges unutilized may not be carried forward.

Four Ltd— Schedule A deficit to be carried forward and set against future rents £1,000.

Question 10

1.

Tugela Ltd Group

Tugela

60% / \ 30%

Modder   Klip

(1/8/81)   (1/10/81)

2. *Tugela Ltd*

	£
Industrial Buildings Allowance	
Factory cost	78,000
Initial allowance 75% × £78,000	58,500
Writing down allowance 2/3 (4% × £78,000)	2,080
	60,580

3.

Tugela Ltd
Corporation Tax Computation
Accounting Period ended 30 November 1983

	£	£
Net loss		79,050
Add:		
Bank deposit interest		2,550
UK dividends		5,800
Group income		3,000
Interest		900
Surplus on sale of government stock		6,150
Stock relief		5,170
Capital allowances		60,580
		163,200
Less:		
Depreciation	17,700	
Debenture interest paid	6,400	24,100
Schedule D Case I loss		(139,100)
Other income accounting period ended		
30 November 1983:		£
UFII		900
Schedule D Case III		2,500
Chargeable gains £6,150 less loss on sale of shares		
in Klip Ltd (part)		Nil
		3,450
Charges: Debenture interest paid 30 June 1983		4,800

Tugela Ltd
Corporation Tax paid and repayable

Original

Accounting Period ended 31 March	1982 £	1983 £
Profits chargeable	20,650	102,000
Corporation tax at 40%	8,260	
Corporation tax at 52%		53,040

Less: Marginal small company relief:

$$\frac{7}{200}(M - P) \times \frac{I}{P}$$

$$= \frac{7}{200}(250{,}000 - 102{,}000)$$

	1982	1983
		5,180
		47,860
Less: Advance corporation tax		22,500
		25,360

Revised
Accounting Period ended 31 March

	1982	1983
Taxable profits	25,450	111,600
Less: S.177(2)		74,400
	25,450	37,200
Less: Charges	4,800	9,600
	20,650	27,600
Corporation tax at 40%/38%	8,260	10,488
Less: ACT paid and carried back (maximum)	6,195	8,280
	2,065	2,208
Corporation tax repayable	6,195	23,152

Repayment of Tax Credit
Accounting Period ended 30 November 1983

Repayment of tax credit 30% × £5,800	1,740

Surrender of ACT
ACT surrendered to Modder Ltd
AP ended 31 March 1983

£22,500 — £8,280 — £6,195	8,025

Modder Ltd

Original	31/3/82 £	31/3/83 £	30/11/83 £
Corporation tax payable	5,720	6,992	5,145
Less: ACT	—	—	857
	5,720	6,992	4,288

Revised

Corporation tax payable	5,720	6,992	5,145
Less: ACT surrendered and paid	—	5,520	3,362
	5,720	1,472	1,783
Corporation tax repayable	Nil	5,520	2,505

ACT Accounting

	£
Accounting Period ended 31 March 1983	
Dividend paid 26.25% × £200,000	52,000
Add: ACT 3/7 × £52,000	22,000
Franked payment	75,000

Accounting Period ended 30 November 1983	
Dividend (including tax credit) being	
Surplus Franked Investment Income	5,800

Modder Ltd

Corporation tax payable:	
Accounting Period ended 31 March 1982	
Schedule D Case I	14,300
Corporation tax payable £14,300 × 40%	5,720
Accounting Period ended 31 March 1983	
Schedule D Case I	18,400
Corporation tax payable £18,400 × 38%	6,992
Accounting Period ended 30 November 1983	
Schedule D Case I	17,150
Corporation tax payable £17,150 × 30%	5,145
ACT paid 3/7 × £2,000	857

(a) *Application of loss of £139,100 of Tugela Ltd*
S.177(2) claim:

	£	£
Accounting Period ended 30 November 1983		
Other income		3,450
Less: Trading loss		3,450
Accounting Period ended 31 March 1983		
Total profits		111,600
Whereof 2/3		74,400
S.254 claim:		
Accounting Period ended 30 November 1983		
Surplus Franked Investment Income		5,800
Less: Trading loss		5,800

(b)

(i) Capital loss available for carry forward:

	£
Loss on disposal of shares in Klip Ltd	26,500
Less: Off-set against profit on British Gas Stock	6,150
	20,350

The allowable capital loss of £20,350 is available for set-off against chargeable gains only, arising in subsequent accounting periods.

(ii)

	£	£
Trading loss as computed		139,100
Less: Applied S.177(2)	3,450	
Applied S.177(2)	74,400	
Applied S.254	5,800	83,650
		55,450

The trading loss of £55,450 is available for carry forward for set-off against traing profits only, arising in subsequent accounting periods.

(iii) Excess charges available for carry forward:

	£
Debenture interest paid 30/6/83	4,800

The excess charges of £4,800 are available for carry forward and for set-off against trading profits only, arising in subsequent accounting periods.

(iv) ACT available for carry forward: Nil

	£	£
ACT paid		22,500
Less: Applied		
Accounting Period 31/3/83	8,280	
Accounting Period 31/3/82	6,195	
	14,475	
Surrender	8,025	22,500
		Nil

(c) If Tugela Ltd were to acquire a further 20% of the issued capital of Modder Ltd, Modder Ltd would become a 75% subsidiary of Tugela Ltd and group relief would be available from the time of acquisition of the additional 20%. This would give an additional means of loss relief in the future and other things being equal would be of benefit to the group.

As regards the proposed contract it would appear advisable that this be undertaken by Tugela Ltd since Tugela has losses which are being brought forward and will be available for relief against the profits of the contract which would need to be realized in Tugela Ltd.

Question 11

1.   *Lindsay Group*

Lindsay

100% /   \ 83.33%

Bigley (1/7/82)   **Cropper** (1972)

2.   *Capital Allowances*
Industrial Buildings Allowance

Lindsay Ltd	£
Disposal of factory February 1982	107,000
Residue before sale	17,400
Balancing charge	89,600
Restricted to allowances given (£60,000 — £17,400)	42,600

New factory
AP ended 31 December 1982

Initial allowance 75% × £55,000	41,250

AP ended 31 December 1982

Initial allowance 75% × £84,000	63,000
WDA 4% × £139,000	5,560
	68,560

Lindsay Ltd
Corporation Tax Computation

AP ended 31 December 1982	£
Profit before taxation	184,142
Add: Depreciation	48,600
Legal expenses—acquisition Bigley Ltd	650
Debenture interest	10,800
Balancing charge	42,600
c/f	286,792

		£	£
	b/f		286,792
Less: Capital allowances:			
Industrial buildings		68,560	
Plant and machinery		71,640	
Stock relief		4,772	
Group income		4,000	
Franked investment income		2,860	
Surplus on sale of factory		65,000	
Profit on sale of investments		3,770	220,602
Schedule D Case I			66,190
Gains on sale of factory—rolled over			Nil
Gain on investments		3,700	
Less: Abatement		1,595	
		2,175	2,175
			68,365
Less: Charges			10,800
Profits chargeable			57,565

Corporation tax payable:

£57,565 × 52% → 29,934

Less: Marginal Small Company relief
(Note: 2 associated companies)

$$\frac{2}{25} \times (75,000 - 60,425) \frac{55,390}{60,425}$$

→ 1,069

	28,865
Less: ACT	11,142
Mainstream corporation tax	17,723

ACT accounting

Dividend paid £200,000 × 14%	28,000
Add: ACT 3/7 × £28,000	12,000
Franked payments	40,000
FII	2,860
Excess of franked payments over FII	37,140
ACT paid £37,140 × 30%	11,142

Cropper Ltd
Corporation Tax Computation

AP ended 31 December 1982	£
Schedule D Case I	26,760

Corporation tax: £26,760 × 40%	10,704
Less: ACT £800 × 3/7	343

Mainstream corporation tax	10,361

(b) Loss of Bigley Ltd available for surrender by way of group
relief to Lindsay Ltd: 6/10 × £63,500   38,100

Profit of Lindsay Ltd available for relief:
     6/12 × £57,565   28,783

(i)   Bigley Ltd can surrender £28,783 of its loss to Lindsay Ltd and carry forward £63,500 — £28,783 = £34,717.

(ii)   In addition Bigley Ltd can surrender the balance of the loss available, £38,000 — £28,783 = £9,317, to Cropper Ltd. In this case Bigley's loss carried forward will be £63,500 — £28,783 — £9,317 = £25,400.

(iii)   Bigley Ltd can carry forward the whole of its loss against future trading profits of Bigley Ltd. There is no opportunity to carry back the loss of Bigley Ltd because of the prior losses.

(iv)   Group relief offers immediate relief and since Bigley Ltd will not be in profit until 1985 should be adopted.

(v)   Carry forward of Bigley Ltd's loss will only be available against future trading profits of Bigley Ltd; a claim for group relief makes possible a set off of a trading loss against a proportion of the chargeable profits of Lindsay Ltd, which include in the year in question chargeable gains.

(vi)   There has been a change in the owership of Bigley Ltd such that if there is a major change in the nature or conduct of the trade in the three years after 1 July 1982 carry forward of losses prior to that date may be denied. This might be a consideration in the context.

Question 12

Castle Ltd
Corporation Tax Computation

	£
AP ended 31 March 1982	
Schedule D Case I	220,000
Schedule D Case III	1,000
Chargeable gains abated:	

$$£13,000 - \frac{11}{26} \times £13,000$$

$$£13,000 - £5,500$$

	£
	7,500
	228,500
Less: charges—loan interest £35,000 — £5,000	30,000
Profits chargeable	198,500
Corporation tax payable:	
£198,000 at 52%	103,220
Less: ACT paid (maximum)	57,300
Mainstream corporation tax	45,920

	£
AP ended 31 March 1983	
Schedule D Case I	300,000
Schedule D Case III	1,200
	301,200
Less: charges—loan interest £33,000 — £7,000 + £5,000	31,000
Profits chargeable	270,200
Corporation tax payable:	
£270,200 × 52%	140,504
Less: ACT paid	81,060
Mainstream corporation tax	59,444

Turret Ltd
Corporation Tax Computation

AP ended 31 March 1980	£	£
Schedule D Case I		62,000
Corporation tax payable		29,200
Less: ACT paid	16,200	
Surplus ACT carried back 1982	956	17,156
Mainstream corporation tax		12,044
AP ended 31 March 1981		
Schedule D Case I		48,000
Corporation tax payable		19,800
Less: ACT paid	9,750	
Surplus ACT carried back 1982	4,650	14,400
Mainstream corporation tax		5,400
AP ended 31 March 1982		
Schedule D Case I		80,000
Corporation tax payable at 52%		41,600
Less: 2/25 (£112,500 — £80,000)		2,600
		39,000
Less: ACT paid (part)	10,800	
Surrendered ACT	13,200	24,000
Mainstream corporation tax		15,000
AP ended 31 March 1983		
Schedule D Case I		120,000
Corporation tax payable at 52%		62,400
Less: ACT paid and surrendered		36,000
Mainstream corporation tax		26,400

Castle Ltd

ACT Accounting

Year ended 31 March 1982		£	£
Franked payments:			
Dividends paid			175,000
ACT thereon			75,000
			250,000
Franked investment income			
£10,500 + 3/7 × £10,500			15,000
			235,000
ACT paid 30% × £235,000			70,500
ACT set-off limited to:			
Profits chargeable		198,500	
Less: Chargeable gains		7,500	
	30% ×	191,000	57,300
Surplus ACT			13,200
Surplus ACT			13,200
Less: surrendered Turret Ltd			13,200

AP ended 31 March 1983

	£
Franked payments:	
Dividends paid	252,000
ACT thereon	108,000
	360,000
FII £10,000 + 3/7 × £10,500	15,000
	345,000
ACT paid, 30% × £345,000	103,500
ACT set-off limited to:	
Profits chargeable £270,000 × 30%	81,060
Surplus ACT	22,440
Surplus ACT	22,440
Less: Surrendered Turret Ltd	22,440

Turret Ltd
ACT Accounting

Year ended 31 March 1980	£	£
ACT paid		16,200
ACT set off limited to 30% × £62,000	18,600	

Year ended 31 March 1981		
ACT paid		9,750
ACT set off limited to 30% × £48,000	14,400	

Year ended 31 March 1982

ACT paid: £38,282 × $\dfrac{3}{7}$ 16,406

ACT set off limited to 30% × £80,000   24,000

Year ended 31 March 1983

ACT paid: £49,000 × $\dfrac{3}{7}$ 21,000

ACT set off limited to 30% × £120,000   36,000

Turret Ltd
Surplus of ACT

Year ended 31 March 1982	£
Surrender of ACT from Castle Ltd	
Maximum ACT set off	24,000
Paid	16,406
Surrendered	13,200
Paid and surrendered	29,606
Maximum set off consists of:	
Surrendered ACT	13,200
Paid (part)	10,800
	24,000
Surplus ACT:	
ACT paid	16,406
Set off	10,800
Surplus	5,606
Available carry back Turret Ltd	
1981 (£14,400 — £9,750)	4,650
1980	956
	5,606

Year ended 31 March 1983

Surrender of ACT from Castle Ltd	
Maximum ACT set off	36,000
Paid	21,000
Surrendered	22,440
	43,440
Less: Maximum ACT	36,000
Carried forward	7,440

Question 13

a   Q and T form a 75% group and the trading losses of Q Ltd for the years ended 30 November 1983 and 1984 may be set off against the profits, as defined for group relief, of T Ltd.

Year ended 30 November 1983

T Ltd	£
Trading profit	10,000
Less: Loss brought forward S.177(1)	5,000
	5,000
Schedule D Case III	5,000
	10,000
Less: Charges	2,000
	8,000
Less: Group relief claimed from Q Ltd	8,000
Profits chargeable	Nil

Q Ltd	
Trading loss	12,000
Less: Surrendered to T Ltd	8,000
Loss carried forward S.177(1)	4,000

Year ended 30 November 1984

T Ltd	£
Schedule D Case III	5,000
Less: Loss relief S.177(2)	5,000
Trading loss	10,000
Less: Utilized S.177(2)	5,000
Loss carried forward S.177(1)	5,000
Add: Excess charges S.177(8)	2,000
Total loss to be carried forward S.177(1)	7,000

Q Ltd £

Trading loss	5,000
Add: Loss brought forward S.177(1)	4,000
Loss carried forward S.177(1)	9,000

Notes

(1) The profit of T Ltd available for group relief in the year ended 30 November 1983 is after deduction of trading losses brought forward. A claimant company's profits for relief are however *before* deduction of losses from subsequent accounting periods. There is therefore no need to apply T's loss for the next accounting period. Profits for group relief are *after* deduction of charges.

Application of group relief gives earlier relief than would application of S.177(2) relief (carry back against total profits) in respect of T Ltd's trading loss for the year ended 30 November 1984.

(2) Unrelieved trading losses in each year are available for carry forward against future trading profits as are the excess trade charges which arise in T Ltd in the year ended 30 November 1984.

(3) Claims for group relief must be made within two year of the end of the surrendering company's accounting period and requires its consent.

b Z Ltd is a consortium company both before and after the Finance Act 1984 and as such consortium group relief for trading losses is available as between the consortium company and the consortium members. Generally, a consortium company is a trading company owned at least to the extent of 75% by UK resident companies none of whom own less than 5% of the ordinary share capital.

Year ended 30 June 1984

Profits of Z Ltd against which B Ltd's loss may be set-off by way of group relief is:

£

$$\frac{24{,}000 \text{ shares}}{80{,}000 \text{ shares}} \times £50{,}000 = \qquad 15{,}000$$

Less: Consortium group relief from B Ltd	15,000

B Ltd	Trading loss	60,000
	Less: applied by way of group relief	15,000
	Loss carried forward S.177(1)	£45,000

Relief must be claimed within two years of the end of the accounting period of the surrendering company with the consent of the surrendering company and all other members of the consortium.

If the surrendering company is a member of the consortium only a fraction of the consortium company's profits, proportionate to the surrendering company's share in the consortium company is available for relief.

APPENDIX 5

TABLE OF STATUTES

INDEX